Final Edition and Me

Covering Late, Great Newspaper Era --

From Letterpress to the Digital Age via Elvis, MLK Jr., Billy Graham, and Murdoch

LaRue Gilleland

Contents

Preface

My newspaper career began at the age of sixteen in 1946 with writing news and selling ads for a weekly. After graduating from the University of Missouri a few years later, I worked for dailies and universities from Honolulu to Boston.

When Martin Luther King Jr. spotted my white face in a Memphis auditorium among African-Americans gathered to hear him speak in the 1950s, he invited me to spend most of the day with him. It may have been because I was a young newspaper reporter. But I felt in the segregated South at that time he did not want to see a stranger perhaps uncomfortable among people of different race.

In the same era, Elvis Presley came to the newspaper where I worked to meet its prize-winning cat. I soon started covering the singer each time he got into legal trouble. This lasted until he was drafted into the army a few years later.

I shared a drink and late night stroll with Bob Hope in Houston, where he contrasted for me his views on comedy and drama.

My journalistic memories include confrontation with an angry U. S. House Speaker Sam Rayburn; an evening with Hawaii's future senator Dan Inouye and his buddies from World War II's most decorated military unit; interviewing presidents Eisenhower and Truman and Truman's daughter Margaret on cruise ships in the Pacific, where she announced to me her plan to change her career from classical singing to writing spy and murder novels; appearing in court to testify about a Tennessee bootleg operation I exposed; interviewing a woman who murdered and sawed her husband into pieces; and conversing at midnight during the Korean conflict with evangelist Billy Graham.

Some personal accounts involve escaping with my wife from a forbidden night club in the old Soviet Union after her tipsy Russian dance partner lost his balance and crashed through a table and watching a half-dozen visionary men and women in Hawaii plan a church where a boy called "Barry" would attend Sunday School before becoming president of the United States. On the West Coast, controversial writer Anna Louise Strong entertained friends and me with stories about her arrest in the Soviet Union and her dancing in China with Mao Zedong. But I failed to measure up to a late-night drink invitation from movie actress Joan Crawford.

My work concluded with preparing young people for media careers at the University of Nevada, Reno, and Northeastern University, Boston, where I headed the School of Journalism as its first director. Two from my classes, including an editor who audited some lectures, led news teams that won Pulitzer prizes.

My students at Northeastern threw a party in 1991 for Ed Bernays, "the founder of public relations," in honor of his 100th birthday, shortly before his death.

I met Rupert Murdoch after he started building his media empire.

Newspapers for generations fulfilled print roles envisioned by the country's builders by exposing corruption and incompetence. Publishers enjoyed healthy profit margins, often rivaling oil companies. When the good times slackened, newspapers such as the New Orleans *Times Picayune,* Seattle *Post-Intelligencer, Rocky Mountain News*, and *Christian Science Monitor*, among others, stopped daily print publication. I competed against two good newspapers that failed, the Honolulu *Star Bulletin* and the Memphis *Press-Scimitar.*

The Boston *Globe,* worth $1.1 billion in 1993, sold for only $70 million in 2013. Amazon founder Jeff Bezos bought the Washington *Post* the same year for the fire-sale price of $250 million, keeping as publisher Katherine Weymouth, a member of the Graham family, the long-time owner.

The term "final edition," as used in this memoir, has two meanings: (1) the last copies of a morning or evening newspaper produced in the same press run, and (2) the last copies produced when a newspaper goes out of business.

Some observers fear final edition, in the latter sense, approaches for all newspapers. I am among those who think newspapers still have a future. Desire by readers for detail, perspective and variety, I believe, will ensure print's future.

In this memoir, I mention three women who shaped my thinking in general. Two, surprisingly, were connected with theater. A college actress taught me how to study. A West Coast actress challenged some of my journalistic assumptions. The third woman, my wife Betsy, encouraged me to moderate ambition with a touch of humility.

I apologize to talented colleagues, inspiring bosses, influential teachers, hard-working students, close relatives, and good friends that I fail to mention.

1

The King and I

In the cluttered press office at Memphis Police Central Headquarters, I stopped typing to take a phone call from my newspaper's night city editor. He had just heard the police radio order Elvis Presley brought in for questioning.

The editor, who kept a police radio tuned low beside *The Commercial Appeal* city desk, told me to check out the report. He knew I'd covered Elvis in trouble in the past.

The assistant police chief's office was down a flight of stairs on the first floor. He confirmed the report. There had been a complaint that Elvis pointed a pistol at a Marine on a downtown street. It was March 1957.

I had Elvis' unlisted phone number, one of many the newspaper compiled on celebrities. I dialed the number about 7:30 p.m. A male voice answered that belonged neither to Elvis nor his manager, Colonel Tom Parker. The voice said he'd pass along to Elvis my name, phone number, and the fact that I was a newspaper reporter, "if I can locate him."

As I worked on other stories more than an hour later, the voice called back. He said Elvis would meet me in an East Memphis residential neighborhood. The man gave an address where I should park my car and wait. He said Elvis would be driving a white Lincoln Continental.

I had first met Elvis two years earlier when he came to the newspaper to socialize with its prize-winning cat, Georgette. This was about the time he gained fame by recording "Hound Dog," "Love Me Tender," and "Blue Suede Shoes," and gained recognition with appearances on Milton Berle, Steve Allen, Ed Sullivan, and other TV shows. I also encountered Elvis after a street brawl that led to Elvis' first arrest. This memoir will later describe those incidents.

As I parked my car under a street light in front of the designated house number, heavy rain began to fall. It was an unfamiliar neighborhood, far from the Audubon Drive house where Elvis lived and the larger Graceland mansion he was about to buy in the city's south end.

After I'd waited a few minutes, headlights appeared in my rear-view mirror. A car parked behind me. I stepped into the rain and hurried between the cars, noting the other was a Lincoln. I jumped out of the rain onto the front passenger seat.

Elvis, alone, leaned back against the door on the driver's side as if wanting to appear nonchalant while ready to react if needed. He looked trim in plaid sport coat and white knit shirt buttoned at the neck. In this era, long before he gained weight, he looked trim.

Recognizing me, he relaxed. "What have I done wrong this time?" he said.

"Police are looking for you," I answered. "Someone says you pulled a gun on him."

"That's all a mistake, sir. It's not what happened," Elvis said.

Although I wasn't much older than he, his polite deference no longer surprised me. He reached across my lap to open the car's glove compartment. He took out a revolver. "Look at it," he said, handing the gun to me. I held it carefully at first. It was heavy, snub-nosed and impressive. It looked like a new .25-caliber "Saturday night special."

But it wasn't real. It was a prop used in a recent movie.

Elvis explained that exiting a downtown pharmacy hours earlier, he stopped to sign autographs for some teenage girls. A young man in uniform, a Marine private, walked up and said, "You rudely bumped into my wife coming out of a restaurant two months ago. She told me all about it. I want to get it straightened out right now."

Elvis said the young man, about 19, "looked like he'd been drinking."

"I told him I didn't know what he was talking about because I'd been in Hollywood at the time making a picture." The singer said it was then that he took the prop pistol from his coat and said, "You don't want to start anything with me, do you?"

The private turned and walked away. He stopped at a nearby pay phone, abundant in those days, and called police.

Elvis told me in his car, "I was smiling when I pulled the gun out. Everybody else standing around there knew it wasn't real."

"It fooled me," I said.

Elvis continued, "It scares me when a guy tries to start trouble. I've had to talk my way out of so many fights I can't even remember them all. The majority of people are nice, decent folks, but a few want to be able to go around saying they beat up Elvis Presley.

"I'm just like they are -- with skin on my bones and blood in my veins -- and I could be beat up just like the next guy. So what would be so big about beating me up?"

To lighten the conversation, I mentioned that I'd received a letter that week from his manager, Tom Parker, with a clipping from a London newspaper. The clipping said Heathrow Airport had been playing Elvis' records over a loudspeaker to scare seagulls off runways.

2

"Colonel" Parker, who had received the honorary title from Louisiana Governor Jimmie Davis, told me in his letter, "I'm not upset over this story as I do not know of any birds having ever bought Elvis' records." Elvis laughed.

I told him I'd given the clipping to Lydel Sims, our newspaper's humor columnist, in case he could use it. Sims put it in his column a couple of days later.

"WE COVER THE NATION"

Thomas A. Parker
Exclusive Management

P.O.
417
MADISON, TENN.

Mr. La Rue Gilleland
Commercial Appeal
Memphis, Tennessee

Dear Mr. Gilleland:

It was so nice of you to call yesterday. Enclosed is the clipping on the seagulls. I thought you would get a kick out of this story.

As I told you over the phone, I was not upset over this story as I do not know of any birds having ever bought any of Elvis' records. Surely, we will not lose any record sales over this story. It is possible, however, that we may even sell some extra records of the same tune used to scare the seagulls, to a good many of the people who have been try to get rid of seagulls.

We could re-title the tune SPECIAL SEAGULL REMOVER.

Sincerely,

Colonel

THE COLONEL

P. S. - Please return the clipping to Colonel Parker. It is the only copy he has for his scrap book. Thank you.

M. Diskin

Elvis and I talked as rain pounded his car. I'd watched him conduct himself well in bad situations before.

While nearly the same age, we embodied different generations. At 23, Elvis had become an icon of the "Boomers," who helped him and Sam Phillips of Sun Records popularize rock and roll. At 27, I represented the last of the "Silent Generation" that grew up on Bing Crosby and Frank Sinatra.

I knew from *The Commercial Appeal's* library of news clippings (we called it "the morgue") that Elvis lived in a cheap, two or three-room frame house in Tupelo, Mississippi, before his family moved to Memphis.

He was graduated in 1953 from Humes High near downtown. He drove a truck for a living and sang in an Assembly of God Church choir before breaking into professional music. That occurred when he visited Sun Records on Union Avenue, two blocks from the newspaper, to spend a few dollars to make a demo record for his mother.

Owner Sam Phillips, liking what he heard, invited Elvis to return to audition with a studio band. That led to Elvis' first professional recordings, "That's All Right, Mama" and "Blue Moon of Kentucky."

In his car, Elvis looked at his watch, then at me, and asked, "What do you think I should do now?" I said, "My advice is to take this toy that scared a Marine to police headquarters tonight. Since I share a desk there with other reporters, I'm willing to go with you. Just tell the inspector on duty the story you told me."

Elvis agreed. "I guess it's now or never," he said.

I followed him downtown in my car, and led him inside the building shortly after midnight. Inspector Joe Gagliano listened to Elvis, looked closely at the pistol, tagged it, and put it in a big yellow envelope on his desk.

He told Elvis to go home. The inspector said he would invite the Marine, stationed at nearby Millington Naval Air Base, to make a formal complaint. If he did, police would instruct Elvis to return. No complaint was ever filed.

Shamelessly borrowing a recent Elvis song title, I wrote for the final edition that he'd pulled a toy pistol on a young man, getting him "all shook up."

Our Elvis Is Quick On Draw —Toy Pistol Scares Marine

(Picture on Page 8, Section II) March 24, 1957

By LARUE GILLELAND

Elvis Presley admitted yesterday he got a young Marine "all shook up" by pulling a toy pistol when the Marine "tried to pick a fight" in downtown Memphis.

The 22-year-old singer said the incident occurred about 10:15 p.m. Friday on Third near Poplar.

Elvis said he was signing autographs for several girls when the Marine walked up to him and said:

"You bumped into my wife as she walked out of a restaurant about two months ago. She told me all about it. I want to get it straightened out right now."

Singer Feared Trouble

The singer said the Marine appeared to have been drinking and that he was afraid "he wanted to start trouble."

"I told him I didn't know what he was talking about because I had been in Hollywood making a picture."

Elvis said he remembered the toy gun, a Hollywood prop pistol, and pulled it from beneath his coat to scare the Marine away.

"You don't want to start trouble with me, do you?" Elvis said.

Pvt. Hershel Nixon, 18, stationed at the Naval Air Station at Millington, told police the rock and roll star pointed "a real gun right at my head and said 'I'll blow your damn brains out, you punk'."

Private Nixon said he was just trying to strike up a conversation with Elvis and mentioned his wife "so I'd have something to talk to him about."

"He pulled the gun—it looked like a 25-caliber pistol—on me for no reason at all," said Private Nixon.

Elvis said the Marine should have realized the gun wasn't real.

"I was smiling when I took it out of my coat. Everybody else standing around there knew it wasn't real.

Elvis, who returned last week from Hollywood after making a motion picture and recording a new song, "All Shook Up," said seven or eight of the toy guns, used in films, were given to him in the movie capital.

Barrels Plugged

Elvis said he and a friend, George Kline, a local disk jockey, had been playing with the prop guns in the singer's home earlier in the evening. He explained the barrels are plugged and the guns shoot blanks.

"It scares me when a guy tries to start trouble. I've had to talk my way out of so many fights I can't even remember them all.

"Majority of people are nice, decent folks but a few want to be able to go around saying they beat up Elvis Presley. I'm just like they are—with skin on my bones and blood in my veins—and I could be beat up just like the next guy. So what would be so big about beating me up?"

Police Insp. Joe Gagliano said he doubted Elvis pulled a real pistol but invited the Marine to come to Police Headquarters today or tomorrow to make a formal complaint.

6

New Role?

(Story on Page One)

Elvis Presley displayed the toy pistol —used in making motion pictures — that caused all the trouble Friday night when a Marine from Millington tried to "pick a fight with me." The singer said he pulled the gun out of his coat to scare the Marine away.

—Staff Photo

7

2

Ozark Boyhood

The foothills where I grew up in Missouri were about three-hundred miles – and a world away – from Memphis and its morning newspaper.

The Great Depression came to the Ozarks in the 1930s with an extra jolt to my parents. Their house burned down.

I remember returning at the age of four with my mother and father from a grocery trip to find our farmhouse in smoking ruin. It was 1934 near Olean, a village of about a hundred people.

My parents blamed a defective stove. They lost everything inside the house, including Buster, our pet dog. My father, Wesley, and mother, Agnes, were fond of part-boxer Buster. They believed he had saved my life the year before.

They said I wandered to a deep pond behind the farmhouse, and Buster followed. Each time I got within a few feet of the water, the dog blocked my path. That's how they found us -- Buster standing between the water and me while I stubbornly tried to go around him.

After their house burned, my parents possessed forty not-too-productive acres, the clothes on our backs, a 1930 Model A Ford, and less than one hundred dollars in the bank. We drove six miles to Eldon, where my father worked as a Rock Island brakeman, and stayed in the small Burris hotel near the railroad tracks.

Years later, the hotel and town inspired writer-producer Paul Henning's popular TV sitcom "Petticoat Junction," where fictional "Hooterville" was located. Hennings based Hooterville episodes on stories he heard from his wife, the Burris Hotel owner's daughter, who grew up in Eldon.

My parents' farm had belonged to my paternal grandfather, John F. Gilleland, long dead. My father sold the land for the Depression-era price of a few dollars an acre.

Eldon was the mid-point on the Rock Island line between St. Louis and Kansas

City. We spent a month or two in Eldon after the fire until the railroad transferred my father to St. Louis.

My parents had married there in 1925 when she was a 19-year-old store clerk and he, eight years older, a steadily employed rail worker. I arrived in the maternity ward of St. Louis Barnes Hospital on February 18, 1930, about four months after the Black Tuesday Wall Street Crash.

During the Depression's nadir, banks failed, Franklin D. Roosevelt replaced Herbert Hoover as U. S. president, freight shipments declined, and the Rock Island declared bankruptcy. Struggling to survive, it placed my father and many other employees on the part-time "extra board." National unemployment bounced for years between fifteen and twenty-five percent.

I attended kindergarten in St. Louis in 1935 after a summer of record-breaking temperatures. My parents disliked the heat, but they complained more about winds from Kansas and Oklahoma that brought remnants of great dust storms that destroyed crops and irritated many people's lungs. Although Missouri suffered less from the dust than farm states farther west, I vaguely remember adults discouraging me from playing outside. The sun increased in redness before dust darkened the skies.

After my sixth birthday, my parents returned to Eldon where I entered the first grade. In addition to the Burris and another hotel, the town had rail yards, roundhouse, engine maintenance shop, depot, stores and churches, and about two-thousand residents, including Rock Island employees.

Ozark highlands began at the town's southern edge. Rugged caves and clear springs punctuated hills that rolled south for more than two hundred miles. They were forested with oak, walnut, hickory, and sycamore trees, interspersed with blackberries and persimmons.

Hard times continued. Hungry people slept under bridges in the country and stood in bread lines in cities. A procession of homeless men "rode the rails" into Eldon. Every few days one knocked at our back door to ask if he could perform a task around the house in exchange for something to eat. My mother often complied by making a sandwich or two.

Older boys living near the railroad tracks climbed aboard parked coal cars at night to toss off loose lumps. Using buckets, they picked up the dislodged coal from beside the rails to heat their parents' houses. If their hauls appeared restrained in size, a rail night watchman usually turned his head.

Although my father received irregular assignments, we never went hungry and we always had a roof over our heads. Dad's income, he told me later, hovered around the town's yearly $2,000 average. I remember two small rented apartments we lived in upstairs in frame houses. Heat came from a wood stove, usually placed in the living room. Vents high on walls permitted some warm air to circulate among rooms.

My parents eventually moved to a brick house on Eldon's Oak Street. They fortunately could afford the coal we shoveled into the basement furnace in winter. A truck periodically dumped the coal through a window into a basement bin.

In summer, cooling of house or car came from open windows. Blocks of ice, delivered to the back door and placed in an "ice box," kept food from spoiling before we could eat it.

Relatives we visited in St. Louis and Kansas City often placed pallets on fire escapes or porches on hot July and August nights to get comfortable enough to sleep. Friends of my parents excitedly described their first encounter with "air conditioning." At a wedding reception they attended in a major St. Louis hotel, a large ballroom had been cooled by placing ice chunks in compartments behind sidewalls along the dance floor.

Radio, our main entertainment, brought music and baseball into the living room. My parents and I often sat facing our Philco radio -- as if we somehow anticipated televised pictures far in the future. At night we heard "Fibber McGee and Mollie," "Jack Benny," and "Edgar Bergen and Charlie McCarthy."

Kids I knew played marbles in front yards and softball and football in any open lot available. At dusk we often engaged in games called "Kick the Can" or "Chalk the Walk." In the latter, one team tried to follow another by deciphering clues left on sidewalks with chalk. The chalk usually had been taken clandestinely from a schoolroom. For a dime on Saturday afternoons we attended the town's only movie house where we saw two films (a Western and a "feature"), a serial episode ("Flash Gordon" was my favorite), a cartoon, and a newsreel several weeks old. Popcorn cost a nickel. The first feature I remember was "Rose Marie," a musical with Nelson Eddy and Jeanette MacDonald.

Women sometimes made dresses from colored flour sacks. It was an era when the town's physicians routinely made house calls to treat the sick.

Overhearing disputes between my parents produced the only sadness I remember from those days. Financial stress may have partly undermined their relationship. The frequency of their quarrels increased. So did my father's consumption of whisky.

One winter night when I was about seven, my parents invited several friends over for drinks and pinochle, a relatively cheap form of Depression-era entertainment. From my bed, I heard voices grow loud. Late in the evening, my father and another man, both drinking too much, got into a quarrel. They threatened each other.

I heard the word "gun." I jumped out of bed and, without anyone seeing me, went to a back room where my father kept a .22 rifle and 20-gauge shotgun. In my pajamas and bare feet, I carried the guns out the rear door and several yards down an alley, where I dropped them into the snow. I re-entered the house and crawled back in bed. The party ended soon after.

The next morning, while dad was away from the house, I retrieved the guns. I told my mother what I had done, and she told him. He asked me if it were true. I said yes. He asked me why. I said I was scared that someone would get shot. To my surprise, he turned, walked away, and never mentioned the matter again.

I worried that the guns, buried for hours under snow, might have received water damage. Although my father hunted quail and other small game often, he never spoke of the guns not working well. Discord between my parents continued for years, eventually ending in divorce.

My father had been married and divorced once before he met my mother. From the first marriage, he had a son named Emanuel about twelve years older than I. Emanuel grew up with his mother in Kansas. I saw my half brother no more than three times in my life. On the last occasion, in 1946, I was about 16. My parents and I drove to Parsons, Kansas, where he lived. By then he had a wife and two daughters. I next heard from him indirectly in 1970 when our dad died. I was 40 then and my brother was in his early 50s. From another state he called the funeral home to inform me that he wanted the man's diamond ring our father wore. I agreed that he, the older son, could have it.

My maternal and paternal grandparents grew up in Missouri. Ancestors on my mother's side, with last names of West, Burd, and Green, arrived at Missouri's Osage River by covered wagon. Brothers William and Isaac West settled there in 1807, shortly after the Lewis and Clark expedition passed about twenty miles to the north. The West brothers made friends with Tuscumbia, chief of Missouri's Osage Indians. The chief protected the West family and their neighbors when Crow, Illinois and other tribes threatened.

A great-great grandfather was Daniel Burd Sr., descended from Virginians who settled Eastern Tennessee. From there, he traveled by wagon for weeks toward the Osage with his wife and their six children, including one-year-old Daniel Jr. Horses pulled them over dirt roads through Tennessee, Kentucky, Illinois, and southern Missouri. A few miles from the Osage River, Daniel Sr. cleared land, built a log cabin, and began farming.

At the age of 54 during the Civil War, he tried to join the Confederate army, but was turned down. His son, Daniel Burd Jr., fought reluctantly on the Union side. Northern soldiers rode onto the father's farm and coerced the son to sign up for duty. Although few blacks lived in south-central Missouri, most of the white population there sympathized with agrarian slave holders.

After the war, Daniel Jr. married a neighbor, Malinda Green. Her parents had been robbed and murdered in their home along the Osage River in the 1840s. It was believed the killers approached their house in daylight and escaped by boat. Malinda and the other Green children discovered their parents' bodies on returning from school.

Daniel Jr.'s son, James Riley Burd, my maternal grandfather, tilled his family's farm before selling it to become a road materials contractor. He married a neighbor, Allie, daughter of Charles Pearson and Sarah West Pearson. James and Allie's son, Maurice Burd, my uncle, conducted genealogical research in which he traced the Burd family back to Margaret Douglas, a granddaughter of England's King Henry VII, in the Fifteenth Century.

Some of Margaret's descendants became the "black sheep side" of the family. One was hanged for treason and another died imprisoned in the Tower of London. Their progeny, finally respectable with last names Howard, Dunn and Burd (also spelled Byrd), settled in Virginia in the 1600s.

On my dad's side, John Gilleland, of Scottish-Irish descent, arrived in Missouri just before the Civil War. The Gaelic term "gille" or "gilly" meant a paid land overseer, hunting guide, or gamekeeper. John Gilleland started a farm near Olean on land purchased from the federal government. He passed the land to his son, born in 1855. The son, John F. Gilleland, and his bride, Josie Wade, daughter of a rural Mt. Rose, Missouri, physician, had two children -- Iva, a daughter, and Alvey Wesley, my father, born 1897.

In my boyhood immaturity, I learned that the name LaRue had been given more often to females than males. I was so miffed that I identified with the country song, "A Boy Named Sue." I finally became reconciled with my name on being told that my migrating ancestors picked it up in the early 1800s on a brief stop in Kentucky's LaRue County, birthplace of Abraham Lincoln.

I attended kindergarten in St. Louis and started the first grade in Eldon. When I was eight or nine, I accompanied my father on a couple of his extra board railroad assignments. On separate trips, I rode in the caboose to St. Louis and Kansas City, about 150 miles from Eldon in opposite directions. The train conductor and my brakeman dad probably violated railroad regulations by taking me along.

Memories of the trips remain vivid. Journey through Ozark foothills and past dairy farms and cornfields took nearly an entire workday, for the train stopped at each small town to unload and take on freight.

At the start of the first trip, I climbed three high metal steps with my dad to the caboose's rear platform and entered the car with wide-eyed wonder. The interior contained at least three or four narrow bunks on which conductor, brakeman, engineer, and (in a bygone era) a "flagman" could sleep. I saw a small woodstove for heating and cooking, a coffee pot, a couple of straight-backed chairs, and a table with oil lantern attached where the conductor checked waybills that listed contents and destinations of boxcars, tank and flat cars. Narrow doors led to a tiny restroom with washbasin and to a storeroom containing signal flags, lanterns and flares.

A few steep steps reached the cupola at the top of the caboose where windows faced all directions so that conductor or brakeman could observe the train in motion and watch for trouble. That included overheated axel bearings, called "hotboxes," which occasionally derailed trains.

From a hard leather bench in the cupola, I looked down the length of the train, more than a half-mile, I thought, to the steam locomotive pulling it. I spent most of the trips there, watching the train gracefully follow curves in the rails. I saw autos and trucks back up at cross roads. White steam from the locomotive shot skyward when the whistle blew.

I savored the black coal smoke that often reached back to the caboose. I imagined myself a conductor with the duty of spotting hot boxes. I never saw one. I sometimes fell asleep on the cupola bench. Slack in couplings between cars produced sharp jolts that usually woke me when the train slowed or picked up speed.

To my young ears, names of the towns along the way had an exotic, almost musical ring: "Meta," "Bland," "Stover," "Cole Camp," "Pleasant Hill," "Lee's Summit," "Raytown," "Owensville," "Argyle," "Gascondy," "Labadie."

In St. Louis my father and I spent the night in a hotel for rail employees. In Kansas City, we stayed at the home of my father's niece, Agatha, and her family. I thought the trips in both directions exciting.

When I was nine, the tallest man in the world visited Eldon. At least, the Guiness *Book of Records* said he was tallest. It was one of the most exciting events I remember in the small town. The visitor was Robert Wadlow of Alton, Illinois. He stood a half inch shorter than nine feet, or about the height a Septuagint account gives for biblical Goliath. He came to town as good will ambassador for a shoe company. The town organized a parade for him.

I watched from a sidewalk with other kids and adults as Wadlow walked down the middle of Main Street, with high school band and several local businessmen accompanying him. The tallest of them did not reach his armpits. Wadlow, someone said, had four brothers and sisters at home of normal size. Despite his nearly five hundred pounds, Wadlow looked lean to me. But he appeared much older than his twenty years, and his shoes looked immense. He smiled and waved to spectators. He walked slowly, as if uncomfortable engaging in so much exercise.

He died less than two years later of a blood infection that began in a lower leg.

My dad occasionally took me small-game hunting. He bought me a .410 shotgun. Sometimes when we returned, my mother cooked squirrel and dumplings. I remember another delicious meal of quail we'd killed, corn and tomatoes fresh from our garden, pie made from wild gooseberries, and tea from sassafras gathered in nearby hills. My mother, father and I also fished for bass, crappie, and catfish in the Osage River, twelve miles from Eldon.

The river got its name from the Sioux-related Osage Indians, who lived along its banks for generations. The Osage River flows from hills in eastern Kansas through much of southern Missouri. It empties into the Missouri River between St. Louis and Jefferson City, the state capital.

A story of lost opportunity from my childhood that I like to tell occurred in 1941 when I answered a knock at the front door. An artist stood with two canvasses he wanted to sell. Because I liked the paintings, my parents invited him into our living room. Appearing about middle aged, he looked distinguished with mustache and carefully combed hair.

After brief conversation, he returned to his car for more paintings, mostly oils and a couple of watercolors. He propped them on furniture and along walls. At eleven years of age, I liked the scenes of men and women traveling in covered wagons and Indians on horseback. My parents focused on two landscapes in vivid colors and fluid lines.

I expressed hope that they would buy them. The prices, as I remember, ranged from about fifty to seventy-five dollars. My mother and father wavered on the brink of purchase, then decided against it -- for that was big money in those Depression days. The artist gathered up his paintings, said a cordial goodbye, and left.

Months later I saw a magazine picture of regionalist artist Thomas Hart Benton. I felt sure I recognized him as the traveling artist. When I asked my mother, she agreed "Benton" may have been the visitor's last name. I learned from the magazine that a controversial nude painting, "Persephone," which my parents and I did not see, cost him his job as a teacher at the Kansas City Art Institute a few weeks before he showed up at our house. At the institute, he had taught other budding artists, including Jackson Pollack.

When later I saw Benton's huge wall murals that decorate the interior of the Missouri State Capitol in Jefferson City, I became even more convinced that I had correctly identified him. Benton's fame steadily increased in future years. He died in 1975 in his studio grasping a paintbrush.

I've often wondered what price those paintings my parents passed up would bring today. "Persephone" hangs in Kansas City's Nelson-Atkins Museum. It's called "the city's Mona Lisa." Artist Thomas Hart Benton was grandnephew of Missouri's famous pre-Civil War senator of the same name.

Like most kids my age I at first had little interest in national or world news events. The earliest news event I remember my parents discussing with excitement was the disappearance of aviator Amelia Earhart and her navigator, Frederick Noonan, in 1937 in the Pacific. "And she's barely forty years old," my mother said. It was clear that my parents admired Earhart's prowess as the first woman to fly the Atlantic solo five years earlier. That her dad worked for the Rock Island in Kansas and Iowa impressed my father.

My first awareness of the power of the press came when I was about eleven. In St. Louis, the *Post-Dispatch* waged a successful campaign against coal-smoke pollution from local industry and home furnaces. When my mother took me on summer visits to her two sisters who lived there, I heard them discuss their hesitation about wearing white dresses or hats because smoke quickly soiled them. In winter, fresh fallen snow grew dingy overnight.

The *Post-Dispatch* campaign against health hazards caused by cheap coal won the 1941 Pulitzer Gold Medal for Public Service. The city's pollution gradually declined as it converted to improved grades of coal and other fuels. A national clean-up trend had begun in Pittsburgh and other cities. In future years ecological organizations appeared throughout the nation, including the Environmental Protection Agency (1970) and the American Coalition for Clean Coal Electricity (2000).

Although my baseball-loving father usually rooted for St. Louis, I shared his excitement as Joe DiMaggio of the New York Yankees hit safely in one game after another in 1941 until reaching fifty-six straight, a record that has lasted until today.

On December 7, 1941, Sunday radio news reports told of the bombing of Pearl Harbor. The next day, my school's principal interrupted our sixth grade class to announce that Congress had declared war on Japan. My classmates cheered. We didn't know the Japanese were celebrating at the same time on Tokyo streets.

The attack on Hawaii occurred before any warning reached officials in Washington. The United States and Germany exchanged war declarations three days later.

As World War II heated up in following months, trains carrying soldiers and munitions on Rock Island tracks east and west through Eldon increased in frequency. My father now worked nearly every day. He was promoted from brakeman to freight conductor. Someone among kids I knew got the idea that we could make money and provide a service to the troops by selling snacks and soda pop when trains stopped briefly at Eldon's small railway station.

Items we purchased for a nickel sold for a dime. The soldiers bought our merchandise by leaning out open windows, for they were not permitted to leave the trains. The soldiers nearly always seemed to be in good humor, and often they tipped us an extra nickel, dime or quarter.

Extra excitement occurred when one troop train came through with blinds drawn on windows of some cars. A rumor said those cars contained scores of young soldiers of Asian descent. We learned later that they were Japanese Americans of the 100th Battalion from Hawaii, heading for training camps, first in Wisconsin and later in Mississippi. As part of the 442nd Regimental Combat Team, it would become the Army's most highly decorated unit. We conjectured later that the military may have ordered blinds pulled on their train for their protection, because of their Japanese ancestry.

Soldiers got off the train in Eldon on only one occasion that I remember during the entire war. But they were too ill to buy anything. They had contacted food poisoning after leaving Kansas City. Rumor, which the kids helped spread, blamed "spoiled mayonnaise."

Along both sides of the train, scores of soldiers lay on the ground moaning and vomiting. It reminded of a scene in the 1939 movie, "Gone with the Wind," when wounded Confederates lay near Atlanta's train tracks. Eldon's two or three physicians came to the chaotic site beside the Rock Island tracks to give emergency treatment. Two soldiers died.

Town adults and kids assisted by running to get water and other items the doctors requested. An auxiliary railroad track through town permitted other trains to pass by.

The seriousness of the situation later prompted local women to copy communities across the country in organizing USO canteens to meet the trains. Participation by youngsters about my age ended.

As time went by, I joined Boy Scouts and others in gathering scrap metal for the war effort. Newspapers from coast to coast promoted the campaign, and one, the Omaha *World-Herald*, won a Pulitzer Gold Medal for doing so. In Eldon, I remember a spacious warehouse where kids and adults deposited piles of metal. Kids collected it door to door. Adults stripped abandoned cars on country roads.

We were told later -- probably falsely -- that a new fighter plane, the P-51, had been named for Eldon High School sports teams, the "Mustangs," because the town collected so much scrap metal for its small size. Whether the P-51 Mustang had an Eldon connection or not, exploits of the plane in World War II became a source of pride for town residents.

Blue stars in many Eldon windows designated family members serving in the armed forces, and occasional gold stars reminded passersby of those who had died. As time went by, gold stars increased in number.

I remember ration cards my parents used for gasoline, food and clothing items. A major hardship, from my boyhood point of view, was scarcity of canned fruit cocktail. I remember paying sales tax for small items with Missouri "mills," oversized plastic coins worth one-tenth of a cent.

While the war ground on, school life proceeded normally. I swam in Lake of the Ozarks in the summer and visited roller skating rinks and drive-in movies with older friends who had cars and ration stamps. With fewer than four hundred students, the local high school was too small to afford football or most team sports -- or so the school board believed. The high school basketball team, however, had enthusiastic town support. Residents showing up for basketball games paid special attention to senior players, for nearly all would enter the armed forces immediately after graduation.

A star player, Harold Clotworthy, captured early by German troops, spent most of the war in an enemy prison camp. He became a town symbol of heroic sacrifice. He returned emaciated after the war and started a successful insurance business.

My parents belonged to the Christian Church, also known as Disciples of Christ, one of the most ecumenical of American fundamentalist denominations. Founded in the early 1800s by former Presbyterians, the Christian Church held its members to one tenet -- the divinity of Jesus. It left members free to follow their own consciences on all other spiritual matters.

I felt comfortable with this church in my childhood and teenage years. On Sunday mornings I listened with pride as the minister invited all visitors to take part in communion, no matter what denomination they represented.

As I grew older, however, I had difficulty accepting the church's anthropomorphic view of a Supreme Being. It was too similar, I thought, to Michelangelo's portrait of God on the Sistine Chapel ceiling. I was happy for the people I knew, including my Nazarene grandfather and uncles, who derived comfort from literal belief in the Bible, heaven and afterlife. But their religious certainty appeared precarious to me – as precarious as someone stubbornly espousing atheism. The atheist and the religious bigot, I thought, both claimed to know too much. Each would benefit from a little doubt. Admitting that some religious questions were unanswerable led me to theologian Paul Tillich's concept of God as "whatever is Ultimate," without further definition.

At 14, I made some money boxing boys my age in preliminary bouts at a carnival that came to town in summers. The bouts preceded the main event between adults. In it, a middle-aged welterweight named "Rocky Kansas" challenged local tough guys, often much bigger than he, to meet him in the ring for a few rounds.

Rocky also organized and refereed the preliminary bouts. That's where I came in. Rocky paired a half dozen boys, including me, for fights lasting three rounds. After each round, the audience tossed money into the ring to be shared by the young boxers. The amount depended on how hard we fought, or how much of a show we put on.

The carnival stayed in town four or five days, and I volunteered to fight every night. I received mostly coins, with an occasional dollar bill. But it added up. The sum at the end of an evening seemed like big money to me. I could hardly wait for the next summer.

That fall I entered a local Golden Gloves tournament. Nobody questioned in 1944 whether I, at fourteen years of age, had lost amateur eligibility by taking carnival money.

The first Golden Gloves event to be staged in Miller County closed Saturday with nine winners. Awards will be presented as follows:

Light Heavyweight: Kenneth Dunstan, 165 pounds, Eldon, won a decision over Lee Smith in a hard fought bout Thursday night.

Welterweight: Herbert Tennyson, 147, Osage, outpointed Luther Henson in a fast-paced contest Friday night. . . .

Junior Lightweight: LaRue Gilleland, 129, Eldon, punched and footworked to decisions over Charles Uptergove on Wednesday, Cletus Stark Friday, and Avery Baucom Saturday night.

The Miller County Autogram
Tuscumbia, Missouri

As a high school freshman, I held a part-time job as janitor in a bank. I worked at night after other employees went home. I remember that occasionally bank managers would test my honesty by leaving a five-dollar or ten-dollar bill on the teller's counter.

Thinking their method a bit puerile, I cleaned around the bills without touching them.

Atomic bombs fell on Japan and World War II ended in 1945 just before I began my high school sophomore year. I lettered in basketball that year as a guard. That turned out to be the peak of my high school sports career. I developed chronic Osgood-Schlatter's condition in ligaments of both knees. Running starts and stops painfully inflamed the condition. I quit playing. I also no longer boxed. But hiking and swimming did not bother me.

Disappointed, I turned to campus politics, theater, and working for a weekly newspaper. I won election in my sophomore year as student council vice president. During a random inspection a few days later, school administrators discovered a bottle of liquor in the locker of the student body president, a senior. It created a town scandal. The school board and Buford W. Robinson, the new high school principal, defrocked the senior and designated me president, the first sophomore so named.

Robinson later became State Commissioner of Education. After retiring from that job, he served as Missouri Senate senior doorman and sergeant-at-arms into his 90s -- the state's oldest employee.

Early in my junior year at the age of 16, I began my first part-time newspaper job on the *Autogram,* a weekly in Tuscumbia, a neighboring town. The town's name came from the Osage Indian chief who protected white settlers, including some of my ancestors, in the early 1800s. I got the newspaper job by convincing the publisher, Charlotte Myers, I could sell some ads because I knew many of Eldon's business owners. Also, with no prior experience, I could be hired cheaply.

LaRue Gilleland, who has been head of student government at Eldon High School, joins the Autogram staff this week as Eldon representative.

Gilleland takes over for Warren A. Kelsay, who has been the Eldon contact man since his return from the service. Gilleland will represent this newspaper in gathering news and selling advertising.

The Miller County Autogram
Tuscumbia, Missouri

On my first visit to the newspaper's back shop, I found an exciting new world. I saw an antique Linotype machine turn hot, molten lead alloy into lines of type. After the type cooled, a flat-bed press applied inked impression to paper.

The Linotype machine, invented about 1885, looked to me to be about the same age of the elderly, itinerant printer operating it. A younger man picked upper and lower case letters from a wooden job-case drawer for creating heads on stories and advertisements. These two printers had no idea their jobs would begin disappearing in a few years. On most days, I wrote short news items, usually requiring someone's careful editing, and I sold ads for an hour or two after school.

The *Autogram* was one of the nation's nearly nine-thousand weeklies located mostly in small towns and suburbs. Their circulations varied from a few thousand to a few hundred copies. In cities, another one-hundred foreign language weeklies regularly appeared.

Wallace Vernon, publisher of the weekly Eldon *Advertiser,* eventually bought the *Autogram.* He also married Marjorie Tompkins, a classmate of mine in elementary and high school. Several years later, the Missouri Press Association, representing weekly and daily newspapers, elected Wallace its president.

In my last summer in high school I convinced Eldon's Boy Scout troop, to which I belonged, to lend a high school friend, Kent Kehr, and me its small sailboat so that we could explore an undeveloped arm of ninety-mile long Lake of the Ozarks and work on outdoor merit badges. The lake was created with construction of Bagnell Dam in 1931 to supply electricity to St. Louis.

I no longer remember whether Kent and I accomplished any serious merit badge work, but we had fun hunting, fishing, swimming, and sailing. We returned the boat in good condition. Kent later attended Colgate University on a scholarship and became a successful St. Louis attorney.

The lake also provided wide-open spaces where 12-year-old black saxophonist Charlie Parker a few years earlier had practiced his music. He'd run away to Eldon from Kansas City where older musicians laughed at his early musical mistakes. He earned money doing errands for stores at the lake and in town. They tolerated him in this Jim Crow region because he was so young. Charlie returned to Kansas City after several months with renewed determination, and became one of the most famous of jazz musicians. He joined Dizzie Gillespie in inventing Bebop. He died of cirrohsis and other ailments at 34 in New York.

The lake developed rapidly in future years, with construction of tourist resorts and fishing camps. Catfish, bass, and crappie drew fishermen from St. Louis, Kansas City and more distant cities. After I left Missouri, sharp-teethed piranha, apparently imported illegally from the Amazon, began to show up in the lake.

AWARDS TO ELDON YOUTH

LaRue Gilleland

ELDON, Mo., May 12 (Special) —LaRue Gilleland, 18-year-old Eldon high school senior, son of Mr. and Mrs. A. W. Gilleland, was judged the best male actor in the Missouri state high school one-act play festival, held at the University at Columbia, May 7 and 8.

Such honors are not new to LaRue, as he has won high recognition in all previous competitive meets. In addition to his dramatic awards, he has received top ratings in interscholastic vocal contests with his baritone solos.

With his personality, he has become one of the most popular and well-liked students of his school; is the high school student president, and editor of the popular school paper.

Graduating from high school this week, LaRue is making plans for further study in dramtics, voice, and journalism.

In my senior year, I won election as Eldon High student body president, thus becoming the first in the school to serve two terms. Like my counterparts in other high schools, I conducted meetings of the student council and performed ceremonial acts, such as coronating the high school queen of beauty and popularity, at a fall festival. The 1948 ceremony attracted a lot of local interest because the queen, Helen Renken, was the third sister in her family to receive the title of high school queen. Her siblings, Juanita and Wanda, preceded her.

Also, I tried acting. I had the lead in a one-act high school play titled "Last Flight Over" by Allen Lemmon. It won a statewide dramatics contest held in 1948 in Columbia, Missouri. Judges also named me the state's best high school actor that year.

The main judge, Irene Freeman, headed the theater and speech department at Central Missouri State College (later University of Central Missouri) in Warrensburg. She offered to arrange a small scholarship for me that paid some tuition costs. With no better offer, I decided to enroll in her college.

When I returned from the state dramatics contest in Columbia, the county Republican Central Committee invited me to present a patriotic reading, "This is America," at a Lincoln's Day dinner at the Masonic Lodge in Eldon. My dad, railway union member and long-time Democrat, expressed doubt that I could comfortably spend an entire evening in a room filled with Republicans. Afterward, he looked surprised and disappointed when I said I'd had fun.

The summer after graduating from high school, I accompanied two school friends, Billy Ray Harrison and Jim Renken, brother of the

Renken sisters, to Detroit to work on the assembly line at Hudson Motor Car Company at Jefferson and Connors. We hoped to earn money for college. We helped assemble "the car you step down into." The phrase referred to a frame design that some other manufacturers soon copied to provide extra passenger safety. The city, with good paying assembly-line jobs, was called the "arsenal of democracy" for its contributions to winning World War II.

We found relatively cheap accommodations in the thriving Brush Park neighborhood not far from downtown. Detroit, approaching two million in population, was riding high before accusations of corruption and drop in property values became prevalent.

My Missouri friends and I learned we probably were not cut out for careers in factory work. Billy Ray Harrison later would graduate from the Air Force Academy. He flew bombers during a military career and retired as a lieutenant colonel. Jim Renken went to work for Southwest Bell Telephone Company and retired as a vice president. His sister, Helen Renken, studied piano and voice at Indiana University, sang in the St. Louis Municipal Opera, and became a successful night club performer under the professional name, "Nancy Knight."

3

Ivy Walls

When I enrolled in Central Missouri State College (later Central Missouri University) in Warrensburg, I was the first in my family to attend college. I earned a limited scholarship by appearing in plays directed by drama professor Irene Freeman. In the first quarter, I performed the role of Nels in "I Remember Mama."

On opening night, a car load of Eldon High students and my high school drama teacher, Ruth Lupardus, surprised me by driving ninety miles from Eldon to see the play.

Professor Freeman taught the Constantin Stanislavski method of acting. We read *An Actor Prepares* and *My Life in Art* by the great Russian director-founder of the Moscow Art Theater, who died in 1938.

Although I passed courses without too much difficulty, I considered my grades to be mediocre until I received help from a college actress. She was a senior with a straight-A record. Her name was Helen Watson. One day I invited her to lunch in the student cafeteria to ask the secret of her academic success.

She said, "I take careful notes, both from textbook reading and lectures. Each night I read through my notes, from beginning to end, for every course. When exams come, I'm ready. I never have to stay up late studying for a test. When other students cram all night, I usually go to an early movie and get a good night's sleep."

I understood how she could read through all notes each day early in the term, but I wondered how she could manage it near the end when, as I put it, "the stack of pages must be very thick."

"If you read your notes every day," she said, "you'll be reviewing them by the end of a term almost as fast as you can turn the pages."

I followed her advice. My grade point average rose dramatically. I even sometimes went to movies on nights before final exams. But, in contrast to Helen Watson, I managed to earn A's in most, but not all, courses.

My college freshmen and sophomore classmates, the last remnant of the "Silent Generation," looked up to juniors and seniors because so many had served in World War II. They had proved they could "get it done." Most males I knew attended college on the G. I. Bill.

After my freshman year, I worked seven days a week during the summer as a lifeguard at a state park beach on a rather isolated arm of Lake of the Ozarks. I shared a barracks with three other lifeguards and the manager of the park's boat marina. The other guards and I began each day cleaning the beach. We then took turns guarding it. Crowds were heavy only on holidays. We most often used a surfboard for rescues.

When off duty, we swam, sailed or read. We had a radio, one of our few entertainments. I remember lying in my bunk one night in late June 1950 listening to the radio describe North Korea's invasion of South Korea. On July 5 the radio said U.S. troops had landed to help the south. As the summer continued, we listened to the radio describe a push by North Korean troops south from the 38th parallel toward Pusan.

On the beach that summer, I decided journalism might be a more practical career for me than acting. For my junior year, I transferred to the School of Journalism at the University of Missouri in Columbia.

The nation's first J-School, it began after the Missouri Press Association vigorously lobbied university trustees and the state legislature. The association's daily and weekly newspaper publishers said they wanted to hire reporters and editors with practical, hands-on training combined with broad liberal education. The new kind of school opened on the University of Missouri campus in 1908. Four years later, Columbia University in New York followed Missouri's lead by starting a graduate journalism program.

I entered Missouri's "J-school" in 1950, because, I thought, I wanted to help write the "first rough draft of history," a phrase I'd heard. At first, the day's news appealed to me far more than accounts of bygone eras. But I soon realized philosopher Santayana and Lord Acton were right: Understanding the present requires knowledge of the past.

Inscribed on a hallway plaque that students passed nearly every day was the "Journalist's Creed" by Walter Williams, the school's first dean. The creed said: "I believe in the profession of journalism. I believe that the public journal is a public trust; that all connected with it are, to the full measure of their responsibility, trustees for the public; that acceptance of a lesser service than public service is betrayal of that trust. . . . I believe that a journalist should write only what he holds in his heart to be true."

Journalism, unlike such "professions" as law or medicine, could not submit to licensing based on educational preparation and adherence to government-approved standards. To escape external control, most journalists agreed with the National Labor Relations Board that called their occupation a "trade." But every journalism student I knew accepted without question Walter Williams' belief that "profession" also can mean receiving pay for a job that provides vital public service and requires a high degree of competence.

Williams' "Journalist's Creed," I became convinced, helped point mainstream

American journalism toward "objectivity" in the early Twentieth Century and away from subjective partisanship. Partisanship began in the colonies in the Eighteenth Century and persisted through the next century's "yellow journalism" period.

Change had been accomplished, at least temporarily, when I entered J-School. At that time, fabricating a story or bending it for political reasons was beyond consideration. Such journalistic integrity declined again afterward. That's when reporter Janet Cooke made up a story for the Washington *Post* about a child heroin addict who did not exist. She appeared to inspire fabricators on several other newspapers. About the same time, many reporters grew comfortable engaging news sources in debate rather than merely asking searching questions.

The Missouri journalism faculty told students they should seek objectivity, a difficult ideal, even if they sometimes failed to attain it. A newspaper's management may take any political position on the editorial page, our professors maintained, if reporters and editors diligently present balanced facts in the news pages. While news media must make money to survive, their first responsibility is informing the public, we were told.

The students I knew chose journalism as their careers for community service. They felt pride at becoming part of the "Fourth Estate," a check on government's legislative, judicial and executive branches. Although they hoped for comfortable lives, none that I knew voiced any fantasies about becoming rich. They assumed they faced careers under deadline pressure for modest but comfortable pay.

Most entered print media, for print hired the largest number of reporters and provided the most time and space for thorough reporting.

Shortly after arriving on the University of Missouri campus, I heard about a talented journalism student one year ahead of me. A former Marine, he performed in campus stage plays while pursuing his degree. People called him "a versatile actor" and "very professional." He took part in productions at the university as well as nearby, all-women's Stephens College. Stephens often hired male actors from as far away as Broadway to take leading roles in public performances opposite its top female theater students.

If a university senior found time to act in plays, I thought, I probably could do the same. So, I went to observe this older journalism student in a stage production. His name was George C. Scott.

Although the name of that play more than a half century ago has escaped my memory, I do recall I recognized immediately that Scott outclassed me in talent. I decided to drop the idea of trying to imitate him. I would concentrate on my J-School courses.

A few days later, I spotted Scott in a journalism hallway and stopped to congratulate him on his performance. His smile and "thank you" had the gracious aplomb of someone already comfortable with his talents being recognized.

He soon left Missouri for Broadway without graduating. He won roles in New York plays for about five years before appearing as a prosecutor stunned by closing testimony in the movie, "Anatomy of a Murder." Later he starred in films "The Hustler,"

"Dr. Strangelove," and "Patton," among others.

The J-School published the *Missourian*, one of two daily newspapers available to residents of the city of Columbia and nearby areas -- perhaps forty-thousand people then. The *Missourian* provided an outstanding teaching tool. It covered local government, politics, business, sports, and cultural events thoroughly. Faculty members filled the newspaper's editing positions, and students did the reporting.

Professor Eugene Sharp, city editor, insisted on detailed accuracy. He intimidated most beginning reporters. He taught us, I thought, why ancient Romans applied the term "editor" to the Coliseum official who decided which wounded gladiators would live or die. But we student reporters eventually lost our fear of Mr. Sharp. We learned he concealed a soft heart.

A debate that Sharp assigned me to cover on November 11, 1951, produced a far-sighted quote. Jesse Wrench, an eccentric, well-loved professor of history, who sometimes wore his long hair in a net, conducted a foreign affairs panel with students from Egypt, Palestine, Syria and Iran before a university and town audience.

The panelists agreed that Great Britain should get out of the Middle East. In my story, I quoted student John Massab of Syria as saying, "If the United States ever takes the place of Britain in the Middle East, the U.S. can expect to receive the same hate from these countries as has Britain in the past." I remembered his words when the United States invaded Iraq in 2003.

Sharp also sent me to interview Blanche Thebom, Metropolitan Opera mezzo-soprano, who arrived in town for a concert. She told me, among other things, that the mental discipline she acquired as a secretary before becoming a singer helped her learn operatic roles. Sharp liked that detail. He told me to cover Thebom's performance before 3,800 people in Brewer Field House the next evening.

Although I had thin knowledge of classical music, I tackled the assignment with gusto. I described her performance of German art songs during the concert's first half and operatic arias in the second half. Then I added, "Miss Thebom wore a brown velvet gown with an off-the-shoulder jewel neckline. Her long hair in braids across her head was entwined with a double string of pearls, and it was easy to imagine her in the great Wagnerian roles she has performed."

Another faculty member, John Philip Norman, assistant city editor, sent me a few days later to cover violinist Nathan Milstein in the same auditorium. I wrote, as I if knew what I was saying, that violinist Milstein played the Sonata in D Minor by Brahms with "beautiful melodic lines."

Not yet discouraged, Norman three weeks later told me to cover a Minneapolis Symphony performance with Antal Dorati conducting.

"The strings opened the program with the brilliant introduction and ensuing turbulent themes of Weber's 'Overture to Euryanthe,' I wrote. "Dorati conducted the overture with a combination of lyricism and triumph."

That was the last classical musical review anyone ever asked me to write.

While a student, I also covered news for the local radio station owned by the Columbia *Daily Tribune*, the city's other newspaper. I helped write early morning newscasts and read on-air copy under the pseudonym "Larry Gil." My real name, I was told, would never work in broadcasting.

The most tumultuous local story I covered for the station was a "panty raid" on women's dormitories and sorority houses conducted by scores of University of Missouri men. Several such raids occurred across the country in 1952 and 1953 at Wisconsin, Northwestern, Minnesota, Vermont, and other campuses. The Missouri raid, probably the most destructive, caused thousands of dollars damage.

I chanced upon the male students on a street corner about 9 p.m. as they gathered into a mob. I followed them as they stormed over the campuses of Missouri University, Stephens College, and across town at Christian College (later called Columbia College). Outnumbered police failed to stop them.

The Missouri men climbed fire escapes and broke into girls' dormitory rooms, where they grabbed panties and bras. I saw men take underclothing off one screaming coed without otherwise harming her.

In some dormitory lobbies, pajama-clad girls formed lines to fight off men trying to enter. Armed with clubs and soda bottles, the girls sometimes succeeded.

About 12:30 in the morning, Columbia Police Chief J. L. Parks addressed the crowd, "Boys, you've torn the Hell out of Columbia. Now go on home and go to bed." The men jeered, but began to disperse.

I wrote a 600-word panty-raid story, long for a radio newscast, before going to bed. After three hours sleep I went before sun-up to the radio newsroom in the Columbia *Tribune* building to help prepare the rest of the early morning newscast. Working with me to put the newscast together was journalism student Mary Prime, who later became an outstanding feature writer and columnist for United Press International in New York.

The *Tribune's* next edition used some information from my eyewitness radio account. Later, when the university expelled fifteen men and suspended 160 others for their roles in the disturbance, I wrote that story for the *Missourian*.

In addition to journalism and required subjects, I enrolled in Philosophy of Science and a few other elective philosophy courses. I also took Introduction to Astronomy, partly because a famous astronomer, Harlow Shapley, graduated from Missouri University in 1911 after working for a Kansas newspaper. Shapley later directed Harvard's astronomy observatory. He proposed accurately that our solar system lay in the Milky Way galaxy's outskirts and that the galaxy's core could be found in the direction of constellation Sagittarius.

My astronomy instructor pitched his class to future scientists rather than students like me trying to fulfill an elective. He surprised me by piling on a lot of mathematics near the end. This time, Helen Watson's study formula did not work so well for me. I passed the course, but my final exam was not pretty.

The Korean War continued when I received my bachelor of journalism degree. I had long advocated a year or two of military or related service for every young person, but Army physicians immediately rejected me. They said a condition called "spondylolisthesis" would eventually require spinal surgery, "probably before you reach the age of thirty."

I received the news with mixed emotions. Glad to look for a job instead of being drafted, I also felt miffed that the Army did not want me. I would later welcome military-related assignments as a reporter. Much later, when I entered college teaching, I supported ROTC programs on campus, in contrast to some faculty members.

But the army physicians were wrong. I never required back surgery.

I headed for Hawaii in 1952, hoping to land my first full-time daily newspaper job in relative proximity to the Korean Conflict. The territory's tropical climate and its efforts to gain statehood also attracted me. I had saved a little money from my jobs as janitor, lifeguard, assembly line worker, and part-time *Autogram* employee. I also received a small "loan" from my parents.

Gingerly wading mud, Gilleland inspects cave-in threatening highway near Wolf River bridge on one of his first reporting assignments in Memphis. (The Commercial Appeal photo)

27

4

The Banyan Tree

Before looking for a full-time job in Hawaii, I visited the outer islands. On the Big Island, I found an isolated beach and swam in the warm Pacific before hitching a ride with two geologists up Mauna Kea. It is a 13,800-foot dormant volcano on which ancient Hawaiians worshipped a snow goddess. If measurement includes its base beneath the surf, the mountain is the world's highest at 32,696 feet.

The geologists' four-wheel drive vehicle rose on narrow asphalt and gravel roads above sugarcane fields, cattle pastures, shrub land, and high snow line. Near the top, the scientists examined samples of volcanic rock. They explained that volcanic activity enlarges the Big Island while pushing the younger, smaller islands of Maui, Molokai, Oahu and Kauai to the north at a fraction of an inch each year. One geologist said he heard that an astronomical observatory and a ski run might be built someday above the clouds on Mauna Kea.

He proved correct. Skiing soon joined surfing as a local sport. By the year 2000, NASA, the University of Hawaii and other institutions built a dozen telescopes, including Keck I, Keck II and Subaru.

After enjoying Mauna Kea's magnificent view toward the east, the geologists and I moved around the top of the volcano until we could see the opposite coastline. Afternoon mists had not yet accumulated. The geologists pointed out farms below us growing millions of dollars worth of Kona coffee trees. Some coffee farms had been started in the early Twentieth Century by Japanese immigrants.

I returned to sea level where I mixed with the town of Hilo's residents in crowded shops and restaurants. The relaxed, unpretentious intermingling of the community's Asians, Polynesians, whites and blacks heightened Hawaii's mystery and beauty in my eyes.

On the island of Maui, I met "Jazz" Belnap, publisher and editor of the Maui *News* in the town of Wailuku. Because I asked him a lot of questions about the island and his business, he invited me to attend a political rally he wanted to cover the next day for his newspaper.

The rally took place outdoors several miles from town on a sugarcane plantation. Hundreds of people attended. They represented plantation workers and various races and social classes. Most women wore long muumuus. A few men and women arrived barefoot.

Candidates for local and territorial offices took turns making campaign speeches. A monitor with a stopwatch sat at a table. Each speaker made his or her pitch in ten minutes. When time was up, the monitor promptly rang a loud bell. Immediately, hula dancers jumped to their feet and musicians picked up ukuleles and drums. They performed longer than each politician spoke. Then the master of ceremonies introduced another speaker. To hear about twenty candidates took nearly the entire day.

As I prepared to leave Wailuku three days later, Belnap said: "No relative of mine appears interested in this newspaper. If you join me in putting it out, work hard, and do a good job, the newspaper could possibly be yours when I retire or die."

I considered his offer overnight. I turned him down because Maui reminded me too much of rural Missouri where I grew up -- except that Maui had palm trees. A country boy from the Osage Valley, I yearned for a city. I thanked Belnap for his confidence and headed for Honolulu.

I often wondered later if I made the right decision. In my middle age, I read about Belnap's death and sale if his newspaper for millions of dollars.

I also pondered wistfully the scientific news generated by several powerful telescopes that opened atop the Big Island's Mauna Kea and Maui's Haleakala volcano. In 2006, the Air Force, the Smithsonian, and University of Hawaii, among others, funded the Pan-Starrs telescope on Haleakala. It was scheduled to look for variable stars in distant galaxies and to track wayward objects in the solar system that someday might strike Earth.

After leaving Maui, I visited Honolulu's downtown public library. I asked a bright-looking reference librarian which of the two local daily newspapers she preferred. She said, "A lot of people would say the *Star Bulletin*, but I like the *Advertiser*. I prefer its local news coverage."

I'd heard the account of the *Advertiser's* press breaking down the night before Japan's attack on Pearl Harbor eleven years earlier, frustrating the newspaper for twenty-four hours from reporting the biggest story in Hawaii's history. The newspaper got back in operation on December 8 by borrowing presses of a local Japanese language newspaper.

I walked outside the library, hailed a cab, and headed for the *Advertiser* building on Kapiolani Boulevard.

The building's beaux-arts style, its tall radio tower on the roof, and its prominent, elegant indoor fountain impressed me. I studied names on the wall directory. I'd heard of only one – Lorrin P. Thurston, president and publisher. Rather than seek out the managing editor upstairs, as most reporting job seekers would do, I decided on a whim to go to Thurston's ground-floor office. His secretary told me he would be back within an hour if I wished to wait.

The publisher, descended from an early missionary family and from the newspaper's founder, had been in charge of the *Advertiser* when the Japanese attacked Pearl Harbor. It was he who had given Hawaii's governor permission to use the newspaper's radio station on December 7 to proclaim a state of emergency.

When I told Mr. Thurston on his return that I was looking for a job, he invited me into his office. He looked at my résumé and said, "A relative of mine has been accepted as a student at Stephens College in Columbia. I've never been there. What can you tell me about it?"

Knowing something about Stephens, I relaxed. I described it as one of the country's oldest and best women's colleges, having begun in the early 1800s -- about the time New England missionaries arrived in Hawaii. I said the college's performing arts program had an outstanding reputation. I explained how Stephens College sometimes hired male professionals to act on stage with female theater majors. I even mentioned George C. Scott – whose name Thurston had not yet heard.

I told about the well-known Stephens equestrian program. I left out the panty raid I'd witnessed on its campus. (I also declined to bring up the legend of the Stephens College "ghost" -- the spirit of a female student presumably roaming the campus since the Civil War while mourning her soldier lover.)

When I paused, Thurston said: "I don't know if the news department has an opening or not, but I'll call up there and see if someone can talk to you." Upstairs, the managing editor asked questions and then said I could have a job covering the "territorial beat," plus occasional general assignments, for sixty dollars a week. I immediately said yes, for that was the most I'd ever earned. My beat included office of the governor and territorial executive branches.

Among those welcoming me to the *Advertiser* newsroom was reporter Bob Krauss. Krauss, a Midwesterner six years older than I, had been covering Honolulu's waterfront and labor activities for several months. At his invitation, we had a couple of drinks under the impressive old banyan tree behind the Moana Hotel on Waikiki beach.

Bob explained that the banyan, a huge type of fig, lives for centuries and expands in size by sending out "aerial roots" that become multiple trunks.

He seemed curious about everything in the islands. Covering the waterfront, he had collected abundant yarns about Hawaii leaders and ordinary people. Born in Nebraska, Bob grew up in Kansas, graduated in journalism from the University of Minnesota, and served in the Navy in World War II. He liked to talk about Polynesians arriving in canoes to settle Hawaii. They came about 500 A.D. from the Marquesas and later from Tahiti. He described Chief Kamehameha I's 1810 consolidation of all the islands under his rule.

Bob also related details of the arrival of New England missionaries about 1820 and their acquisition of prime land. He explained how descendants of missionaries served on interlocking boards of Hawaii's Big Five firms that controlled the sugarcane and pineapple industries. Four of the firms -- Alexander & Baldwin, Castle & Cooke, C. Brewer, and Amfac -- also owned the Matson Navigation Company and Waikiki's Royal Hawaiian and Moana Hotels.

From the banyan tree, Krauss and I walked to nearby Lau Yee Chai restaurant, where we ate Chinese food and he interrogated me about my ambitions. I detected a bit of

Under a Waikiki banyan tree, Gilleland listens to veteran newsman Bob Krauss describe Hawaii's early settlement. There Gilleland also met founders of the church where a boy called "Barry" attended Sunday school before becoming U. S. president. (photo: Bob Krauss)

impatience on his part that I had not yet set journalistic goals. He soon revealed that he had done so carefully.

When we left the restaurant, Krauss pointed out some paintings on velvet by Edgar Leeteg of Tahiti on display at a Waikiki art shop. The portraits, mostly buxom Polynesian women or aged men in native dress, carried price tags up to several hundred dollars -- too much for my pocket book. In rich colors and appearing almost three-dimensional, the paintings were unlike any I had ever seen, although cheap imitations soon became prevalent.

Krauss described Leeteg as a Midwesterner, born in St. Louis, who migrated to Tahiti during the Depression. Honolulu art gallery owner Bernard Davis discovered Leeteg and promoted him as "the American Gauguin." Within months of my introduction to his paintings, Leeteg died at age 49 in a Tahiti motorcycle crash.

Every time I walked through Waikiki I stopped to admire his work.

A few weeks after the dinner at Lau Yee Chai's, the *Advertiser* assigned Krauss to write a five-day-a-week column called "In One Ear." His column gained immediate success. He entertained readers with his local stories, both serious and humorous. He described his own adventures in the islands, such as walking around Oahu's 125-mile perimeter with no money in his pockets -- and, in those days, no credit card.

While still a bachelor, he wrote tongue-in-cheek that Hawaii mothers "have it easy" and complain about hard work only to get husbands to wash dishes. Thirty women threw down gauntlets, offering chores in their homes to put Krauss to a test. He accepted the challenge of a woman with four small children. Getting ready for the task, he complained to his readers that a mother has nine months to prepare while he had only one weekend.

He described his household tasks and admitted dismay at fixing dinners, cleaning rooms, changing diapers, and "taking little girls to the men's room" during a trip to the zoo. In 1956 *Time* magazine featured his plight. His readers loved him. Krauss eventually married, had a daughter of his own, and wrote thousands of columns and fourteen books about Hawaii and the Pacific. He died at 83 in 2006.

Lorrin P. Thurston, the Honolulu *Advertiser* publisher who hired me, inherited the newspaper from his father, Lorrin A. Thurston. Lorrin A. came from a missionary family that shaped much of Hawaii's history. He served one of Kamehameha's successors, King Kalakaua, as interior minister before drafting what was called the "Bayonet Constitution." Thurston and a militia armed by plantation owners put the constitution in place in 1887. It stripped the king of most of his executive powers. Queen Liliuokalani, with diluted authority, followed Kalakaua to the throne.

In 1893, backed by Marines and sailors from an American ship, Thurston and pineapple grower Sanford Dole led a "Citizens Committee of Public Safety" that overthrew the queen and ended the royal kingdom. They set up a temporary republic. Also prominent in the queen's ouster was William Owen Smith, another missionary descendant, who had served in her cabinet.

Thurston saw future annexation of the islands by the United States as a way of avoiding duties Hawaiian companies paid on sugar shipped to the mainland. Thurston headed a delegation to Washington, D. C., to testify before Congress. Their presentation led to official United States recognition of a provisional Hawaiian government under control of island haoles (Caucasians). Lorrin A. Thurston declined the provisional government's presidency. Instead, he bought a newspaper – the morning Honolulu *Advertiser*. Sanford Dole became the islands' provisional president.

As one of its first acts, the provisional government put down a revolt by Oahu residents seeking to reinstate Queen Liliuokalani. The government placed her under house arrest for eight months. During confinement she wrote the classic Hawaiian song, "Aloha Oe" (Farewell to Thee).

Congress made Hawaii a United States territory in 1900, and all its citizens became U. S. citizens. Dole's title changed from provisional president to territorial governor. A Hawaiian Homes Commission Act assigned about two-hundred thousand acres of former royal Crown lands, a fraction of the total, for lease at nominal fees to kanakas, commoners with fifty percent or more Hawaiian-Polynesian blood.

A marriage that joined William Owen Smith's family with the Thurstons produced Thurston Twigg-Smith, the publisher's nephew. He'd soon be my boss.

I had been with the newspaper a few days when I first heard his name. Gossip around the office said "Twigg," as he was called, would join the newsroom. A Yale graduate, he had worked five or six years in all other newspaper departments "to learn the business from ground up." He would serve a while in the newsroom, according to rumor, before succeeding his uncle, Lorrin P. Thurston, as publisher.

When I reported for work early one morning, Twigg sat at the copy desk, not yet functioning for the day. He was talking to Raymond Coll, the longtime editor in chief. Coll was nearing retirement. Twigg, in his 30s, greeted each newsroom staff member in a friendly, relaxed manner.

Trim, of medium height, he had a crew cut and twinkling, confident eyes. He displayed a subtle sense of humor and a quick mind. After graduating from Yale, he earned a Bronze Star as an army officer in Europe in World War II. He also held the rank of major in a Hawaii National Guard artillery unit he helped organize after the war.

He learned quickly. In only a few weeks, Twigg started making decisions as city editor and, for the most part, did a good job.

When I began covering state offices in what was called the "territorial beat," Oren Long served as Hawaii's governor, the tenth since Governor Dole in 1900. President Eisenhower, on winning the 1952 national election, appointed Samuel W. King to be Hawaii's eleventh governor.

As a reporter, I called on the governor's office in old Iolani Palace, which King Kalakaua built in the late 1800s and Queen Liliuokalani had occupied. Governor King, who dealt with a lot of reporters in his career, received me with business-like courtesy. King had represented the territory as Republican delegate to Congress in the 1930s before serving as a World War II Navy captain.

My early stories about him as governor included his cabinet appointments. Among them, he named Neil Blaisdell, a pineapple company executive, to be director of public welfare. King recommended to President Eisenhower that Farrant L. Turner be named Secretary of Hawaii.

Islanders liked Turner. He had commanded the famous Japanese-American 442nd

Regimental Combat Team in World War II as a lieutenant colonel. As Secretary of Hawaii, with an office in Washington, he acted as liaison between the governor and the U.S. president and his Secretary of Interior.

Generally mild mannered, Governor King minced no words in my presence about his dislike for Jack W. Hall, regional director of the International Longshoremen's and Warehouse Union. Hall was under federal indictment. The governor felt sure Hall was "a communist." King said Hall should be convicted in a federal trial that had dragged on in Honolulu for months. Hall and union associates, called the "Hawaii Seven," were charged with violating the federal Smith Act by conspiring to overthrow the government by force or violence. Their union included workers on shipping docks and on sugar and pineapple plantations. Most were Filipinos and Japanese.

The Hawaii Seven case was Hawaii's counterpart of the West Coast trial of ILWU boss Harry Bridges. Also making headlines at the same time were hunts for "subversives" on the mainland by Senator Joseph McCarthy and by the House Un-American Activities Committee.

When not in court, the tall, thin Jack Hall, then in his mid 30s, occasionally could be seen walking around Waikiki or going in and out of the ILWU's local union building at 451 Atkinson Drive. That's where I met him.

I first went to the ILWU building because the union let a local jazz band use it at night or on Sundays for public concerts. I liked to attend the concerts, which featured Dixieland. I wrote a story about the band, and the newspaper displayed it prominently. Jazz performances drew many Honolulu residents whose love of music overpowered any political reluctance to enter an ILWU building.

I formed no firm opinion about whether Wisconsin-born Jack Hall violated the Smith Act or not. But he impressed me by initiating classes to teach ILWU members the history of their union. Organizations of all kinds, good or bad, I thought, would probably benefit if members knew their own histories.

A jury convicted Hall and the Hawaii Seven in 1953. But the defendants disappointed Governor King by winning on appeal. The U. S. Court of Appeals said the federal prosecution had focused too much on defendants' beliefs rather than any overt acts. The U. S. Supreme Court issued a similar decision in the Harry Bridges case on the mainland.

5

Ike, Harry, Margaret

City editor Twigg-Smith occasionally sent me to intercept cruise ships at sea to interview celebrities and other visitors before they disembarked at Honolulu.

I most often met the SS Lurline, a Matson Company ship, and the SS President Wilson of the American President Line. (It was a Lurline radio operator, just prior to December 7, 1941, who first heard ominous messages from a Japanese fleet approaching Hawaii.)

At daybreak eleven years later, a newspaper photographer, an older reporter and I boarded a tugboat that took us to meet the arriving Lurline several miles out to sea. We carried a ship passenger list.

As the Lurline drew near, it slowed slightly to permit us to jump from the tugboat through an open hatchway in the big ship's hull several feet above the water. Because most cruise passengers by that time had left their cabins in anticipation of arrival, finding specific persons was sometimes difficult, but we usually succeeded. We had at least two hours or more to do our jobs before the ship docked.

The newspaper designated me to be its only reporter sent to a ship when interviewees ranged from ordinary people to some entertainment celebrities, such as Don McNeill of the network "Breakfast Club" show. When U.S. presidents were on board, I accompanied an older, more experienced newsman. The senior reporter usually wrote the main story, but gave me opportunity to ask a few questions and write sidebars. This occurred when newly elected President Dwight Eisenhower and ex-President Harry Truman arrived on separate occasions.

Truman, in my presence, defended his firing of General Douglas MacArthur early in the Korean conflict for criticizing the president's reluctance to bomb Manchuria. Truman said he thought striking Manchuria might draw the Soviet Union into the fighting.

I told President Eisenhower I had covered his appointees Oren Long and Samuel

King and that the people of Hawaii liked both governors. He smiled without appearing overly impressed with my judgment. On other subjects, Eisenhower repeated the pledge he'd made during his 1952 election campaign to go to Korea to negotiate the war's end.

After asking the presidents what I considered my allotment of questions, I went off alone, on separate occasions, to find their wives, Mamie Eisenhower and Bess Truman, and the Trumans' daughter, Margaret. Mamie and Bess mostly talked about places they looked forward to visiting in the islands.

I obtained my best quotes from 29-year-old Margaret, fresh from concerts and TV appearances as a singer. Aboard the Lurline I found her reading a magazine on a deck chair not far from her cabin. She wore expensive tailored slacks and a colorful flowered blouse. She was more attractive, I thought, than news photos taken at her vocal concerts and TV appearances.

I introduced myself as a reporter who wanted to ask her some questions. When I told her I had met her father and mother earlier that morning, she smiled and said, "Pull up a chair."

Foremost in my mind as I sat down was her father's threat two years earlier to beat up a Washington *Post* music critic who disliked one of her performances. "She's often flat," the critic had written.

I avoided that topic. It was old news. I decided to focus on Margaret's future. But she insisted on asking me the first questions.

"How long have you been a reporter?" "Do you like it?" "Do you meet every ship?" "Where did you go to college?"

When I said "at Mizzou," she said, "You're a Missourian?" as if surprised to find another in mid-ocean so far from home. I said I also had attended Missouri's Eldon High School. "I know Eldon," she said. "It's an easy drive from Independence, where I grew up."

When I finally got to question her, she said she had been a history major at George Washington University in the nation's capital and that she planned to write books, including histories. She said she still loved music but writing books interested her more.

This was the first I'd heard of her plan to change careers. She said a history of the White House topped her list of topics. Next, she mentioned biographies of first ladies and crime and espionage novels.

The thought of Margaret Truman creating convincing spy stories surprised me until I remembered that her father had overseen creation of the Central Intelligence Agency only a few years earlier.

Although I doubted the president had ever shared any top secrets with her, she had probably heard numerous White House conversations about espionage and national security. With a half-serious grin, she said, "I also may write about a recent Missouri University journalism graduate who's caught snooping around Washington politicians." We both laughed, she louder than I.

Margaret later married E. Clifton Daniel, a reporter for the New York *Times*. He became the newspaper's managing editor under executive editor Turner Catledge.

In later years, she wrote more than thirty books, including successful murder and spy mysteries. Titles included *Murder in the CIA, Murder at the Pentagon, Murder at the Library of Congress, Murder at the National Cathedral, Murder at Union Station,* and *Murder at the Kennedy Center,* among others.

I was flattered at first on reading *Murder in the CIA,* for Margaret portrayed the long-time boyfriend of the protagonist, a female government agent, as a University of Missouri journalism graduate. But he was very handsome and employed by a magazine, not a newspaper. His name in the novel was Vern Wheatley.

Each time the Lurline tied up in Honolulu, the Matson Company invited all local newsmen and newswomen aboard to gather in the "Barnacle Club" on a lower deck. Attendants served us free coffee, Bloody Marys and snacks. The club's printed rules said members and guests should "keep conversation elevated -- at least as high as the table top."

6

Banzai

Hawaii provided my first military-related assignment. When the aircraft carrier Philippine Sea returned briefly from the Korean conflict with a damaged twenty-ton propeller, my newspaper dispatched me to Pearl Harbor about daybreak to board the ship.

I was told to observe and report a risky maneuver. For the first time, the carrier's forty planes would be launched while the ship was at rest rather than heading into the wind at sea to provide extra lift.

To repair the propeller, the heavy carrier had to be moved to a dry dock and reduced in weight. Removing planes by cranes would consume too many hours. The Navy, with a war to fight, wanted to hurry. Catapult launching would take less than an hour. The planes were F4U Corsairs and Douglas AD attack bombers.

Prior to the launch, I enjoyed a leisurely cruise on the carrier's deck through Pearl Harbor waters until it reached its destination -- the facility where the USS Enterprise and other ships had been repaired often during Pacific action in World War II.

Aboard the Philippine Sea, I was permitted to mix with crew and pilots as long as I adhered to certain safety rules. I heard an air operations officer say, "The planes have been idle several days, and anything can happen." Late in the morning a loud speaker announced, "Command all stations for launching aircraft."

Commander A. J. Holderman adjusted his crash helmet and said, "This is a good trick, taking off while the carrier isn't moving." Then he climbed into the first F4U Corsair. Extra pressure was fed to the hydraulic catapults. While hundreds of crew members, a few photographers and I stood watching, the catapults yanked the planes into the air at 52-second intervals. It all appeared routine until the last plane, an attack bomber, raced off the bow.

Its engine stalled.

Exclamations went up from the crash crew.

38

For a suspenseful moment, the plane dipped toward the waves until Lt. H. E. Wolking got the engine started again. With inches to spare, the plane gradually rose above the water and flew away. All planes landed at Barber's Point on Oahu to await the ship's repair.

With renovated propeller, the Philippine Sea returned to battle. After the war, the Navy began replacing hydraulic with more powerful steam-driven catapults. Years later I read that the Philippine Sea had been cut up for scrap.

Peace negotiations began near Korea's 38th parallel between North Korea and China on one side and the United States and United Nations on the other. While these negotiations plodded along, the French in Indochina, two-thousand miles to the southwest, tried to re-establish the century-long colonial grip on Indochina that they lost in World War II. The Honolulu newspapers covered Korea well while giving relatively little attention to Vietnam until the battle of Dien Bien Phu, which ended France's dominance in Indochina since the late Nineteenth Century. Military action there soon would draw the United States into another war.

A key element in the French plan called for turning Dien Bien Phu, a small airfield near a rice-growing village in mountains west of Hanoi, into a secure military base for defeating the communist Viet Minh.

I interviewed a number of military officers stopping in Honolulu en route to and from Korea during and after that conflict. One, Capt. Zach Dean, a P-38 pilot, was the last American prisoner of war repatriated at Panmunjom after the July 27, 1953 armistice. He had been shot down near Pyongyang. He complained to me that he had endured long interrogations over two years by Korean and Chinese captors. They also forced him to read works by Karl Marx and Mao Tse Tung six hours a day. It was the worst part of the ordeal, he said.

Power for Peace

The H[...]

To Reach All Departments
Telephone 52977

LAST REPATRIATED PRISONER—Capt. Zach Dean, a 34-year-old air force pilot who was the last Allied prisoner to reach American soil after the Korean prisoner exchange, arrived in Honolulu yesterday from Japan with his wife. After his plane was shot down in North Korea, he was a prisoner for more than two years. Capt. and Mrs. Dean are en route home to Douglas, Kans. (Advertiser photo.)

Forced to Study Red Books, Says Ex-POW

By LaRUE GILLELAND

Capt. Zach Dean, 34, the last American prisoner and the only air force pilot the Reds repatriated at Panmunjom, told reporters at Ft. DeRussy yesterday he was forced to study Communist literature "six hours a day for 18 months" in a Chinese POW camp.

Capt. Dean was captured by Communists on April 22, 1951 when his F-51 jet plane was shot down about 50 miles northeast of Pyongyang. The pilot was held prisoner for two years and four days. He arrived in Honolulu yesterday morning with his wife from Tokyo, where she was a former Red Cross social worker.

A TALL, soft-spoken man from Douglas, Kansas, Capt. Dean said he and other Allied prisoners-of-war were put in classrooms where they had to read and discuss books by Mao Tse Tung, Howard Fast, Marx, Engels and Stalin. He said the Communists had an "extensive library" for the prisoners to use.

They were told, he said, that the Red totalitarian government is actually "benevolent" in the long run. That its aim is to make the world a happier place to live.

What affect did this instruction have on Capt. Dean? "I learned not to trust anything they said," he declared.

CAPT. DEAN SAID these classroom lectures and discussion periods were discontinued about six months ago after "a Russian diplomat" asserted in the UN that Allied prisoners were not being forced to study Communist literature.

Capt. Dean, an Air Force pilot for 15 years who flew a P-38 in the southwest Pacific during World War II, said among the other things, he suffered from dysentery while he was a prisoner.

What kind of medical care did he get? The blue-eyed, 177-pound pilot knocked ashes off his cigarette and said, "It wasn't very good."

After he walked across the prisoner exchange line in Korea on April 26, he was placed under hospital treatment in Japan. He is the last of the recently freed sick and wounded POW's to leave Japan.

HE SAID HE WAS a friend of Cpl. Susumu Shinagawa of Kauai, another American prisoner who returned to Hawaii the first of this month. "We were in adjoining camps for some time," he said.

Capt. Dean told of one humorous incident during his bleak captivity. That was in the summer of 1951 when Allied prisoners in his camp sent the Reds a signed petition asking them to spare the life of a pet pig called "Elmer." Elmer was the only pig out of several inside the camp that had not been killed for food. He was a favorite of the prisoners.

It was about this same time that the Communists were putting on their "Save the Julius Rosenbergs" campaign. As a joke, the Allied POW's sent the Reds a petition which read, "Save Elmer." The Communists, not wishing to cause an unnecessary disturbance among the POWs, allowed them to keep Elmer. However, Capt. Dean added, the pig died of pneumonia a week later.

THE SON OF a Kansas oil man, Capt. Dean and his wife Abigail, whom he met on Okinawa, will return to Douglas after they spend a "three or four day honeymoon here," as he put it.

He explained that he was sent to Korea only a few days after they were married in Tokyo on Dec. 14, 1950. Several weeks later, while out to bomb a North Korean railroad tunnel on his 70th mission, he was blasted out of the air by ground fire.

"This is the first opportunity we've had to be alone since I was captured," he said.

40

Shortly after the armistice was signed on July 27, 1953, Yu C. Yang, South Korea's ambassador to the United States, made a stopover in Honolulu. He told me that he feared the armistice would lull America and the United Nations into a false sense of security.

When Japanese-Americans of World War II's most highly decorated military unit assembled on Oahu for a reunion dinner, they invited the newspaper to send a reporter as their guest. I received the assignment.

Members of the 100th Battalion, 442 Regimental Combat Team had suffered high casualties and won hundreds of combat medals despite widespread discrimination directed at them because of their ancestry. Known as the "Go for Broke" unit, it had fought through Italy and France and rescued a U.S. "Lost Battalon" in France's Vosges Mountains.

During the war, the federal government placed mainland relatives of many of the soldiers in barbed-wire concentration camps. Instead of giving the Nisei battalion a "1st," "2nd," or "3rd" designation customary throughout the Army, the government called the unit the "100th Battalion," distinguishing its racial makeup, some said.

The Army appointed a Caucasian as the Japanese-American unit's top commander. Despite bravery of the 100th in helping capture Rome, the unit was diverted from joining other American soldiers in that city's liberation ceremonies.

At the battalion's reunion I attended in 1953, these men laughed a lot, offered toasts and told stories. They spoke with pride of wartime service to their country. They gave genial applause to a brief speech by Secretary of Hawaii Farrant Turner, their commanding officer during much of the war. He was the only Caucasian other than me that I remember at the banquet that night.

At low tables where scores of Nisei veterans and I sat, waiters kept everyone's sake glass filled. It was my first taste of Sake. I liked it. Every few minutes, one of the Nisei stood up and made a toast. Shouts of "Banzai," "Banzai!" filled the room -- the traditional exclamation in Japanese before an "honorable" surprise attack.

I saw Daniel Inouye at the next table raise a glass with his one arm remaining from World War II. I asked him if he remembered kids trying to sell snacks a decade earlier when the train taking his unit to basic training made a stop in Eldon, Missouri. He said in his direct, cordial manner that he remembered traveling through Missouri, but reminded me he saw little because of orders to keep blinds pulled.

As a lieutenant, Inouye led a charge on a German machine gun nest in Italy, receiving a massive wound to his right arm. He used his left hand to pry loose a grenade gripped firmly in his right fingers. With his left hand he tossed the grenade toward the Germans and wiped out the nest with his submachinegun. Medics later amputated his right arm.

On release from a hospital back in the states, he decided, with one arm, to study law in college, instead of medicine and surgery. He entered a barbershop for a haircut to be told, "We don't serve Japs."

Mr. Inouye served in both houses of Hawaii's legislature before becoming the new state of Hawaii's first delegate to Congress in 1959, and he began more than forty years of distinguished service as a Democratic U.S. senator. He received the Medal of Honor for his combat record. He co-founded a bank.

After observing so much good will among 100th Battalion veterans, I found myself a few days later amid a cantankerous group of mental hospital physicians. I sometimes questioned the mental health of these mental health practitioners. A group of unhappy staff members at the Territorial Hospital at Kaneohe wanted to get rid of their young medical director, Dr. Robert A. Kimmich. I wrote stories about the dispute and covered a hearing at which opponents presented charges against him.

Two hospital physicians opposing him had resigned. Three remaining physicians wanted him replaced. They said, among other things, that he often instilled distrust of older staff immediately upon welcoming new members at the airport. One said Kimmich tried to get a new physician inducted into the army by writing a letter to his draft board.

Kimmich survived the scrutiny, despite the hearings and my stories about them. He kept his job, probably learning a little patience in his efforts to improve the hospital staff.

Three years later he published a detailed account in a medical journal of the history of Hawaii's treatment of the mentally ill. His research went back to days when the royal kingdom locked up some of its insane with prison inmates and placed others under care of the natives' priestly Kahuna. The Kahuna treated the sick of mind or body with herbs and a massage technique called "lomilomi."

In my spare time, I swam and worked out at Honolulu's newly-built Central YMCA on Atkinson Drive, near the ILWU hall, two or three times a week. It was the first place I lived in Honolulu before getting a small apartment in nearby Waikiki.

I maintained membership in the Y and became casually acquainted with a long-time, middle-aged resident named Stanley C. Van Dyke. I'd often seen him in the lobby or lounging beside the outdoor pool. Cordial and distinguished looking, he walked with two canes with which he moved along rather well.

Sitting beside the pool where I often swam, he sometimes asked questions about my newspaper job. When I inquired about his background, he gave courteous but evasive answers. I learned only that he had been "in business" in California. He appeared always to be alone. I never saw him swim.

About six months after meeting him I came across a surprising two-paragraph item inside the newspaper while sipping my morning coffee. It said Van Dyke's corpse had been found. A fisherman discovered the body, clothed in swimming trunks, in the surf off Honolulu's Ala Moana Park. The story identified Van Dyke only by name and YMCA address.

On arriving at work, I told the wire service editor I thought United Press should be asked to check out Van Dyke in California. The editor took my suggestion.

The next day a UP story about Van Dyke appeared at the top of the front page. It described him as a former oil company executive who had been president of the Pasadena Chamber of Commerce and chairman of Pasadena's annual Tournament of Roses football game and parade. A private plane crash had injured his legs a few years earlier, the story said. His fall from prominence came after Pasadena police arrested him on a charge of chronic alcoholism. The UP story said he had been divorced twice and had a college-age daughter living on the mainland.

The Honolulu coroner said Van Dyke died of drowning, but could not determine whether he had committed suicide. Police said that three months earlier, in what they called a swimming accident, he had been pulled from the surf near the same spot where the fisherman spotted his lifeless body.

My short stay at the YMCA prompted a short article about Allan Robertson, the executive secretary of the Central YMCA in Honolulu and a brief history of the YMCA.

Four Familiar Letters:

Many Men View YMCA As True Life Philosophy

By LARUE GILLELAND

Above a noisy street corner in nearly any big American city towers, an inconspicuous building from which hang four familiar letters—YMCA.

To thousands of persons who elbow their way past the structure, the letters stand for a hotel without private baths or a gymnasium where a business man can get a workout after office hours. To others the sign recalls a similar building they may have seen in any one of 77 countries.

* * *

BUT TO MANY MEN, such as Allan Robertson, executive secretary of the Central YMCA on Atkinson Drive, "YMCA" means a philosophy of life.

Mr. Robertson, who was born 41 years ago in Winnepeg, Canada, manages the $1,205,000 Central YMCA which opened in 1951 as one of the most modern Ys in the world. Under his direction, membership in the first year jumped from six to 1800 persons.

Mr. Robertson

"The YMCA should offer young men clean rooms away from home and provide them with good athletic equipment, but if they don't catch something else, something spiritual, we're not offering much more than a body building club," Mr. Robertson declared.

* * *

MR. ROBERTSON started making up his mind regarding his careeer at the age of 10 when he visited a YMCA camp on Turkey Foot Lake in Ohio. As a result, he holds one of the few jobs calling for the cool tact of a hotel manager, a minister's desire to perform service to humanity, and an interest in sports.

One of his favorite topics is the story of the YMCA. He enjoys telling how a 23-year old country boy went to work in a London drapery store in 1841 and was appalled at the way city boys lived.

To drapery store clerk George Williams, wicked, stale-aired London contrasted sharply with the out-of-door life he had known back on the farm.

* * *

"THAT WAS DURING the middle of the industrial revolution when London was tense and nervous with its overstuffed population," Mr. Robertson said.

The country boy had a great deal of religious zeal and it didn't take him long to see that London offered young men a chance to gratify about everything except intellectual, athletic and religious desires.

One day the clerk got 11 of his friends together in an upstairs room and they all agreed to form an informal association to promote "the spiritual and mental improvement" of other young drapery clerks.

George's roommate got to his feet, cleared his throat, and said he had a good name in mind for the organization.

"Let's call ourselves the Young Men's Christian Association," he said.

* * *

MR. ROBERTSON said, "It's significant that in 1869, just 25 years later, another group of men in Hawaii met at the home of Peter Cushman Jones and founded the Honolulu Young Men's Christian Association."

Mr. Robertson is responsible for directing the many services his organization offers to people.

Men and women from all over the city gather each week at 401 Atkinson Drive to learn a gamut of skills from how to develop a good photograph to a new tango step. Men practice almost everything from weaving baskets to improving their crawl strokes.

* * *

THE CENTRAL YMCA sponsers Father and Son clubs, a health service, cultural programs and an attractive chapel, all of which make the red neon sign out in front stand for much more than a body building club.

44

One day, heading for an interview at Honolulu Academy of Arts, rain greeted me as I stepped outside the newspaper building. Another man, heading for a destination beyond the academy, offered to share his cab. During the ride I found he could be a character out of a James Hilton novel. He had suffered amnesia for eighteen years.

He regained his memory several days earlier in a Honolulu hospital. He said he had difficulty realizing the year was not 1934.

When he woke up, he said, the last thing he remembered was living in Burbank, California. Automobiles suddenly appeared bigger and more streamlined. Clothing, especially women's, looked different. World War II had come and gone. In the past few days, he said, authorities had traced him to several parts of the world. But they had found none of his relatives or friends in Burbank.

When brought to the hospital, he said, he had some money in his billfold. X-rays showed that during or before his long amnesia he had received more than one severe blow to his head. He had improved enough in the hospital that physicians permitted him to travel about Honolulu for a few hours during the day, with plenty of hospital identification in his possession. They wanted him back at night for a while.

I thought I had stumbled across a better story than I expected to get at the Academy of Arts. When I told him I worked for a newspaper, he became upset. In the cab's back seat, he begged me not to write about him, for he said he could not yet cope with it emotionally.

Our cab arrived at the academy. I gritted my teeth, got out of the car, and said, "I won't even ask you your name." I shut the door and walked off.

A tiny newspaper story announced the scheduled stopover in Honolulu of young evangelist Billy Graham en route to South Korea to speak to American troops. The evangelist was rapidly becoming a world figure. The story caught my attention because I remembered that I'd heard about him for the first time from Bob Scrivner, my high school classmate. That had been about three years earlier when we both returned to Eldon from separate colleges for a Christmas holiday. The evangelist's career, Scrivner said, influenced his decision to study for the Southern Baptist ministry.

I told editor Twigg that if no one had been assigned to cover Graham's Honolulu visit, I'd like to do it. I figured Bob Scrivner would be pleased, if I ever saw him again. Twigg did not like the idea. He made it plain he did not want me to divert attention from my regular beat.

I decided that I'd do the story on my own time. I did some library research on Graham and came across his picture. Among a few newspaper clippings, I found one in which President Truman called Graham a "publicity seeker."

The evangelist arrived in Honolulu by Pan American. Photographers and hula dancers in grass skirts greeted his plane, as they did most tourist flights. The dancers covered the necks of passengers, including Graham, with flower leis.

He stayed at the Royal Hawaiian Hotel and planned to dine with friends at a Waikiki Beach restaurant.

Leaving work about 9:30 p.m., I learned from a Royal Hawaiian desk clerk that Graham had not yet returned to his room. I listened to a few tunes by the hotel's Hawaiian combo until I saw the evangelist enter the lobby. I introduced myself as a reporter and said I wanted to ask questions for a story. I told him I'd first heard of his work from a high school friend who credited his decision to go into the ministry to Graham. That seemed to please him. The evangelist said he had soft drinks in his room if I'd like to talk on his lanai.

The lanai, on an upper floor, overlooked moonlit Waikiki Beach, the ocean, and lights of an occasional ship moving along the horizon. We had a friendly conversation for more than an hour. I asked about his trip to Korea. At one point he emphasized his conviction about infallibility of the Bible and importance of his mission to "save souls." He touched on numerous other topics. He said his only speaking engagement on his trip would be a radio broadcast to the mainland.

Then, remembering President Truman's complaint, I asked my first probing question, "As you gain fame, do you ever worry that your personal ego might conflict with your religious mission?" He seemed comfortable with the question.

"It is a constant concern of mine," he said. "Yes, I admit that as a human being I enjoy the approval of others, but I ask God not to let that interfere with my work for Him. I pray about it regularly."

Then he said he had a more immediate concern -- a newspaper photo that might appear showing him with hula girls when he got off the plane in Honolulu. "Back home there are some people who wouldn't understand such a picture," he said.

I had learned from Bob Krauss that the lineage of scantily clad hula dancers could be traced back to Hawaii's ancient religious ceremonies. They had been dedicated to pagan gods and conducted by Hawaii's Kahuna priestly class. I explained to the evangelist that publication of the photo was mostly out of my hands but that I'd look into it.

Since the presence of hula dancers bothered Graham, I asked if he ever had to deal with women who sometimes congregated around male celebrities. He said, "I knew from the start of my calling that I could never let even the slightest hint of immorality enter my life. I never permit myself to be alone in a room with any woman except my wife. I always make sure other people are around."

It was after midnight when Graham and I shook hands cordially as I left the Royal Hawaiian Hotel. I pitched my story on his excitement about visiting Korea and his eagerness to talk to American troops. Twigg, or some other editor, cut the story drastically. The version that appeared in print stressed Graham's concern about the photo with hula dancers, a fact I had included but downplayed deep in the story.

Graham's photo with hula dancers did not appear anywhere.

On page 181 of his 2007 autobiography, *Just As I Am*, Graham seems to recall this event writing: *"When we were on the ship returning from Japan and Korea in early 1953, we met a*

Jewish businessman named Jack Lewis. He invited us to a party he was giving, during which a woman performed a hula dance. When she found out who I was, she apologized, fearing she had offended me. I told her I had been to Hawaii before and knew it was part of their ancient culture."

On days off, I often ordered a Singapore Sling at one of the tables in the shade of the Moana Hotel's banyan tree, a favorite spot. I watched waves roll in from the Pacific while listening to Hawaiian musicians perform in a nearby, open pavilion.

I pondered the Moana's colorful past. Mrs. Leland Stanford, co-founder of Stanford University, died mysteriously in one of the hotel's rooms in 1905, not long after it opened. She was a rich widow in her late 70s. Strychnine was found in her body. The case was never solved. Later, the rich and famous from throughout the world stayed at the Moana. The room where Mrs. Stanford died disappeared in a fancy lobby expansion.

On one occasion, as I prepared to sit near the banyan tree, four or five people appeared to be ending a meeting at the next table. A man glanced at me over his shoulder and remarked, "You'll like the music." My chair was so close to his table that I soon found myself conversing with its occupants. The leaders were Robert Rich, who first spoke to me, and Rosemary Thompson. They said they were organizing a "Unitarian fellowship." They had held previous meetings elsewhere.

I asked, "What's a Unitarian?" They said Unitarians followed a liberal religion that took hold in New England in the late 1700s. With roots in Judeo-Christian traditions, they said, Unitarianism embraces diversity of thought among people seeking to understand the universe and place themselves in harmony with it.

"We question scientific and religious answers," Mr. Rich said. "We keep in mind that Albert Einstein predicted human beings will never fully succeed in knowing the real nature of things."

The group explained to me that a fellowship is usually the first step in establishing a church. Typically, lay men and women conduct the fellowship, sometimes for years, until it gains enough members to become a church and hire a minister. When not debating scientific, religious and social problems, they said, their main "ritual" is "service to humanity."

I mentioned I was a reporter and asked if any coverage of the fellowship's formation had been carried by local newspapers. A small story had appeared, they said.

Because I showed interest, my new acquaintances took turns dropping famous names associated with Unitarianism in the past. They smiled as they observed my surprise. They mentioned Paul Revere, John Adams, John Quincy Adams, Thomas Jefferson, Louisa May Alcott, Joseph Priestly, Charles Darwin, Alexander Graham Bell, Charles Dickens, Ralph Waldo Emerson, and Henry David Thoreau, among others.

Ruth Iams added to the list Cartoonist Thomas Nast and Publisher Horace Greeley "just for your benefit, since you're a journalist."

She was right. I was impressed. I remembered from J-school courses that New

York *Tribune* founder Greeley helped lead the 19th Century's anti-slavery movement before writing his editorial advising adventurous young men to "Go West." Cartoonist Nast designed the plump Santa Claus that became familiar to children. He also created the elephant and donkey symbols for Republican and Democratic parties.

I later attended some of the Unitarians' Sunday evening meetings in space provided by a Congregational Church on Queen Emma Street. Fellowship members, I observed, dared to think big. They talked, among other things, of a time when their group might serve as headquarters for like-minded people across the Pacific. The first step would be to reach out to a handful of Unitarians on Wake Island, two-thousand miles away.

For several weeks, programs featured Catholic, Protestant, or Jewish laypersons or clergy outlining their beliefs. A session with a visiting Buddhist went so well that I proposed to Robert Rich and other leaders that the fellowship consider holding a joint meeting with the local Buddhist temple. The Unitarians agreed and delegated me to approach Ernest Hunt, the Western Buddhist Order's local leader, to make arrangements.

He greeted me in his office. We set a date for a Sunday evening at the Soto Zen Temple on Nuuanu Avenue. Rosemary Thompson (she later became Rosemary Mattson, wife of a Unitarian minister) publicized the event. She planted stories in both local newspapers, radio stations (television was just arriving in the islands), and in the fellowship newsletter she edited. Nearly a hundred people showed up, the most until then to attend a Unitarian-sponsored event in Honolulu.

In his talk to local Buddhists and Unitarians, Hunt outlined tenets of his faith. He pointed out that Gautama Buddha had attained enlightenment in India while seated under a bodhi tree, a species related to banyan. He saw similarities in Gautama and Jesus, who lived about five hundred years apart. Both expressed concern for the poor, sick and downtrodden. Hunt concluded, "As all roads up the mountain lead to one top, and from that top all who arrive see the same view, so many and various are the ways to truth."

Both local newspapers covered the event and described it as the "first time in Hawaii's history that a Buddhist sect and a Christian denomination had met together."

I wrote a brief story about the combined service and the Unitarians' first year in Hawaii that appeared on page 30 of the December 1953 *Christian Register* (precursor of *UU World*).

After I moved from Hawaii, the fellowship developed into First Unitarian Church on Pali Highway, eventually associated with the Unitarian Universalist Association, headquartered in Boston.

A boy called "Barry," later to become U. S. President Barack Obama, attended Sunday School at the Honolulu church.

His parents married while attending the University of Hawaii, and he was born August 4, 1961 in Honolulu. Both local newspapers carried his birth announcement placed by the state health department, a customary practice.

His father, whom Barry described as "non-religious," came from Kenya. His mother grew up among Baptists and Methodists in Kansas. She was called Stanley Ann Dunham until she dropped the first name. When she divorced Barack's father, he enrolled in Harvard for graduate work. Ann remarried.

Barry spent his first four grades in Catholic and state schools in Indonesia while living with his mother and stepfather. The stepfather was a surveyor for a while, and she worked with micro-finance programs to stimulate Indonesian village industries, first for the U. S. Agency for Industrial Development and later with the Ford Foundation. Barack returned to Honolulu at age ten to live with his grandmother, a Bank of Hawaii vice president. His mother divorced again and joined Barack in Honolulu. She earned a Ph.D. in anthropology from the University of Hawaii.

Her son completed fifth through twelfth grades at prestigious Punahou School in hills overlooking Waikiki. She supplemented Barack's education, she said, with correspondence courses and Martin Luther King speeches. After her death in 1995, the University of Hawaii established an endowment fund in her honor.

His grandmother, Madelyn Dunham, lived into the next decade. A funeral service for her was held at the Honolulu church in December 2008.

I got to know several kanakas, native Hawaiians of Polynesian descent, including cab drivers. They made up only about fifteen percent of the Hawaiian population. Although they originally settled the islands, the kanakas were eventually outnumbered by Japanese, Chinese and Filipinos imported to work on sugarcane and pineapple plantations.

Along with surfing, dance, and the medicinal benefits of eating poi, the kanakas I knew talked occasionally about whether sovereignty lost in 1893 might be regained someday, and who should be able to lease or own island land.

Most kanakas I knew did not approve of the drive for statehood. It was led by newspapers and Democratic and Republican parties. As long as Hawaii remained a territory, kanakas held hope for reversal of the U.S. annexation of the islands that occurred after the overthrow of Queen Liliuokalani.

The native Hawaiians resented that only one-fifth of land designated for them a half century earlier had been awarded, a violation of the land law's intent. The territorial legislature and an agency called the Hawaiian Homes Commission controlled land leases.

Leases for 99 years, when they could be obtained, cost only about a dollar a year. Most had been awarded to large haole-owned sugar plantations and other businesses, such as Dole plantations and the Big Island's Parker cattle ranch. Kanakas debated whether leases should go to persons with less than fifty percent Polynesian blood. Kanakas feared that leasing on the basis of highly diluted parentage would result in their eventually losing all the land.

A kanaka I observed often was Duke Kahanamoku, then in his sixties. The former Olympic gold-medalist swimmer still gave impressive Waikiki surfboard performances, a sport he popularized throughout the world. The son of a policeman, he had been elected local sheriff, a position he held for years. He often visited the beach on days off, stopping sometimes at the Moana Hotel for lunch or dinner.

I proposed to City Editor Twigg-Smith one day that I expand my territorial coverage to include more news about native Hawaiians. He pointedly made it clear the idea did not interest him. His reaction surprised me. It was not until much later that I realized he may have known something I didn't. A group of kanakas had moved beyond mere talk to organizing a pro-sovereignty movement. Perhaps Twigg, whose ancestors helped overthrow Queen Liliuokalani, did not want me digging for stories that might hinder eventual statehood.

While many Hawaiians in the sovereignty movement opposed statehood, others sought self-government on reservations similar to that won by Native American tribes on the mainland.

Twigg eventually inherited control of the Honoluulu *Advertiser* and became its publisher.

On a visit to Maui soon after, he met a young boy who questioned why Twigg's grandfather, Lorrin A. Thurston, "stole" the lands of native Hawaiians. The encounter spurred Twigg to write a book, *Hawaiian Sovereignty: Do the Facts Matter?*

In it, Twigg said his grandfather helped remove the monarchy to make way for U. S. annexation to benefit all the people in Hawaii. Twigg argued that after Polynesians settled Hawaii, the royal family, not commoners, controlled most of the land.

The land dispute continued through the Twentieth Century. A congressional act in 1993, the centennial of Queen Liliuokalani's overthrow, finally acknowledged the role played by the United States. The federal government made a token settlement. It provided kanakas land parcels on most islands, including two hundred acres near Hilo, where resort hotels stood, and nearly six hundred acres on Oahu's Barber's Point, site of a military base.

A stronger bill aimed at righting old wrongs began moving through Congress in 2010, with the blessing of President Obama. One provision would enable Hawaiians to govern a chunk of the islands, as done by more than five-hundred Native American tribes on the mainland.

In 1992, Twigg sold the *Advertiser* to the Gannett Company for a reported $250 million. He retired to Kauai. With later consolidation by a Canadian firm, Honolulu's two newspapers became the *Star-Advertiser*.

7

L. A. Smog

During my second year in Hawaii, I began to doubt it was the place for me over the long run. Influenced partly by Twigg's history of working in various departments, I took a job at the Los Angeles *Times*. It was in the Advertising-Dispatch Department. I thought getting experience on a large newspaper in a department other than news might prove valuable someday. It did.

Another enticement: the *Times* provided me with a car. It was a new Ford Mainliner sedan, for job and personal use. I had never driven a new car before. That was a big deal in 1954 when I was single and in my twenties.

Although my job ranked at the bottom of the publishing food chain, it enabled me to observe a growing, efficient newspaper empire from the inside. The *Times*, controlled by the Chandler family for three generations, was rapidly becoming a major force in national and international journalism. It already ranked near the top in circulation, advertising linage, and profits. Its circulation would soon exceed a million copies a day.

My job was easy. Duties included distributing advertising proof sheets to businesses and picking them up when corrections were made. On occasion, a store or shop would ask my opinion about an editing change in an ad. I felt confident because I had answered similar questions working as a teenager for the weekly *Autogram* in Missouri.

I also sometimes collected overdue payments for advertising, especially from Sunset Boulevard nightclubs. I usually saw the interior of these clubs for the first time when they were nearly empty, except for a manager or cleaning crew. Night club managers that I dealt with were always cooperative. They recognized the *Times* as a powerful institution.

Although I had no connection with the *Times* news department, I read each day with admiration the work of its talented reporters and editors.

Shortly after starting at the *Times*, I sent Twigg at the Honolulu *Advertiser* the following tongue-in-cheek, first-person report, which he published.

The Honolulu Advertiser
Hawaii's Territorial Newspaper

COMICS   •   FEATURES

HONOLULU, HAWAII, FRIDAY, OCTOBER 8, 1954.

Beverly Hills Cops Are Tough

Ex-Honolulu Reporter Henceforth Will Shun Marilyn's Back Alley

By LaRUE GILLELAND

HOLLYWOOD, California, Oct. 5 (via Airmail)—The moral of this story is never let the Beverly Hills, Calif., police catch you snooping in Marilyn Monroe's back alley. They caught a former Honolulu reporter doing it this week, and I thought I was going to end up in jail. Told a wild fib to keep out of it.

It happened this way: Was cruising through the West Los Angeles smog early Tuesday morning when the thought occurred that Mr. and Mrs. Joe DiMaggio's "honeymoon house" was only a few blocks away.

* * *

THE LATEST editions told how right then Marilyn was sleeping off some sedatives in her bedroom upstairs while Joe sat in the living room below thinking how to handle the knuckle ball she'd pitched at him—her divorce suit.

The proximity of this homey scene naturally aroused my curiosity. So I turned off Sunset Boulevard, drove about three blocks and pulled up in front of 508 North Palm Drive, Beverly Hills.

Looking at their attractive, steep roofed house, one could almost picture the domestic scene inside.

* * *

STANDING AROUND in a huddle on the grass were the photographers and reporters. They had been waiting there for two days. They were arguing over whose turn it was to fix a buffet lunch at noon.

"Heck," I thought, "these guys could hang around out here for hours while the DiMaggios went in and out their back door."

Decided to take a look. Besides, I'd never seen a movie star's rear alley before.

* * *

IT LOOKED like any alley. There was Marilyn and Joe's trash can and an alley cat. But, as I stared up disappointedly at a pair of pulled curtains on the second floor, I stumbled onto something else. A cop.

Worst of all, he was a Beverly Hills cop. They're tough. But I knew my rights. I hadn't broken any laws, I said to myself, and I'd tell him off quick like.

* * *

"YOU LIVE around here?" he snarled.

"Uh, no," I answered.

Question—"You got some kind of important business back here?"

Answer—"Uh, no."

Q.—"Then you must be lost."

A.—"No."

Q.—"What are you doing here?"

A.—"Uh, nothing."

Q.—"Perhaps a night or two in jail will sharpen your memory!"

A.—"Well, you see, officer, I work for a daily paper here in the city (that much was the truth) and I just picked up some advertising copy from a man a few houses down and I'm taking a short cut to my car parked over on the street."

"Let's see this . . . whatever it is," he said.

* * *

BY CHANCE, I did have copy for a furniture store ad with me and showed it to him. Surprised, I suppose, that my tale hung together as well as it did, he let me go.

But I've learned my lesson. I'll never get caught snooping around Marilyn Monroe's rear alley again. And, anyhow, she keeps her bedroom window curtains pulled shut.

Twigg, a patron of the arts, sent me a modest but welcomed check and asked for another story. It was about an acquaintance of his, Samoan-born John Kneubuhl, former director of Honolulu Community Theater.

Since moving from Honolulu to Hollywood, Kneubuhl had been writing movie scripts. My story angle for Twigg stressed how Kneubuhl's latest script, "An Island Affair," a South Sea extravaganza, would not be made anywhere near the South Seas. To avoid delays caused by the Pacific's rainy season, the movie would be filmed in Argentina. Twigg liked that angle.

I sometimes visited the First Unitarian Church of Los Angeles to hear the Rev. Stephen Fritchman. He'd been described as an advocate of civil liberties and world peace. His carefully-crafted sermons did not disappoint, although I disagreed with his position that the United States should set an example for other nations by unilateral disarming. I attended his sermons and other church functions often enough to become fairly well acquainted with him.

I learned that after graduating from Ohio Wesleyan University, Fritchman had served as religion editor of the New York *Herald Tribune*. His newspaper experience gave us something in common. He worked for the *Herald Tribune* while earning a divinity degree from Union Theological Seminary.

He had become a close friend of Linus Pauling, winner of the Nobel Prize in chemistry and a contributor to the discovery of the DNA Double Helix. Linus Pauling sometimes came to hear Fritchman speak.

At a church social function, Fritchman introduced me to a 70-year-old woman he described as "a famous journalist you probably should know." She was Anna Louise Strong. Daughter of a Nebraska Congregational minister, she had been a spokeswoman for a brief 1919 strike of Seattle ship workers that spread to other unions. Impressed with her work, Author Lincoln Steffens advised her to travel to the Soviet Union as a journalist.

There, she served as Moscow correspondent for International News Service in the early 1920s and helped Mikhail Borodin, a former adviser to Sun Yat Sen, start the Moscow *News*, that city's first English language newspaper. She interviewed Trotsky and Stalin. She married a Russian journalist who died a decade later. She covered the Spanish Civil War in the 1930s.

She also made a number of trips to China. She spent six months during its civil war in 1945-46 with Mao Zedong and his troops and lived among them in caves at Yanan overlooking the Yellow River.

Mao's army settled in Yanan after the "Long March," a year-long trek through rough terrain in 1934-35 to escape entrapment by Chaing Kai-shek's Kuomintang army. Yanan lies just north of Xian, where the ancient Silk Road ended. It's also where China's First Emperor hid his famous Terracota Warriors about 200 B.C.

Mao and his army lived in caves. He assigned Anna Louise Strong a typical cave, refurbished with homemade-brick floor, white-washed walls, and a cast-iron stove for heating and cooking. While she interviewed Red Army generals and danced with Mao and Zhou Enlai at Saturday night parties, Chaing's planes flew over, occasionally dropping bombs.

After Anna Louise returned to Moscow in 1949, the Soviets jailed her briefly on a charge of being an American spy.

I saw Strong on a number of occasions in Los Angeles in 1954-55. She puzzled me at first. For someone with her many adventures and wide notoriety, she had a soft-spoken, almost diffident manner. She was cordial to me, I thought, because she felt a motherly interest in a 25-year-old journalist who still had a lot to learn.

Although she gave me a copy of her book, *The Chinese Conquer China*, she described her adventures in communist countries with no hint that she wanted to proselytize. A few days later I read a New York *Times* column by Harrison Salisbury that referred to Strong's arrest in Moscow. He conjectured that the Soviets took her into custody for visiting Marshal Tito in Yugoslavia on the eve of a falling out between Tito and Stalin. When I asked her about Salisbury's story, she said she doubted her visit with Tito had anything to do with the incident.

"I've never known the real reason," she told me. "I had last talked to Tito five years earlier. I was in my hotel room in Moscow when the arrest was made. They jailed me for five days before releasing me on the Polish border."

She added, "I was not a spy. I hope eventually to come across some of my old friends in Russia who can explain it. But that still hasn't happened." She also dismissed conjectures I'd heard that Stalin may have disliked some of her writings that portrayed Mao Zedong as ultimately more important than Stalin to the spread of world communism.

I asked her about Mao. She described him as "a good conversationalist with a sense of humor." He liked to dance.

Two of her remarks stuck with me: Mao did not oppose capitalism per se, she said, and he doubted that a war would ever occur between the United States and China or the Soviet Union.

She quoted Mao as saying, "It's neither the people nor the ordinary capitalists in America who raise fears of such a war. It's the monopolistic capitalists who do so. Cooperation among the peoples of all three countries will prevent World War III."

I later associated Mao's reference to "monopolistic capitalists" with President Eisenhower's warning about a "military-industrial complex."

Strong described Mao's skills on the dance floor. She said he danced to Western and Chinese tunes with Mrs. Mao and others in a Yanan cave designated for social events. But she said he sat out most dances because so many people wanted to chat with him.

"When he took the floor, it was with easy definiteness, as if he gave the 'party line' to the band. Some people have said he has no sense of rhythm; with this I disagree. He had a firm and delicate sense, and the rhythm was his own."

She added, "He kept the friendliest contact with the music, yet never slavishly submitted. As a partner, you had to pay close attention, yield watchfully, and move at slight indications. But if you got his rhythm, he brought you out -- bang -- with the band at the finish. It was in several ways a triumph to dance with Chairman Mao."

Anna Louise returned to China in 1959. She died there in 1970.

As part-time diversion from my day job, I reverted to my old interest in theater. In doing so, I learned something new about journalism – from an actress. She was Roxanne Arlen.

I acted occasionally at Geller Theater on Wilshire Boulevard in Beverly Hills. My newspaper job did not interfere with night rehearsals or productions.

Although most Geller actors, like me, were amateurs, Roxanne and some others were professionals. They had contracts with major studios that sent them to Geller for additional acting experience when not making movies.

I acted with Roxanne in Maxwell Anderson's "Elizabeth the Queen," a good play, and Garson Kanin's "The Live Wire," a dud.

In "Elizabeth the Queen," I played the court jester. The director told me, with innocent exaggeration, that the role rivaled "King Lear's fool."

For "Elizabeth the Queen," the theater filled each night. Beverly Jacques, an excellent actress, had the title role. Most cast members and I felt Beverly had a promising theater career ahead. But I never heard of her after her fine performances as the Geller queen.

Roxanne, in her mid-twenties, was under Warner Bros. contract. She modeled for glamour magazines and acted in such films as "Gypsy," "The Best Things in Life Are Free" and Ben Hecht's "Miracle in the Rain." She got her first major stage role by replacing Jayne Mansfield for a tour of "Will Success Spoil Rock Hunter."

She had been married and divorced while still a teenager. The daughter of a Michigan-attorney father and school-teacher mother, she said she had taken a few courses at the University of Detroit. She had a sharp mind. She read serious novels and good newspapers. She could expound on Stanislavski's acting theories.

During Geller rehearsals, she and I occasionally took coffee breaks at a nearby restaurant. She socialized with an older Hollywood crowd I did not know. I dated a bright female bookkeeper named LaVonne, who had moved from Iowa to California.

Over coffee, Roxanne told me stories about actors, directors and agents, including some she went out with. But I remember best our conversations about news media.

She complained that her walk, which she insisted was natural, led the press to call her "the Wiggle." Most published stories about her mentioned her sexy walk and her 36-22-35 measurements. Despite that, she hoped soon to be recognized as a serious actress.

She appeared interested when I talked about my journalistic ambitions. I said that after several more years of newspaper work, I hoped to take graduate courses in philosophy and combine them with journalism. "There are philosophical issues related to media that have not been adequately explored," I said.

"Like what?" she asked.

"Problems in ethics and epistemology," I said.

"What's epistemology?"

"That's a fancy term for analyzing what we know and what we merely think we know," I said.

"I guess I can see how that would worry a newspaperman. Where do ethics come in?"

I said, "Some ethical issues occur when the government's obligation to withhold sensitive information conflicts with media's responsibility to publish. Or when aggressive reporting violates someone's privacy. Or an editor pays a source for information. Or a reporter quotes someone without identification. Or an advertiser attempts to influence news judgment."

"Anything else?"

I responded that news should be presented as objectively and unemotionally as possible. If democracy is to survive, I pontificated, the public must be adequately informed.

I said I feared that someday media could feed audience biases by focusing too much on opinion rather than fact. "Important information could be subordinated to mere entertainment – to the theatrical," I said. "As when a writer calls you the Wiggle."

Her reaction was not what I expected.

"How could a reporter think as you do?" she asked. "At first, I hated newspapers calling me the Wiggle. But I recovered and grew more resilient. Flawed publicity is sometimes better than none."

Roxanne recognized a paradox. "If news didn't contain an element of entertainment, few would read it," she said.

She had a point. I had not adequately considered the difficulty of defining an effective balance between what is entertaining and what is important. I would wrestle with the paradox for years to come, both as reporter and as a journalism educator.

Roxanne liked to talk about Stanislavski's acting method. She pointed out that the famous Russian director insisted each member of his cast be familiar with the "entire psyche" of any character the actor portrayed. Stanislavski's actors had to create a complete "inner life" for every role, including attributes that were good and bad. That meant the cast invented background not provided by authors. But a cast member's inventions had to remain logically consistent with action on stage.

Roxanne's discussion of Stanislavski's conviction that every psyche contains both "good and bad" stayed with me. I recalled it later when interviewing accused felons -- and political leaders.

Roxanne, after leaving California, appeared in "Who Was That Lady I Saw You

With" and other stage productions in Philadelphia and New York. She moved to London, where she died more than three decades later at age 58. The monicker, "the Wiggle," followed her to the end.

I later had the lead in another mediocre Geller production, "Out of the Frying Pan," by Francis Swann. It's probably an indication of my talent that the theater went out of business soon after I performed that play.

Gilleland, moonlighting from his Los Angeles newspaper job, rehearses a scene from "Elizabeth the Queen" with Roxanne Arlen at Geller Theater in Beverly Hills in 1954. He appeared in two stage plays with her. She taught him he still had much to learn about journalism.

After Los Angeles, I took a job in Tulsa as summer-replacement newscaster for KVOO-TV and KVOO-Radio. Using the name "Larry Gil," my assignment included filling in for television and radio newscasters taking vacations.

Democratic Senator Robert S. Kerr, Oklahoma's former governor, owned the station. He had become wealthy as part owner of Kerr-McGee Oil Company. Gene Autry got his start singing and playing guitar on Kerr's radio station about the time I was born.

Senator Kerr visited the TV newsroom once during my summer there. In a TV interview I conducted with him, he described his early life on Indian Territory near the Oklahoma town of Ada and his proposal for a huge navigation system, including locks, in Oklahoma on the Arkansas River.

"It would be important for barge traffic, flood control, recreation, and wildlife conservation," he said.

Kerr pointed out that hydraulic-engineer Hans Einstein of the University of California-Berkeley, son of famous physicist Albert Einstein, supported the idea. The younger Einstein calculated that the biggest obstacle -- the Arkansas River's heavy silt deposits -- could be controlled.

After Kerr's death a few years later, the Army Corps of Engineers fulfilled his vision. It built the McClellan-Kerr Navigation System on parts of the Arkansas, Verdigris and White rivers.

From Tulsa, I moved to Memphis.

8

Down in Dixie

Memphis, a busy news town perched on a bluff overlooking the Mississippi River, was a good place to work.

It was the nearest big Southern city to my home in Missouri. I liked Memphis' size -- about a half-million people then -- its relatively mild winters, its history, and the penchant of its people to celebrate their colorful past. In Jim Crow country, the city was strategically located for covering the national racial integration controversy. The first segregationist White Citizens Council had been formed nearby in Indianola, Mississippi in 1954.

I arrived in Memphis the next year, shortly after the death of Boss E. H. Crump and the U. S. Supreme Court decision in Brown vs. Board of Education. The court's decision would not end school segregation without a long civil rights fight, especially in the South.

The City of Memphis got its start in 1819, when Andrew Jackson helped found it. He did so after leading American troops to victory over the British in the battle of New Orleans in 1812 and before his election as U.S. president. He gave Memphis the name of its ancient Nile counterpart in Egypt.

Twenty-one years later itinerant printer Henry Van Pelt arrived in the river town to start a conservative Democratic newspaper, the *Weekly Appeal*. Van Pelt's editorials appealed for unity among his readers in preserving a "Southern way of life" and attaining commercial independence from the North. Two new owners acquired the newspaper in 1847 and called it the *Daily Appeal*.

Boiler explosions and other steamboat accidents on the Mississippi often made big news. An explosion on the side wheeler Pennsylvania near Memphis in 1858 killed about half the four-hundred-fifty people on board, including Samuel Clemens' brother Henry, a crew member. Samuel was piloting another boat when he heard of the accident. The future Mark Twain hurried to Memphis to comfort his dying brother. After witnessing tender medical and nursing care Henry and other badly burned victims received, Samuel Clemens was quoted as saying, "God bless Memphis."

When the Civil War began, newspaper editors John McClanahan and B. F. Dill equipped an artillery unit for the Confederates. They called it the "Appeal Battery." Memphis women presented it with a silk battle flag. The battery fought at Corinth and Vicksburg until captured.

Thousands of Memphians watched from the river bluffs as a superior Union naval force sank eight of nine Confederate gunboats defending the city. Memphians then stood by as Union troops occupied the city in 1862.

Meanwhile, the *Appeal* fled. McClanahan, Dill and sixteen newspaper employees loaded type, paper, ink, and a heavy 20 by 9 by 6-foot press on a railroad box car. Pulled by a locomotive, the press headed south across the state border. Moving through Mississippi ahead of Union armies, the newspaper continued to publish during stops in Hernando, Grenada and Jackson. When the editors ran out of newsprint, they published on wallpaper.

As Northern soldiers entered Jackson, the *Appeal* staff and equipment crossed the Pearl River on a flatboat to reach mules and wagons waiting to pull them to Meridian, Mississippi. In one version of the escape, Northern cannon shells splashed on both sides of the fleeing boat.

Gaining fame for stubbornness and luck, the newspaper became known as the "Moving Appeal." Its reputation enabled it to attract enough subscriptions and advertising to survive in nearly every Southern community where it stopped, whether for a few days or several months.

Continuing to flee, the *Appeal* published in Montgomery, Alabama, and four Georgia communities, including Atlanta. There it spent a year. The newspaper covered Atlanta's last defensive gasp when Confederate suicide charges and rebel yells failed to stop Sherman's troops that crossed Peachtree Creek in July 1864. Sherman's soldiers finally caught up with the "Moving Appeal" near Columbus, Georgia. There they put a halt to its three-year odyssey.

Back in Memphis, a Confederate cavalry under General Nathan Bedford Forrest made a night-time raid. It surprised patrons of the then-elegant Gayoso Hotel by riding horses through the lobby. Although failing in its mission to capture top Union officers and release Southern prisoners, the cavalry took five-hundred captured Union troops with them as they fled the city.

When the war ended a few months later, the *Appeal* and its staff returned to Memphis and resumed publishing.

Recalling the battle of Peachtree Creek, a Cincinnati newspaper said, "We remember well the copy of the *Appeal* issued at Atlanta on the morning of the battle . . . It was full of fight." A Nashville *Banner* writer predicted that "a hundred years from now the *Appeal's* story will read like a romance."

S. C. Toof, a foreman at the *Appeal* from the 1850s through the Civil War, established Graceland, a farm named for his daughter, eight miles south of downtown Memphis. Elvis Presley bought the property a century later.

A flood fifty miles wide south of Memphis in 1872 devastated hundreds of Arkansas and Mississippi farms and plantations. Repeated overflows of Mississippi and tributary rivers prompted *Appeal* editorials calling for improved levees and federal help in flood control.

The *Appeal* prospered, and its circulation reached about five-thousand in 1876, larger than the *Avalanche* and other local competitors.

Soon Yellow Fever, which had broken out every few years in the lower Mississippi Valley, hit hard in Memphis and its population, then fifty-thousand people. About half fled. Of those remaining, more than five-thousand died of the disease. The death toll included eighteen of the *Appeal's* forty-one employees.

The newspaper kept publishing. It reported mass burials of Yellow Fever victims in unmarked graves. It reported a child found trying to nurse its dead mother and a brothel madam who cared for the sick. It congratulated police officers who remained on duty.

In those days, no one knew Yellow Fever's cause. But some *Appeal* editorials came close to the mark. They recommended covering open sewers and cisterns, avoiding night air, burning barrels of tar, disinfecting objects with carbolic acid, taking castor oil with quinine in it, and staying away from Arkansas swamps. It was not until 1901 that a team headed by Dr. Walter Reed in Cuba proved the theory that mosquitoes carry Yellow Fever.

Mergers of three newspapers – the *Appeal*, the *Avalanche* and the *Commercial* -- resulted in appearance of *The Commercial Appeal* in 1893. Editors insisted from the start on capitalizing the "T" in the name.

The new newspaper's appearance in the same year that a U.S.-backed faction overthrew Hawaii's monarchy encouraged a new jingoism in its editors. They advocated American expansion in the Pacific and Caribbean -- at Spain's expense. When the battleship Maine blew up and sank in Havana harbor in 1898, *The Commercial Appeal* joined others calling for war with Spain and occupation of Cuba and the Philippines.

Meanwhile, a few blocks away from the newspaper, the Memphis Cotton Exchange rose on Front Street by the river. The large cotton market made fortunes for many floor traders (called "factors") and plantation owners in Tennessee, Arkansas, and Mississippi. On the exchange floor, five-hundred pound bales of cotton were sold to textile mills in this country and abroad, based on samples cut from the bales and graded for quality. Railroad boxcars and river barges carried the bales of "white gold" from Memphis to their destinations.

Editor Charles P. J. Mooney led *The Commercial Appeal* during the Spanish American War and the rise of E. H. Crump as the city's powerful political boss in the early 1900s.

Mooney successfully urged farmers to diversify crops to avoid soil depletion and overproduction of cotton.

Crump, a city commissioner, won election as Memphis mayor in 1909. Although he held that office only six years, he dominated Memphis politics for four decades, personally selecting key occupants of local and state offices. His reputation as an urban political boss soon rivaled his contemporary, Tom Pendergast of Kansas City. Editor Mooney disapproved of Crump because his political machine failed to enforce prohibition, and it permitted a red-light district to flourish. Clarence Saunders, Memphis' originator of Piggly Wiggly and other self-service grocery stores, contributed to Crump's opposition.

In World War I, two newsroom employees, a reporter and a news clerk, were among the American soldiers who died in combat. After the war, relations between Crump and Mooney grew temporarily cordial, for both disliked the Ku Klux Klan's attempt to meddle in city politics. Although Crump and Mooney considered white people to be racially superior, they generally opposed violence toward blacks.

A campaign against the Klan by newspaper editorials, bolstered with cartoons by J. P. Alley, won *The Commercial Appeal* the Pulitzer Gold Medal for Public Service in 1923.

Accurate, detailed reporting of devastating floods in 1927 by *The Commercial Appeal's* Mississippi-born reporter Turner Catledge enhanced his reputation so much that the Baltimore *Sun* hired him away from Memphis. He soon joined the New York *Times*, and rose to become its managing editor, executive editor and vice president.

Memphis grew and prospered. A new Peabody Hotel, replacing one erected immediately after the Civil War, opened downtown on Union Avenue in 1925. It became famous for ducks that swam in a marble lobby fountain and marched twice daily on a red carpet to catch the elevator to and from their top floor "penthouse," near the Skyway nightclub. Peabody hotels in Little Rock and Orlando soon imported their own ducks to entertain patrons.

The 31-story Sterick Building, erected in 1930, stood for years at the corner of Third and Madison as the South's tallest structure. Large department stores – including Goldsmith's, Lowenstein's, and Gerber's – anchored a prosperous downtown.

When Crump finally decided in the late 1930s that the city's high crime rate and poor national image hurt business, he ordered a cleanup. Newspaper editorials grew more tolerant of him. Under Crump's orders, police closed bars and cracked down on prostitutes. The city's murder rate declined. A local ordinance made loud noise a misdemeanor. Defective car mufflers and honking auto horns, except in emergencies, became illegal. Memphis soon called itself "the nation's quietest city."

But Memphis liked some kinds of loud sound – live music. The city would give birth to blues and serve as midwife to jazz and rock and roll.

Meanwhile, Edward Wyllis Scripps, owner of the Cleveland *Press*, had gained controlling interest in 33 newspapers and formed America's first large chain, by 1914. He called himself a "damned old crank" and promoted progressive democracy to benefit middle and lower classes.   He received help from his brothers and his sister, Ellen.

E. W. Scripps started United Press (later United Press International) and founded the Scripps Institute of Oceanography at La Jolla, California. After his death in the 1920s, his son, Robert P. Scripps, and business partner, Roy Howard, continued to expand as the Scripps-Howard League that included the New York *World-Telegram.*

The chain bought *The Commercial Appeal* in 1936. Scripps-Howard combined it with the Memphis *Press-Scimitar*, an afternoon daily. With their own news-editorial staffs, *The Commercial Appeal*, a morning daily, and the *Press-Scimitar* competed editorially from separate floors of the Memphis Publishing Company building at 495 Union Avenue.

Years later, when I headed the journalism department at the University of Nevada-Reno, I would know E. W. Scripps' grandson well. He was E. W. Scripps III, a Nevada alumnus. His son would be one of my students.

Scripps-Howard hired Frank Ahlgren, formerly of the Duluth *Herald* and Milwaukee *Journal*, as *The Commercial Appeal's* editor-in-chief. The newspaper's circulation grew in Memphis and spread in eastern Arkansas, the Missouri panhandle, western Tennessee and northern Mississippi. More than four-hundred full and part-time correspondents gathered news in those areas. Readers increasingly called *The Commercial Appeal* "the Old Reliable."

Ahlgren edited the Memphis newspaper during World War II. After the war, a symbol of patriotic pride for many Memphians stood atop a pedestal on Central Avenue for years. It was a B-17 bomber, "the Memphis Belle." The Memphis Belle was one of the first U. S. heavy bombers to survive twenty-five missions over France and Germany. Its patriotic symbolism ranked in Memphis with a statue of Confederate General Nathan Bedford Forrest that stood in a city park.

Editor Ahlgren offered me a job in 1955 on condition that I agree to work several weeks on the copy desk before receiving a reporting assignment. The newspaper needed help on the desk, he told me, and editing copy would be a good way to learn the city. I agreed.

Ahlgren's copy editors insisted on accuracy. They took pride in catching factual and grammatical errors, deleting needless words, and writing bright, succinct heads.

As I grew familiar with the city, I learned, among other things, that blacks could sit only in the balconies of movie theaters, as in much of the South. They could not vote. They could visit the city zoo one day a week, and on that day whites had to stay away. Jim Crow laws separated whites from blacks at lunch counters, drinking fountains, and rest rooms.

Meanwhile, White Citizens Councils spread from Indianola, Mississippi, to other nearby towns. Some called the councils "Ku Klux Klan chapters that have discarded their white sheets." The councils responded they merely wanted to improve local communities, including schools.

This was the era when newspapers routinely referred only to "Negro" or "Negroes." Common use of terms "African-American" or "black" came years later. In this memoir, the word "Negro" appears only in quoted material, including mine, from that prior era.

All editors and reporters at the newspaper were white, except for an occasional part-timer hired to cover all-black school sports. The notion that the *The Commercial Appeal* someday would hire a full-time black reporter or copy editor in the city room seemed remote. That someone of African-American descent would become the nation's president in my lifetime was inconceivable.

One of the first stories to come across the copy desk after I joined it in the summer of 1955 told of the murder of Emmett Till, a black teenager. The 14-year-old Chicago boy had wolf-whistled at a white woman in the nearby town of Money, Mississippi. He had gone to the small town to visit an uncle. Probably everyone on the copy desk edited stories in the next few weeks about two white men who dragged the boy from his bed at 2 a.m. They took Emmett to a wooded area of Mississippi's Tallahatchie County where they beat him and shot him to death.

Police charged Roy Bryant, the white woman's husband, and J. W. Bryant, his half brother, with murder. After a five-day trial a month later, a jury deliberated only sixty-eight minutes before acquitting both men. Years later, near the end of their lives, they confessed their crimes to *Look* magazine.

Several slayings violating civil rights in that era went unsolved for years. Notable victims included NAACP field secretary Medgar Evers in Jackson, Mississippi; Johnnie Mae Chappell, a black mother in Jacksonville, Florida; and three abducted civil rights workers -- James Chaney, Andrew Goodman and Michael Schwerner, all in their 20s -- in Philadelphia, Mississippi.

It took fourteen years to get a conviction for the 1963 bombing deaths of four black schoolgirls attending church in Birmingham, Alabama. The explosion was so loud that nine-year-old Condolezza Rice, a playmate of one of the dead, heard it at another church across town. She later became Stanford University provost and Secretary of State under President George W. Bush.

A miscegenation law in the 1950s made it a misdemeanor for whites and blacks of opposite sex to sit on the same car seat. A Memphis Press Club incident emphasized this for me.

After work, I often walked across Union Avenue to the club. It provided a bar and restaurant for reporters, editors, and other employees of *The Commercial Appeal* and *Press-Scimitar*, plus associate members. Press Club members had an easy-going, friendly relationship with the club's employees, both white and black.

As I sat at the Press Club bar late one night, a violent thunderstorm began. A weather bureau broadcast predicted possible tornados. The Press Club manager said he planned to close early and asked me if I would drive a young, black female bartender home, for he knew she lived in the general direction of my neighborhood. I said I would.

What I remember most about that dark, windy night was my discomfort when she and I walked to my car. After hesitating, I opened the back door and she climbed in without saying a word. We both knew we could be arrested if police saw her sitting in front.

During the 25-minute drive to her house, I tried to make light-hearted conversation by asking the bartender whether she'd grown up in Memphis (no, she came from a small town in Arkansas), and if she lived with family members (she shared an apartment with a sister). When we reached her apartment building, she stepped out and said, "Thanks. See you back at the Press Club."

Later, a carload of Ku Klux Klan members shot and killed Viola Liuzzo, a 39-year-old white Unitarian-Universalist housewife from Detroit, as she drove a 19-year-old black male in her car toward his home near Selma, Alabama. He was a Southern Christian Leadership Conference volunteer. In the trial of her murderers, the defense referred to Viola as a "white nigger." She was described as deserving to die because she chose to be alone at night in a car with a black male.

Her death came just two weeks after a mob beat to death Boston Unitarian Universalist minister James Reeb for taking part in a Martin Luther King inspired march from Selma to Montgomery.

More Unitarian Universalist clergy took part in the march than clergy from any other denomination.

The copy desk chief assigned me one day to make up a routine page inside the paper. I designed the page after selecting some stories and a couple of photographs. One photo showed the president of a local white women's organization giving a check to officers of a black charity. The day after the photo appeared in print, the copy desk transferred a phone call to me from an angry white female reader.

"How dare you picture a white woman with niggers," she said. "You damned Yankee! Why don't you go back up North where you belong!" I said I was sorry she felt that way, but made no apology for the picture.

After a few weeks on the copy desk, I moved to the night police beat.

9

Police Beat

My routine in the new assignment duplicated that of police reporters at most morning newspapers throughout the country. Reporting for work in the newspaper newsroom shortly before 6 p.m., I first telephoned several hospital emergency rooms to obtain names and conditions of victims admitted in the last few hours from traffic accidents, shootings, or other emergencies.

I then drove to the office designated for reporters in central police headquarters at Second and Adams. There I had access to another desk and phone. Each evening I visited nearby offices of homicide, vice squad, and traffic divisions, and the assistant police chief. The assistant chief directed the police department at night after the chief went home.

During the day, another reporter called on the same offices. I visited each at night to gather details for new and follow-up stories. I also checked the Shelby County Sheriff's office, a few blocks away. When a significant story broke during the evening -- homicide, robbery, drug bust, major fire, or fatal accident -- I drove to the scene if an approaching deadline made that necessary. When time was short, I telephoned the newsroom from the scene, either dictating the story word for word from my notes or giving information to someone on the rewrite desk who organized it.

The first time I telephoned the city desk to say, "Get me rewrite," hoping not to sound theatrical, I reported the antics of an African lioness roaming Memphis streets. Her name was "Countess." Countess escaped her backstage cage about 8:30 p.m. during a circus performance. I heard about it when a scared pedestrian spotted the lion and called police.

Countess strolled downtown several minutes in the rain. Deciding she didn't relish her freedom, she returned to the Memphis Auditorium and jumped through a glass door to get back to her cage. She suffered a minor shoulder cut. I reported how the show proceeded with the audience of 4,500 unaware of her disappearance or return.

More serious police stories introduced me to Mid-South misfortune and crime. Some that I remember writing:

- A 12-year-old boy killed by a truck as he rode his bicycle to visit the zoo;
- A 28-year-old man who ended up in jail after he skipped church choir practice to rob a pharmacy;
- A former sheriff's deputy and his wife who arranged dates in their home for an 18-year-old prostitute with whom they split earnings;
- A 17-year-old male who stabbed to death a 41-year-old divorcee when she withdrew sexual favors -- after welcoming him in prior visits;
- A 21-year-old bridegroom, arrested hours after his wedding, for making obscene phone calls to older housewives;
- A father who seduced his 15-year-old daughter after convincing her incest was not sinful by reading her the Genesis story of Lot and his daughters;
- A Marine Corps pilot who died when his parachute failed to open after his plane went out of control at 3,000 feet just north of Memphis;
- A burly Texan in flashy cowboy duds and wide-brimmed hat who robbed a liquor store and left the scene in a taxi. It took police seven minutes to spot the big hat and capture him;
- A woman murdered by a rejected lover within three days of her divorce from Grand Ol' Opry singer-fiddler Floyd Taylor "Lightning" Chance. The lover shot Dora Chance as she sat in a car when she told him she would not marry him. He used the same gun to kill himself.

I remember one story about a young woman who clubbed her husband to death and dismembered his corpse with a handsaw. I interviewed the 28-year-old murder defendant, Mary Imodean Stout, in jail. She told me, "Sawing him was the most terrible experience any human ever went through."

The auburn-haired factory worker described hitting her husband Floyd in the head with a claw hammer because she grew tired of "his refusal to find a steady job." Then she rolled him onto a plastic tablecloth.

"I'm sure he was dead when I started sawing. He made no movement. I was completely numb at the time, like a dead person myself."

I thought of the scene in Hemingway's *For Whom the Bell Tolls,* which I had just read, when Fascists cut off Spanish Loyalist heads.

Mary Imodean said she put her husband's head in a pillowcase before enclosing it in a gunnysack. She sawed off his legs and placed each in a "gray, knit looking, fleece-lined cloth." His torso and arms went into another gunnysack.

She made four trips with the bundles to the trunk of her car parked in the driveway about twenty-five feet from her back door. "The bundles were heavy. It was hard for me to do from the beginning. It will be hard for me to the end," she said.

About 2:45 a.m. she drove "like a maniac" about 90 miles north to an Obion River bridge from which she tossed the bundles containing head and legs. Because of approaching headlights, she left the bridge and drove twenty more miles to a creek into which she dropped the torso. She returned home about 6 a.m. She cleaned up the house as much as she could, and reported to her job.

Fishermen found her husband's body parts within a week. Air pumped into water-shriveled fingers made prints possible. Mrs. Stout, quickly arrested, signed a confession.

I later received a summons to appear in Criminal Court to answer questions about my jailhouse conversation with her. But because she stuck to her guilty plea I did not have to testify. She received a life sentence.

MRS. STOUT CALLS SAWING UP HUSBAND TERRIBLE EXPERIENCE

Wife Of Memphian Will Be Arraigned Here Today On Murder Count

'I'M SURE HE WAS DEAD'

Made Three Trips To Auto Carrying 'Heavy' Bundles —'Drove Like Maniac' To Dispose Of Parts

(Additional Story on Page Five)

By LARUE GILLELAND

Mrs. Imodean Tredo Stout looked down at the slender hands yesterday with which she had butchered her husband's body and said softly:

"Sawing him was the most terrible experience any human ever went through."

Calm During Interview

The auburn-haired factory worker was calm during an interview at County Jail shortly after being charged in the grotesque hammer-and-saw death of Floyd Brown Stout, 33, in their home at 1163 Peach at 1 a.m. June 20.

She will be arraigned in City Court at 9 this morning on a charge of murder.

Mrs. Stout confessed she hit her husband on the head with a claw hammer during a quarrel in a hallway. Then she said she sawed off his head and legs and carried them in the trunk of her car to Dyer County where she tossed them in a creek and river.

"I'm sure he was dead when I started sawing," she said as she put her hands to her eyes to block the tears. "He made no movement."

"I was completely numb at the time, like a dead person myself."

Head In Gunny Sack

Homicide Capt. W. W. Wilkinson said the 28-year-old woman wrapped her truck driver husband's head in a white cloth and placed it in a gunny sack.

She placed the legs in a "gray, knit looking, fleece lined cloth."

She wrapped the torso in a plastic tablecloth which she had placed under him before disjointing the body.

She said she made three trips with the bundles from her front door to the car parked in a driveway about 25 feet away.

"The bundles were heavy. It was hard for me to do from the beginning. It will be hard on me to the end."

She said she took no special precautions to keep neighbors from seeing her.

'Drove Like A Maniac'

After locking the body in the trunk, she "drove like a maniac" to a bridge near Bogota and threw the head and legs into the Obion River.

Then she drove to a creek about three miles east of Halls and dropped the body into the creek.

She said she didn't dispose of the body in the river because she saw car lights approaching.

She said she left home about 2:45 a.m. and returned about 6 a.m. She said she tried to clean up the house and then reported to her job at Kimberly-Clark Corp. where she is a packer.

'He Would Have Killed Me'

"I slept as well since then as I did before when I had to be in the house with him. He had threatened me a month and a half earlier. I was afraid of him. He had told me during one of our quarrels that he would kill me."

Mrs. Stout, who was wearing a print dress with a green palm design, said: "I believe he would have killed me later in the night if I hadn't killed him first."

"Me and Floyd were awful mad that night, madder than we had ever been."

She said they had been quarreling over bills he had been charging and because he had refused to get a steady job.

"He turned his back on me

(Continued on Page 2, Col. 4)

(Continued from Page One)

and started out of the kitchen. My temper got the best of me. I picked up a claw hammer in the kitchen and struck him on the head after he had gotten into the hallway. He fell to the floor."

The torso was found in the creek June 21 by a fisherman. Mrs. Stout became a suspect when the FBI in Washington identified fingerprints as her husband's. Air had to be pumped into the water-shrivelled fingers so prints could be made.

Mrs. Stout was arrested at her home Saturday night. She signed a confession before Memphis police, Dyer County Sheriff Ted Pitt and John Cribbs of the Tennessee Bureau of Investigation.

She said she did the crime alone. Sheriff Pitt said yesterday dragging operations for other parts of the body would have to be delayed due to high waters in the area. The sheriff said he had learned another fisherman spotted a bundle in the Obion River several days ago. He threw the bundle back in the water because of its "foul odor," the sheriff said.

Captain Wilkinson yesterday requested persons in the area to be on a lookout for the legs and head and "call us immediately" if found.

Mrs. Stout, who has no children, described her "unhappy" married life.

She said, "I loved my husband when I married him in 1954. I planned to spend the rest of my life with him and did my part in trying.

"If he had faced his responsibilities, I would have respected him as much as any woman ever respected her husband. But he made my life miserable. I had to take things from him nobody knows about but me."

She said she owned her home

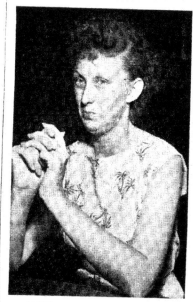

ACCUSED OF MURDER—Mrs. Imodean Stout, 28, of 1163 Peach, who was charged yesterday with murdering her husband, described at County Jail how she killed Floyd Brown Stout, 33, and dismembered his body before disposing of it in a river and creek. —Staff Photo by Lloyd Dinkins

and had a good credit rating when they were married.

She said he charged parts for his truck in her name and had been delinquent in paying a jewelry store for her wedding ring. She said she was embarrassed when the store later called her at work demanding payment.

Mrs. Stout said her husband, whom she met at a downtown cafe where she had stopped one night for a cup of coffee before attending wrestling matches at the Auditorium, had often refused to work for a week at a time.

"I hadn't missed a day of work this year. I often even had to buy his cigarets."

Captain Wilkinson had several books she had been reading in his office. They were taken from her house during the investigation.

The titles were: "The Case of the Runaway Corpse" by Erle Stanley Gardner, "Man Missing" by Mignon G. Eberhart, "Tell Her It's Murder" by Helen Reilly and "Murder of the Well Beloved" by Margot Neville.

I did, however, testify in another case. It involved illegal gambling and bootlegging.

A Memphian could take a legal bottle of liquor, on which taxes had been paid, to a restaurant or night spot where the bartender tagged it and prepared mixed drinks ordered by the bottle's owner. Otherwise, liquor could be sold by the drink only in private clubs, such as the Memphis Press Club.

My involvement in the bootleg case came when residents of the Memphis suburb of Oakville told the newspaper that intoxicated motorists regularly created traffic dangers as they drove from the site of Sunday afternoon dice and card games. The games and liquor sales took place in a neighborhood outside a house far from the main road.

When Oakville residents said the Sheriff's Office ignored their complaints, my editors told me to investigate. They assigned a photographer, Lloyd Dinkins, to accompany me. In my car, Lloyd and I followed two Oakville residents to a narrow dirt road that led to the action. After telling our guides goodbye, Dinkins and I formulated a plan.

He climbed a hill from which he could point a telephoto lens toward the house without being seen. I drove to a guarded gate. The guard permitted me to pass when I waved money and said I wanted to buy whisky. In a big yard outside a house, about seventy-five men tossed dice in several small groups. All were black. Another man sold bottles of illegal booze.

I bought a half pint. I asked the seller if he ever worried about sheriff's deputies. "That's the chance you take," he said. "Deputies come around periodically. It looks like a track meet when these boys scatter." I moved among the gamblers, giving photographer Dinkins on the hill time to do his job.

No one showed any interest in me until I tried to horn in on a game. That aroused suspicions. My presence no longer welcome, I left.

Back at the office, I wrote my lead, using a rare first-person angle:

Dice games and bootlegging flourish openly beside a narrow, dead end road in residential Oakville. Negroes run the illegal operation, and a white man apparently can buy corn whisky any time. I did.

70

Dice Games And Bootlegging Brazenly Open In Oakville

(Picture on Page 15)

By LARUE GILLELAND

Dice games and bootlegging flourish openly beside a narrow, dead end road in residential Oakville.

The illegal show is run by Negroes, but a white man apparently can buy corn whisky anytime.

This reporter bought a half pint there yesterday. It was easy. The price was $1.25.

No one in the crowd of Negro men showed any suspicion until I tried to horn in on their crap game. They were rolling dice on the ground six feet from the road.

The spot is on Frisco Road 200 yards east of Tchulahoma Road in south Shelby County.

Residents Are Upset

There were about 75 Negro men there at 3 yesterday afternoon when I was driven to the place by the Rev. J. C. Hulme, pastor of Oakville Methodist Church, and Gene Wood, a service station owner and layman at Lucy Baptist Church in Millington.

They and many other Oakville residents are upset because the gambling and bootlegging is not curbed.

The Rev. Mr. Hulme said he called the sheriff's office two weeks ago and was told "there's nothing we can do because our squad cars are too busy investigating accidents." He said the officer he talked to refused to identify himself.

H. E. Crowson of 3478 Tchulahoma Road, a layman at Oakville Memorial Baptist Church, said the gambling and bootlegging has existed "every week end since I moved here three years ago."

Sheriff E. H. Reeves could not be reached for comment.

Chief Deputy Hugh Bertschi balked at questions: "I don't have anything to say."

Afraid Of Arrest?

When a Negro whisky salesman was asked if he was afraid of being arrested by sheriff's deputies, he said:

"That's the chance you take. Deputies come around periodically. It looks like a track meet when these boys scatter."

What did he mean by "periodically?" "Oh, once or twice a week."

Felix Miller, assistant night jailer at the sheriff's office, said: "Our squad cars check that road pretty regularly. But they can see you coming and flush like a covey of quail. We get a complaint every now and then."

Robert T. Stone, Federal Alcohol and Tobacco Tax office group leader, said: "I am not familiar with this case. If any Oakville resident makes a complaint at our office in the Falls Building, I assure you there will be an investigation."

Dinkins' photographs accompanied my front-page story.

SUNDAY SPORT—Three dice games in one huddle of players took place yesterday on Frisco Road in Oakville. Staff photographer Lloyd Dinkins caught the unsuspecting players in action with a telephoto lens from about 100 yards away. Oakville residents are disturbed because they say gambling and bootlegging occur here every week end.
(Story on Page One)

Deputies soon found Lee Vick, 31, who sold me the bottle, and charged him with violating liquor laws.

I received a summons to appear in court in the Lee Vick case. On the witness stand I made it plain that *The Commercial Appeal* did not want the defendant to become a scapegoat. I said, "My aim was not to cause Lee Vick to be prosecuted for what many men do in Oakville, but to inform our readers that bootlegging and illegal gambling have existed there so long."

My testimony, I believe, helped Vick receive only a small fine and no jail time. Sheriff Ed Reeves in court said, "The situation is regrettable and certainly not condoned by me. It will be stopped."

Sheriff Reeves, however, could not keep his promise. He was killed a short time later. He made the mistake of using an electric pump at his home to clean his partially-filled swimming pool. A neighbor also died trying to rescue the sheriff. I wrote the story after interviewing Reeve's wife, emergency crew, and deputies at the scene.

"My husband was down in the pool at the deep end trying to get the water out so he could paint it," Mrs. Reeves told me. "He was using the pump in about three feet of water. Tom Bryan, his good friend, watched from the pool's edge. I was on the telephone when I heard Mr. Bryan yell for help.

"I ran outside and saw Ed lying in the water. I thought he had a heart attack. I climbed down the ladder and had just started to reach for my husband's head when another neighbor, Melwyn Dan, jumped over me into the pool. He grabbed Ed, then fell back in the water, too.

"Mr. Bryan turned off the pump with a switch near the edge of the pool and ran into the house to call an ambulance. If I had touched my husband first, the electric current would have killed me, too."

Gilleland interviews the wife of Tennessee sheriff Ed Reeves on the night of his accidental death, 1955.

73

I occasionally discussed issues with a Mississippi-born assistant city editor, whose racial views were more conservative than mine. He based his argument that blacks were inferior to whites partly on the "fact" that blacks failed to invent the sail despite using boats for centuries on African lakes and rivers.

One night that editor telephoned me at the police press office to say that a couple of citizens claimed to have seen two sheriff's deputies beat up a black man for no apparent reason just outside the city-county line. They said the deputies used clubs and placed the victim in the back of a squad car while he bled profusely. The editor said the sheriff's office had already denied the report to a reporter checking on it from the city desk.

The editor asked me if I had ever been in the squad car parking lot at night. I had. He asked me to describe its layout. The part of my description that interested him most was the lot's dim lighting. The editor said, "A shift change has occurred since we received the call, and it's doubtful deputies would drive around in a car with a bloody back seat. I want you to see if you can find that car. Go to the parking lot and check back seats for fresh blood. If you find any, we'll confront the Sheriff's Office again."

For the first time as a reporter I questioned an assignment. "Are you sure this is a good idea?" I asked. The editor insisted.

Besides wanting to keep my job, another factor in my giving in was my surprise that this editor showed concern about a black man's welfare. I went to the dimly lit parking lot, entered an open gate, and saw several squad cars. No one else was there. Nervously, I opened a car's back door, leaned far in, and carefully felt the seat. I did this again and again, car after car.

Only three vehicles remained to be searched when a squad car's headlights approached the gate. I crawled flat on a back seat and closed the door. The incoming car parked about fifteen yards away. I could hear doors slam and a couple of deputies walking my direction. Two visions flashed through my mind: receiving a beating with billy clubs and being charged with a trespassing crime. If the former occurred, I hoped the newspaper would pay hospital bills. If the latter, I hoped the paper would defend me in court.

I could hear the officers' voices as they walked by. I listened until they had gone. I hesitated before looking in the last two squad cars. I decided to finish the job, but quickly. I did so without finding anything of interest. I walked out of the lot, apparently unseen. For the next few days the city desk assigned another reporter to pester the sheriff's office about the reported beating, but no evidence of it ever surfaced.

I saw police guards slug prisoners, both white, on two occasions. Each time I thought the prisoner asked for it. One prisoner spat at a guard. Another kicked a guard in his shin.

The newspaper wanted a story about closure of an old East Memphis precinct police station called Barksdale that once housed horses for the city's Mounted Patrol. In covering the assignment I found a retired police lieutenant who helped capture "Machin Gun Kelly" in the 1930s.

Kelly's full name was George Kelly Barnes. He was a contemporary of hoodlums Bonnie and Clyde, John Dillinger, and Baby Face Nelson. All operated in other parts of the country until shot dead by police. Memphis-born Kelly had more education than they, having attended Mississippi State University for about a semester.

Kelly became "Public Enemy No. 1" for armed bank robberies, Prohibition-Era bootlegging, and kidnappings. Kelly's second-wife, Katherine, bought the gangster his first machine gun and served as his unofficial underworld public relations agent. She circulated stories, often exaggerated, about his crimes.

His downfall came after kidnapping a wealthy Oklahoma oilman that he eventually freed for $200,000 ransom. By remembering sounds, including overhead plane traffic, the oilman helped police pinpoint a Texas farm as the place he had been held hostage for a week by Kelly. Kelly also buried some of the ransom money on the farm. Investigators traced Kelly from the farm to Memphis. That's where A. B. Randle enters the story.

I found former police lieutenant A. B. Randle basking in retirement at the age of 76 in his Memphis home. He recalled working out of Barksdale station.

Seated in his favorite chair, he described for me the cool, early morning in September 1933 when he approached the back door of a house on Rayner Street. He, three other police officers, and three FBI agents acted on a tip that had been traced to Katherine's loose tongue.

Kelly, Katherine, and two gang members occupied the house. Officer Randle, carrying a 44-caliber revolver, entered the back door with Sgt. William Raney. Other police covered the house. All occupants were asleep, except Kelly. Randle said Kelly, in his underwear and suffering a hangover, appeared in a hallway, surprised and unarmed. Randle said he and Raney confronted Kelly. Hearing their order, "Don't move," he obeyed. "That's how it was," Randle told me. "Without his machine gun, he wasn't much."

Randle said the awakened Katherine put her arms around the subdued Machine Gun Kelly and said, "These G-men will never leave us alone," thus coining a term for FBI agents that endured for years.

From 1933 until his death in 1954, Kelly served a life sentence in Alcatraz and Leavenworth prisons. He sometimes performed "altar boy" duties during prison church services. Kelly died behind bars of a heart attack at 54, in contrast to Dillinger, Nelson and the Clydes, all killed by police bullets. Katherine Kelly, paroled in 1958, became a bookkeeper.

My future wife, Betsy, who grew up in Memphis, remembered as a girl reciting a home-grown doggerel with other children:

"I kept a little monkey
Way out in the country;

I fed him on ginger bread.

**One day Machine Gun Kelly
shot him in the belly,
and now my monkey is dead."**

Meanwhile, I wrote a story about Boris Morros, Russian-born musician and movie producer, implicated in a 1957 spy case against Jack and Myra Soble. Morros had fled the 1917 Bolshevik Revolution because the new regime resented his "czarist connections." In the 1920s he directed music for vaudeville and silent movies in Memphis. He later helped produce such Hollywood films as "Carnegie Hall" and "Lysistrata."

I quoted sources that conjectured he might be a double agent. That turned out to be wrong. I learned later that he had been a U. S. plant inside the Russian secret police for years. He fled the Soviet Union for the last time when he couldn't deliver on its request that he secure an American formula for jet plane tires. Russian tires sometimes exploded on landing.

After returning to America, he testified against the Sobles. The government convicted the Sobles of belonging to a conspiracy that passed secrets to Soviet agents in New York, Paris, Zurich and Vienna. Mr. and Mrs. Soble served prison terms of seven and four years, respectively.

When I noticed many of the same faces again and again in court on public dunkeness charges, I asked City Court Judge Beverly Boushe about them. He estimated the number of Memphis and Shelby County drunks arrested regularly at more than a hundred.

The judge recalled an elderly man seen frequently in his court. Charged on one occasion with setting his mattress on fire while smoking and drinking in bed, the defendant said, "Judge, there's not a word of truth to that. The bed was on fire when I got into it."

In juvenile court, twelve teenagers appeared on the same day in an assortment of cases to testify about beating up people -- even strangers. Typical was a 16-year-old who told of hitting another boy "just for excitement." His victim, 14, received a concussion when his head struck the sidewalk, and he spent three days in a hospital. The boy had been assaulted while standing in front of a theater with his girlfriend.

His older attacker told the juvenile judge, "I had nothing against him. I didn't even know him, but I hit him."

More instructive was this quote: "My mother never asks me where I'm going, and I never tell her."

I learned early why authorities insist on notifying next of kin before releasing names of the dead to news media. After receiving information from a hospital emergency room about a car accident that killed a male driver, I telephoned his house to get full name, age, occupation, and family survivors. The wife answered. She had not heard of the accident. Her voice broke into sobs when I told her why I called.

I felt awful. Despite her sorrow and confusion, she managed to give me the facts I needed. I thanked her and apologized. Although that situation was unusual, I found most people cooperate in providing information about a recently deceased loved one, because they want the last story to be accurate.

10

Blues Highway

On days off, I sometimes drove my car south from Memphis to glimpse sites prominent in the history of blues, jazz and rock. I followed Highway 61, "the Blues Highway."

After crossing the Tennessee border into the Mississippi Delta, the highway cut though clumps of trees and cotton and soybean fields that rolled east from the Mississippi River past the city of Oxford to the Alabama border. At Oxford stood the University of Mississippi and William Faulkner's stately home. Other writers who had lived in the Delta area included Tennessee Williams, Eudora Welty, Shelby Foote, Richard Wright, Hodding Carter, and John Grisham.

Highway 61 passed at least two of several crossroads claiming to be the legendary spot where musician Robert Johnson "sold his soul to the devil" on a dark night about 1930. Myth says he did so to acquire guitar-playing prowess. It "made him the most important jazz musician who ever lived," according to Eric Clapton. Johnson died in 1938 when he was only 27.

My drive soon brought me to the towns of Clarksdale and Tutwiler. Clarksdale is about 75 miles from Memphis, and Tutwiler is reached by detour a few miles farther.

In Tutwiler in 1903, W. C. Handy waited for a train on a small railroad platform. He turned his attention to another black man seated nearby playing slide guitar by moving a closed pocketknife across the strings. The guitarist caressed flatted 3rds and 7ths in a way that Handy had not heard before -- and Handy had played and listened to a lot of music.

A cornetist, Handy directed a black Clarksdale band called Knights of Pythias. His musicians performed tunes containing African rhythms and themes from old spirituals, but nothing quite like the 12-bar pattern played by the lonely guitarist seated beside the Tutwiler railroad track. He told Handy his music was called "blues" and that it mimicked the melancholy call and response chants of plantation field hands and prison chain gangs.

After listening for a while, Handy caught the train to Clarksdale, but he remembered the incident. He soon moved his band to Memphis where they took up residence. He performed in Pee Wee's and other Beale Street saloons a few years before writing his first blues tune. He named it "Mr. Crump" and played it at a political rally during E. H. Crump's 1909 campaign for mayor. Crump liked the song.

Handy, after election memories faded, changed the song's name from "Mr. Crump" to "Memphis Blues" in 1912. He sold it for a hundred dollars, something he regretted when it became the first blues "hit." The tune's beat, some said, inspired dancers Vernon and Irene Castle to invent the fox trot.

Handy decided to establish his own sheet music publishing company. Needing money, he obtained a loan from John Ross, a white Memphis businessman with a reputation for philanthropy. Ross owned real estate, including rental properties, and an agricultural feed business on Front Street. He contributed support to a number of organizations for young people, especially crippled children, and he competed as a driver in some of the Mid-South's earliest cross-country auto races. He directed county and state relief organizations during the Depression, and served several years as a federal probation officer.

Handy published "Jogo Blues" in 1913. Remembering the loan he'd received, he dedicated the song to John Ross. Handy rewrote some themes from "Jogo Blues" a year later, and they became "St. Louis Blues." He wrote "Beale Street Blues" in 1916.

The day W. C. Handy died at 84 in New York on March 28, 1958, I was working in *The Commercial Appeal* newsroom. The wire editor and the copy desk chief, sitting nearby, recognized Handy's death as a front-page story. They discussed whether to run his picture -- and, if so, where. I listened with interest. I remember one editor saying the front page had never carried a black person's obituary photo. They agreed on a compromise. A front-page story about Handy would jump inside where his photo would be placed.

At Handy's funeral in New York a day or so later, police estimated 25,000 people filed through the Harlem church containing his casket, and another 150,000 gathered on nearby streets to pay their respects.

Clarksdale, where Handy first organized his band, contained a small, nondescript hotel that previously had been a hospital. I visited it on one of my Blues Highway excursions. Blues Singer Bessie Smith died in the hospital in 1933 of injuries received in a head-on car collision with a truck. She had been driving from Memphis to Clarksdale after performing at a Beale Street nightspot. Some blacks complained that if she had been white she would have received quicker treatment -- and might have lived.

A few years later, the hospital was converted to Clarksdale's Riverside Hotel. The hotel management, catering to black clientele, preserved "Room 2," the former hospital emergency room where Bessie Smith died, as a memorial to her. Hotel guests at one time or another included musicians Bo Diddley, B. B. King, Ike Turner, Muddy Waters, Howlin'

Wolf, John Lee Hooker, and Jackie Brenston. They often held impromptu jam sessions in Room 2.

A couple of old timers in Clarksdale told me that music history was made in the lobby in 1951. Band leader Ike Turner on guitar and saxophonist Jackie Brenston composed "Rocket 88" for a band called the Delta Cats. Some music historians called it the first rock and roll tune. To record it, the young composers drove an old car to Sun Record Company in Memphis. After that success, Ike Turner married his singer, Tina.

Sam Phillips started Sun Record Company at 710 Union Avenue, two or three blocks from *The Commercial Appeal's* front door. Elvis made his first record at Sun three years after "Rocket 88" had been produced there. Later at Sun, Jerry Lee Lewis recorded "Great Balls of Fire," Johnny Cash recorded "Folsom Prison Blues," and Carl Perkins recorded "Blue Suede Shoes."

In Tupelo, a hundred miles east of Clarksdale, stands a two-room birthplace of Elvis Presley. Elvis' truck-driver father said he built the tiny house, later a museum, for a few hundred dollars. When Elvis was 13, his family moved to Memphis where he attended Humes High School, practiced his guitar, and listened to rhythm and blues recordings by black musicians on Beale Street and radio station WDIA. *The Commercial Appeal's* rear parking lot opened onto Beale Street, about three blocks from W. C. Handy Park and the shops and cafes adjacent to it.

Occasionally I worked the rewrite desk, a favorite assignment. A diversion in the busy desk's routine was taking calls from readers, often in bars, hoping to settle arguments. Among questions I remember: "How far away is the moon?" "When was the first auto accident in Great Britain?" "What time does the midnight service start at St. Mary's Cathedral?" and "Are there more male or female birds in the world?" The newspaper's handy, nearby reference library helped settle some, but not all, arguments.

The rewrite desk's main tasks included turning out stories on deadline from notes phoned in by reporters and cleaning up copy written on an earlier shift. One evening an editor handed me a story a reporter turned in before going home. The reporter had interviewed movie actress Joan Crawford, visiting Memphis alone and staying at the Peabody Hotel. She had just finished a movie, "Autumn Leaves," in which she had a romance with an emotionally disturbed younger man. She then made a business trip to Memphis as a PepsiCo board member. The company's chairman, Alfred Steele, was her fifth husband.

My editor pointed out "a hole" in the reporter's story and told me to call the actress at the hotel for missing information. It was about 9 p.m.

Joan Crawford answered the phone. I introduced myself, explained why I was calling, and took notes as she gave the facts I needed. I casually asked if she'd been in Memphis before. She had been. She said she found the city "charming" and said she planned to visit "a couple living in the nearby Clarksdale area." I mentioned the Blues

Highway and Clarksdale's contributions to music. She asked me how long I'd been with *The Commercial Appeal.* I told her.

We chatted a few minutes more, and, in a voice I thought reminiscent of her role in "Mildred Pierce," she said, "I've got a bottle of vodka here in my room. If you're interested, you might care to pick up some orange juice when you get off work -- and come by to have a drink."

The notion of having a drink with Joan Crawford dazzled me. I told her I'd be glad to bring the orange juice. I even fantasized to myself about what she would be wearing. I hoped that, whatever it was, it included her stylish shoulder pads I'd noticed in movies. After a few more pleasantries, she asked, "What time do you get off?" My ego deflated.

"I, uh . . . at 1:30 in the morning." I quickly explained I could pick up the orange juice and be at the Peabody before 2 a.m. Her tone changed. Clearly, she had no interest in that late hour. She told me so. I said I'd enjoyed our conversation, and we hung up.

The shoulder pads would remain a mystery.

The next night at work I told some colleagues about my conversation with the actress. One said, "Gilleland, you idiot! You could have gone. If you had told us at the time, any one of us would have covered the rewrite desk for you. Even top management would have approved your visiting Joan Crawford."

I long regretted my botched opportunity to socialize with the glamorous Academy Award winner. In her 1936 movie, "Love on the Run," Joan Crawford played an heiress who got mixed up with a poor, young newspaper reporter. They met when he arrived uninvited at her hotel room. I saw the movie more than once.

After work, copy editors and reporters liked to gather at the Memphis Press Club on Union Avenue across Union Avenue from the newspaper. They flavored their food and drink with discussions of the day's news and works of modern novelists. I mostly listened to the literary talk. Ernest Hemingway topped the Memphis newsmen's list of favorite authors at that time, followed by William Faulkner, Joseph Conrad, and Thomas Wolfe.

Like its counterpart in many cities, the Press Club had associate members. They supported the club with higher dues than journalists paid. Associate members were mostly business and professional people. They brought friends or clients to the club for dinner or drinks because they liked its off-beat atmosphere and lively conversations.

An associate member who hobnobbed often with reporters and editors was professional golfer Cary Middlecoff. He'd been a dentist in Memphis and the Army before beginning his professional golf career. He joined the Press Club when he was 34, shortly after winning the 1955 Master's Tournament at Augusta, Georgia. He beat Ben Hogan in that tournament by seven strokes.

Cary and his wife Edith often dined at the club. I sometimes found them sitting at the bar when I got off work. He'd ask what I'd been covering that day. He and his wife always seemed interested, no matter what kind of story I related. They also liked to talk about local politics, jazz and blues. We compared notes on sites we'd visited along the Blues Highway.

I remember Cary buying a round of drinks at the club on a crowded evening shortly after he won the U.S. Open in Phoenix in 1956.

He seldom talked about himself at the Press Club unless someone put a pointed, personal question to him. I asked one night how long he thought he'd compete on the golf tour. He answered, "As long as I still enjoy it. When I can't put the ball in the cup, I'll go back to putting fillings in teeth."

He retired from golf competition five years later after winning a total of forty tournaments, including another U.S. Open, and being inducted into the World Golf Hall of Fame.

11

Elvis and Georgette

A handsome domestic cat walked through the Memphis newspaper where I worked in 1956 as if it owned the place. Most reporters and editors in *The Commercial Appeal* newsroom paid little attention to it. They had no idea the cat soon would become famous.

Occasionally, the tabby-coated animal jumped atop a reporter's desk. It would sit and watch him or her type before springing to a neighboring desk.

"Whose cat is that?" I asked Louis Silver, a veteran reporter working near me. He explained that several weeks earlier the cat had appeared half-starved amid the huge printing presses in the ground-floor production department. The animal apparently had walked in from an alley or from nearby Beale Street.

Louis said production department employees soon adopted it. They named the cat "George" for George Edmonds, the first pressman to share his sandwich with it.

George, the cat, became a favorite for its mouse-catching prowess. George searched for prey among noisy presses that stood a couple of stories tall and among the stacked rolls of heavy newsprint. One day, when hunting was unusually good, George pranced about with two or more dead mice in its mouth -- or so the admiring production department employees bragged.

As the heavy presses roared each night, producing five editions, George liked to sleep nearby. A city edition, on the streets about dinner time, was followed by Arkansas, Mississippi, Missouri, and West Tennessee editions an hour or more apart. A final edition, after midnight, went to Memphis homes. When the noise of the presses stopped, the cat usually woke up.

A couple of months after I first met the animal in 1956, the newspaper printed a humorous little story about how "our office cat" had surprised everyone -- and embarrassed some -- by giving birth to kittens. The story emphasized that protective production department employees quickly changed the cat's name to "Georgette."

One of the pressmen came up with the idea of entering Georgette in the working cat division of the big upcoming Memphis and Mid-South Cat Fanciers Show. It would be held in the ballroom of the city's fanciest hotel, the Peabody. Georgette immediately began receiving regular grooming, and her handlers added ice cream to her sandwich and mouse rations.

Georgette appeared ready when the weekend of the big show arrived. Because she had grown accustomed to shouting newspaper workers and roaring presses, the hotel ballroom's milling crowd of patrician felines and their owners didn't bother her one whit.

She out-performed all working-class contestants. Plunked into a maze designed to test "mouseability," Georgette flitted through an obstacle course to four mice in a protective cage in a minute and forty-eight seconds. Her closest competitor, Zephyr Awning, reached the cage in two minutes, and Camshaft Flywheel covered the route in three minutes and ten seconds. Judges announced Georgette the working class champion.

She then breezed through the rest of the show, unruffled by pedigreed competition. She emerged with six ribbons, including short- hair best of color, all breeds best of color -- and best-of-show.

The Commercial Appeal ran a Sunday morning front-page story and photo of Georgette, proudly looking over her ribbons. Associated Press and United Press International also distributed the story. It described Georgette's Cinderella rise to fame and how she liked to sleep near noisy presses. It also described the production department's elation, quoting George Edmonds as saying, "I knew our Georgette was a lady."

Pressman Zeke McKelvey boasted he had "invested at least 140 bottles of milk in her."

Time magazine put an item about Georgette in its "People Section." Georgette, as I remember, received a couple more lines in the magazine's People Section that week than did actress Marilyn Monroe.

Before long, another story about Georgette appeared. She was expecting again. As her pregnancy progressed, children from throughout the world wrote the newspaper to ask if they could adopt one of her kittens.

Meanwhile, the cat periodically visited newspaper departments -- retail advertising, classified advertising, circulation, business, and composing room. She even came back to the upper-floor newsroom.

One day as I worked, she walked across my desk. She jumped to another desk just as the elevator door opened and 21-year-old Elvis Presley stepped out with a couple of his buddies. Having not yet seen him in person, I recognized him from his photos.

I assumed he and friends had walked the two or three blocks from Sun Records at 706 Union. That's where proprietor Sam Phillips boosted Elvis' career months earlier by recording "That's All Right, Mama" and "Blue Moon of Kentucky." Although still friendly with Phillips, Elvis had recently signed with RCA to do "Heartbreak Hotel." Meanwhile,

Sun recorded "I Walk the Line" by Johnny Cash, "Crazy Arms" by Jerry Lee Lewis, and "Blue Suede Shoes" by Carl Perkins. These singers and Elvis knew each other well.

On entering the newsroom, Elvis looked around and asked, "Is that Georgette?" The singer had come to meet Memphis' other new celebrity.

I paused in my typing long enough to watch Elvis bend down, pet the cat, and say something to her. Then he noticed a noisy teleprinter pounding out wire service copy nearby. He stood looking at it with curiosity. Assuming he had never seen such a machine before, I got up to give him a brief explanation of how Associated Press, United Press International, Reuters and other news services distributed information to their media clients. He asked a few questions and said, "Thank you, sir," as I walked away.

The "sir" struck me as polite but quaint, since I was not much older than he. In a few minutes, Elvis and his friends left.

I would next encounter Elvis in a courtroom -- after his arrest in a street fight. It was several months later, seated in his car under a street light, that I informed him that he was sought by police.

A week after Elvis' newspaper visit, we received bad news about Georgette. She started acting sickly, and Edmonds took her to a veterinarian. X-rays showed Georgette suffered a broken pelvis, probably in her alley-cat days, or perhaps in a clash with a car. The vet had to perform surgery and she could never have kittens again.

Georgette recovered. She reigned again over the production department, performing her job well until dying a few years later at an estimated age of ten or eleven.

She left an estate. During her illness, her friends took up a collection to pay the veterinarian bill. When she was discharged and all bills paid, $4.10 remained. Two fans added 90 cents to make it an even $5 deposited in the newspaper credit union. After her death, the money went to a children's charity.

It was eight months after Elvis Presley visited Georgette that I wrote my first story about him. I told how he rocked two men in a fistfight and then rolled over them in a courtroom.

The fracas began when Elvis pulled into a Memphis service station to check his car's air conditioning. When he got back in his car, a couple of salesmen from a dealership next door approached and started joking with him about how he should trade his Lincoln for a Ford. The service station manager interrupted to tell Elvis to move the car, and Elvis said he would.

Some high school girls spotted Elvis and surrounded his car while three of them asked for autographs. The station manager came outside again and ordered Elvis to leave. Elvis hesitated because several girls stood in front of his car.

While he fumbled with the ignition, the manager said, "I don't give a damn if you're Elvis Presley," reached through Elvis' open car window, and hit him on the back of the head. Elvis got out and knocked the station manager down. An employee ran up to help his boss. Elvis punched him just as a police car rounded the corner.

Police stopped the fight and arrested all three men. They were ordered to appear in court on assault and battery charges.

**Georgette, prize-winning newspaper cat, became such a well-known Memphis celebrity that Elvis Presley came to newspaper to meet her.
(The Commercial Appeal photo)**

AFTER THE FIGHT—Police booked Aubrey Brown (left), singer Elvis Presley (right) and Edd Hopper, who declined to pose for a picture, after a fight early last night at a downtown service station. After his release by police, Presley went home to relax and play with his new pet.

—Staff Photos

My city editor told me to be there. That morning Elvis fans crowded the courtroom. After trying a dozen defendants for public drunkeness, the judge called the singer's case. Witnesses and even police officers backed Elvis' story. A patrolman added that he saw the station manager draw a pocketknife with a three-inch blade as he got up from the ground after Elvis' punch. After the judge gave Elvis' two opponents stern lectures and small fines, he dismissed the charge against Elvis. Spectators cheered.

I followed Elvis as he made his way down a crowded courthouse hallway to the front door. There, a little woman, perhaps seventy-five or more, stepped up to him and said, "I'm just an old lady, but I like you, too." Elvis reached down, took her face in his hands, and said, "You look like you're twenty-five years old to me."

I used that quote to end my story. Elvis and Colonel Parker, his manager, apparently liked it. They sent me a Christmas card.

Audience Flips As Our Presley Wins In Court

(Pictures on Page 31)

By LARUE GILLELAND

Teenage idol Elvis Presley barely managed a shy grin as he walked from a packed courtroom yesterday after rolling to a second and legal decision over two filling station men he rocked in a fist fight.

City Court was crowded with giggling girls and curious adults who applauded with gusto when Acting Judge Sam Friedman told Presley:

"The testimony points to the guilt of the other men. I'll dismiss you."

Opponents Fined

The rock and roll singer had been charged with assault and battery and disorderly conduct.

His opponents in Wednesday's fight at the Gulf Station at Second and Gayoso were fined.

Edd Hopper, 42, of 3225 Cicalla, station manager, paid a $26 fine. He appeared in Court with a bandage over an inchlong gash near his bruised left eye where Presley hit him.

Aubrey Brown, 21, of 262 South Pauline, a big six-four station attendant, was fined $15. Disorderly conduct charges against both men were dismissed.

Cameras flashed and girls screamed, "Oh, there's Elvis," as the 21-year-old Presley started into the courtroom. There were 207 women and girls waiting for him.

Accompanied By Father

He arrived with his father, Vernon Presley, just as the morning court session was getting under way at 9:10.

Dressed in a rust-colored sport jacket and open-collared shirt, he took a seat in the last row and quietly watched the judge try 12 persons on public drunkenness charges.

Then his case was heard.

The judge said he gave Hopper a heavier fine because the case against him was more serious than against Brown.

Three patrolmen who broke up the fight testified Hopper struck Elvis first as the singer sat in his $11,000 Continental Mark II parked in front of the station's gasoline pumps.

They said Hopper pulled a knife on Presley after he jumped out and punched the station manager.

Judge Friedman asked Presley, who likes to spar with boxing gloves at home, to give his version.

Presley said he was alone and driving along Gayoso when something went wrong with the air conditioning unit. Fumes were coming up in the car making his "eyes water."

"I pulled into the station and asked the men to look at my car," he testified. "When I got back in it some Hull-Dobbs salesmen came over and started kidding me about trading my Continental for a Ford."

Agreed To Move

He said Hopper asked him to move and he replied, "Yes, sir, I will."

Three girls then rushed over and asked for autographs.

"I was writing my name, and trying to hurry, when Mr. Hopper asked me to move again. There were people in front of the car and you don't just drive off suddenly when people are friendly and talking to you."

"I signed the autographs and was turning on my key when he reached in the window and hit me on the head with his hand.

"I was more or less stunned because I wasn't expecting that. I started to get out of the car and he pushed me back. Then I jumped out and hit him and he pulled a knife on me.

"Then that other gentleman, Mr. Brown, ran to me and said, 'You can't do that to him,' and swung at me. I don't remember whether I got hit or not but I hit him. Then the policeman stopped the fight."

When the judge dismissed the singer's charges, people in the courtroom applauded. Judge Friedman pounded his gavel and said, "Stop this applause! This is a courtroom, not a show."

Earlier the judge told photographers they could shoot pictures in the courtroom but that he wouldn't permit flash bulbs.

Presley said he planned to leave last night for Biloxi, Miss., for a short vacation before appearing Sunday, Oct. 28, on Ed Sullivan's television show in New York.

When he walked into the street from the courtroom, motorists waved and yelled at him and pedestrians begged him to let them be photographed with him.

'Still My Friends'

"These people are still my friends," he said as a half-dozen screaming girls, all about 15, asked him for autographs.

A mounted policeman rode up on a horse and Presley said, "Say, you ought to come up to the house and see my mules. I've got two Mexican burros. Come and see them."

A little woman, about 65, stood in front of him and said, "I'm just an old lady but I like you too."

Presley reached down, took her face in his hands.

"You look like you're about 25 years old to me."

As he drove away in his car, she turned to another woman and said, "Isn't he a dandy?"

Police Back Story

Patrolmen Tom Yeager and R. E. Ferguson said Presley's story was correct. Patrolman Yeager said, "His car was completely surrounded and he couldn't pull away. I was trying to clear some girls away from the front of the car when Hopper said, 'I don't give a damn if you're Elvis Presley' and reached into the car and struck him."

Patrolman Yeager said Presley got out and knocked Hopper back about 10 feet with a blow. He said Hopper then drew a pocket knife with a three-inch blade.

"I saw the open knife in his hand. I jumped between Presley and Hopper and told Hopper to go into the station. I was not holding Hopper when Presley hit him."

Mr. Hopper testified the pocket knife wasn't open and that Presley's car had his gasoline pumps blocked about 20 minutes. He claimed officers held him when Presley struck him.

Mr. Brown said he tried to hit Presley but missed. He said Presley had been asked to move in a "nice way" but had refused.

Advice From Court

Judge Friedman told Presley: "I realize your position and that crowds follow you wherever you go. I will give you this advice—in the future try to be considerate and co-operate with businessmen. Avoid crowds where business will be interrupted."

To Hopper and Brown he said: "You should have called police to move Mr. Presley if, as you have said, he stayed longer than a reasonable time. The law does not permit you to strike any man."

THE COMME

MEMPHIS, TENN., S

Amidst Cheers And Applause Elvis

FATHERLY ADVICE—Vernon Presley (left) gave advice to his 21-year-old son during the trial of Elvis and two gasoline station attendants in City Court yesterday. Charges against the rock and roll singer were dismissed.

THE AFTERMATH — After the proce found himself more popular than ever as he

A Legal Knockout In City Court

THE LINEUP—The three principals in the fight at Gayoso and Second took the oath before acting Judge Sam Friedman. Edd Hopper (left) and Aubrey Brown (center) were fined for their parts in the fist fight.

omen and girls jammed the court. Miss Mary of 215 West Edwin stands alongside the singer.

I wrote my last newspaper story about Elvis when the Army inducted him in 1958. I thought army service might be good for him, especially if he associated with bright officers, or others, who could broaden his horizons.

My impression of Elvis was that he was curious and intellectually restless. Grade school teachers, after apparently failing to stimulate him, called him "average." My observation was that he had an alert mind. He grasped concepts that interested him. He easily memorized and accurately recalled many songs.

I was not impressed with the friends I saw huddling around him, including young bodyguards that some dubbed the "Memphis Mafia." Colonel Parker was a smart man, from my perspective, but I got the impression that Elvis and his manager seldom discussed anything other than the music business.

Elvis served in Germany, and was honorably discharged as a sergeant in 1960. With his solid, above-average baritone-tenor vocal range, he returned to recording songs, appearing in public concerts, and making movies. He married Priscilla Beaulieu, whom he had met in Germany.

The stretch of Highway 51 bordering Graceland was renamed "Elvis Presley Boulevard." On the boulevard, I passed Graceland daily going to and from Whitehaven, the suburb where I lived a few miles south of Memphis. No matter what time I drove by, including late night or early morning, I saw Elvis fans milling around, often staring quietly though steel bars of his driveway's front gate. The fans -- sometimes many, sometimes few -- were always there, whether he was home or not.

Elvis died unexpectedly at 42 at Graceland. Traces of many prescription drugs were found in his body.

12

Let Me Call You Sweetheart

About the time I was writing news stories about Elvis Presley I interviewed 73-year-old Alice Whitson Norton, a songwriter at the opposite end of the musical spectrum. When she was sixteen back in 1901, more than half century before I met her, she and her older sister wrote the lyrics to "Let Me Call You Sweetheart." The sister, Beth Whitson, had already published several poems.

In what may have been her last newspaper interview, Alice described for me the night when she returned from a date with a high school boy about her age.

"He was tall and handsome. He had just brought me home from a party in Goodrich, Tennessee," she said. "Beth challenged me to write a song with her. She and I sat on a hammock between two tall cedars in our yard.

"We completed the lyrics right there. The most difficult line for me was 'Let me hear you whisper that you love me too.' It took forty minutes to write that line. The rest was rather easy.

"Of course, we didn't know the song would become a favorite of millions. I was full of youth and romance then. Now I'm just full of romance."

In 1904, Beth teamed up with composer Leo Friedman to write "Meet Me Tonight in Dreamland" for the opening of a new park at New York's Coney Island. When Friedman read Alice and Beth's lyrics to "Let Me Call You Sweetheart," he decided to set them to music as well.

The famous song was published in 1910. Beth lived until 1930. Alice died in Nashville a few years after I interviewed her. She gave me an autographed copy of her song.

The Commercial Appeal considered any major event in Little Rock, more than a hundred miles west of Memphis, almost a local story. So, Little Rock held the attention of Memphis in September 1957 when Arkansas Governor Orval Faubus vowed to use the National Guard to prevent nine male and female black teenagers from integrating Little Rock's Central High School. Faubus did this despite the U.S. Supreme Court's 1954 Brown v. Board of Education ruling making public school segregation illegal.

Central High had a good reputation in academics and sports. The governor kept the Guard at the school even though a Federal Court judge denied a plea from the Little Rock school board to postpone integration. Ironically, the Arkansas governor several months earlier permitted towns of Hoxie, Fayetteville, and Charleston, Arkansas, to integrate their white schools.

News media converged on Little Rock from around the world. According to an anecdote producing chuckles among Southern journalists, a British newsman arrived in Little Rock and asked, "I say, ol' boy, precisely what is it you don't like about this integration thing?"

While Kenneth Johnson of *The Commercial Appeal's* Little Rock bureau performed the hard work of covering the Little Rock showdown, my editors instructed me to come up with a story putting the crisis into historical perspective. I drove to Little Rock to see the school as part of my research. The long, handsome structure of yellow brick and stone, several stories high, accommodated about 2,000 students. My front-page story on September 8, 1957 began:

The conflict between federal and state authority in Little Rock is dramatic but not new. Americans have experienced remarkably similar incidents before -- once in Memphis.

I described how threatened use of Tennessee National Guard in 1938 arose from conflict between Memphis political boss Crump and Governor Gordon Browning. Facing re-election, the governor said he would use national guardsmen to stop Crump from "stealing" an election with "invalid votes" for Browning's opponent, Prentice Cooper.

A federal judge ordered the National Guard, stationed in Dyersburg and other nearby towns, not to enter Memphis. Governor Browning sputtered, "The idea of letting a federal judge deter me from handling state troops as I want is silly and absurd." But he withdrew the troops two days before the election, which he lost by a landslide.

In the story I also described two squabbles elsewhere in the country when federal authorities prevented governors from prevailing despite their use of National Guard troops. Those incidents occurred in Texas in 1931 over how much oil should be drilled and in Pennsylvania in 1809 over who should possess a captured British ship. My story gently implied that Faubus also would fail in Little Rock.

A few days later Governor Faubus bowed to pressure and replaced National

Guard with Little Rock police. But tensions continued. A reporter quoted the Rev. James Wesley Pruden Sr., prominent Arkansas Southern Baptist minister and spokesman for the segregationist Capital Citizens Council, as telling a mob, "That's what we gotta fight -- Niggers, Communists and cops."

Daisy Bates, a black newspaper publisher's wife who headed the Arkansas NAACP, mentored the nine black teenagers. She motivated them so well that they enrolled at Central High even after school officials told them they could never participate in sports or other extra-curricular activities.

As they entered the school, hundreds of white adults, and some white students, cursed them and protested so angrily that the nine had to be escorted out the back door for their safety.

Little Rock's mayor and the U.S. Congressman Brooks Hays of Arkansas asked for federal intervention. In Washington, President Eisenhower responded by ordering more than a thousand soldiers of the 101st Airborne to enter Little Rock. They escorted the students to class.

Governor Faubus appeared on TV to complain, "We are now an occupied territory." After receiving a vote of confidence from citizens, he ordered Central High and Little Rock's three other high schools closed for 1958-59. Students lamented their "lost year." Although he cancelled all classes, the governor permitted Central High's football team to play scheduled Friday night games to add to its streak of 32 straight wins. A federal court re-opened the schools the next year, this time integrated.

The crisis ruined the political career of Brooks Hays, who had served in Congress sixteen years. Resentful that he'd invited federal troops to Little Rock, segregationists organized a write-in vote that swept Hays from office.

The Little Rock crisis spurred racist activity in Memphis and elsewhere in the South. I wrote a story about the burning of a five-foot wooden cross in the middle of the night on the front lawn of a black family. The family had bought a house on Azalia Street in a white Memphis neighborhood. The old Ku Klux Klan symbol was wrapped in burlap and soaked in kerosene. Perpetrators were never found.

A small object in space soon pushed Little Rock from the nation's front pages. The Soviet Union put up Sputnik I in October 1957. It shocked *The Commercial Appeal* newsroom and the rest of the nation.

The basketball-sized communications satellite sent signals to Earth from beyond the ionosphere for the first time. Americans worried that a nuclear attack by Soviet ballistic missiles might be imminent.

I called engineers at the newspaper's radio and television stations, WMC and WMCT. They told me they had picked up Sputnik's signals on frequencies used by amateur radio operators.

"It's obvious they want to be heard," one engineer said. He interpreted that to mean an attack was unlikely. A month later, Sputnik 2, carrying the dog Laika, went into orbit.

The Soviet versus U. S. space race began, with imported World War II German scientists helping both sides. A Congressional decree gave birth to the National Aeronautics and Space Administration, NASA. The United States and other nations soon put their own communications satellites into orbit. They changed everyday life with improved weather forecasting, global positioning maps, easier banking and credit card transactions, orbiting telescopes, and eventual creation of the Internet, which would soon have a serious impact on the daily newspaper industry.

Schools increased emphasis on science and mathematics -- for a while.

Although public nervousness about Sputnik soon declined, frequent exercises across the country tested military readiness to react to possible nuclear attack. Early morning phone calls awakened physicians, nurses and dentists belonging to National Guard medical battalions to report to local armories. I wrote how the Memphis units loaded trucks and ambulances with medical supplies, tents and cots and headed for suburbs to get ready to treat the "injured."

The 215th Medical Battalion set up tents in open lots in nearby towns of Collierville and Somerville just as a make-believe "nuclear blast" over downtown Memphis "killed" about half the city's population. The battalion consistently received yearly ratings of "ready" to treat thousands of "wounded" survivors.

Nuclear bomb "duck and cover" exercises in schools turned out to be even more sobering to watch. Children hid beneath their desks. Their facial expressions showed they realized the exercise was no game.

After reaching this peak of activity, frequency of emergency tests by schools and National Guard units gradually declined around the country until the end of the century. They resumed in a few places after the September 11, 2001 attack on New York.

Editor-in-chief Frank Ahlgren, impressed with stories he'd read by a young reporter at the *Arkansas Gazette* in Little Rock, recruited him for *The Commercial Appeal*. He was Wesley Pruden Jr. Although he was son of Little Rock segregationist clergyman Wesley Pruden Sr., most of the younger man's feature and news stories Ahlgren liked had nothing to do with civil rights or school integration.

When Wesley Jr. showed up for his first day at *The Commercial Appeal*, he looked much younger than the rest of us. He had graduated from Little Rock's Central High School four or five years before the desegregation crisis and started working almost immediately for the *Gazette*. He took a few college courses in Little Rock.

After he settled himself at a desk near mine, I walked over and said, "Welcome aboard." I immediately thought to myself, "Gilleland, it's dumb trying to sound nautical in the cotton belt." Wesley shook hands cordially. He said he looked forward to living and working in Memphis.

Before long, Wesley, reporter William Boozer and I, all bachelors, agreed to share a rented house in Whitehaven, a Memphis suburb.

Among excellent writers on *The Commercial Appeal* were Wesley, Henry Mitchell, Michael Grehl, Lydel Sims, and William Bennett (not the future Secretary of Education). Bennett would soon head the newspaper's state bureau in Nashville.

Henry Mitchell covered many topics, from theater to gardening, and his prose often sounded poetic. In a regular entertainment column, "Dixie Dailing," he wrote one day about Roxanne Arlen, my old theater acquaintance in California. He interviewed her by telephone a few hours before she appeared on the June Allyson network television show. In his column, Henry sympathized with her anguish that agents and writers focused more on her wiggle and bust size rather than on her acting ability. Roxanne then was in her late twenties.

Henry added, "I did not tell Roxanne that she doesn't have to worry -- in a few years her problem will be over. But seriously I admire her good sense. A woman with a large bust has a certain exaggerated value in television for a time and then she's finished. A good actress is always in demand, or at least has a marketable talent. In this area, as in others, art has survival value." Henry later joined the Washington *Post* as a columnist.

Photographers Robert Williams, Lloyd Dinkins, Lou Lowry, and Barney Sellers won many awards for *The Commercial Appeal* using their bulky, nine-pound Speed Graphics, soon to become classic collectibles when replaced by smaller, more versatile cameras. Williams could catch an entire story in one flash-bulb moment.

Calvin Alley, editorial page cartoonist, was son of J. P. Alley, who held the job a generation earlier. J. P. Alley helped the newspaper win the 1923 Pulitzer Gold Medal for an anti-Ku Klux Klan campaign. He also created a cartoon panel called "Hambone's Meditations" that featured a witty, black sidewalk philosopher. After succeeding his father, Calvin Alley drew a popular syndicated cartoon strip called "The Ryatts" and continued the panel on "Hambone." Calvin Alley was Editor Ahlgren's brother in law.

At our house after work, Wesley Pruden Jr., Bill Boozer, and I sometimes conversed on such serious topics as women, about whom we all admitted failures, and the Civil War, about which we all liked to read. We agreed that we regretted the disappearance of the best qualities of the Old South.

Wesley asked me point blank one day where I stood on racial issues. He listened politely as I voiced my opinion that blacks had been mistreated for generations. I probably went on too long. He made no comment. Although I felt sure he disagreed with me, I never heard him express racist views. He also denied that his father had referred to "Niggers, Communists and cops" during the Little Rock crisis. His father did not use such language, he insisted, although I doubted him.

Wesley Pruden and Bill Boozer seldom socialized at the Memphis Press Club, where I went often after work. I kept much later hours than they did.

Wesley left *The Commercial Appeal* in the 1960s to work for the *National Observer*.

The *Observer* sent Pruden to cover the Vietnam War and other foreign assignments. He joined the far-right Washington *Times* in 1982 and became its editor-in-chief ten years later. On its editorial page, he sometimes referred to his fellow Arkansans, Hillary and Bill Clinton, as "Bonnie and Clod," and he provoked controversy by objecting in his newspaper to President Obama's bowing before the Japanese emperor.

Remembering our Whitehaven conversations years later, I sometimes mused that Wesley, who never completed a college degree, became editor-in-chief of a newspaper nearly every politician in the nation's capital felt obliged to read, and I, who never completed my Ph.D., ended up directing a major university's journalism school. He kept writing columns for the Washington *Times* after officially retiring in 2008.

I occasionally got an opportunity in Memphis to cover politics. I wrote about Democratic convention delegates' caustic criticism of Tennessee Senator Albert Gore Sr., father of the future vice president in the Clinton administration. The elder Gore unexpectedly withdrew from the vice presidential nomination in 1956. He did so during heat of a party battle in Chicago. I wrote that former Memphis mayor Watkins Overton, a convention delegate, complained he and other delegates did not know Gore intended to pull out of the race until his last minute announcement on the convention floor. "Gore's action let our fellow Southern states down," Overton said.

The Democrats in Chicago finally gave the vice presidential nomination to Estes Kefauver, also of Tennessee. Kefauver's 1949 election as senator had ended E. H. Crump's domination of Memphis and state politics. In the national 1956 election, Kefauver went down to defeat with Adlai Stevenson in an Eisenhower-GOP landslide.

Another politician, U. S. House Speaker Sam Rayburn, lost his temper with me in the Memphis Airport in 1959. He had arrived on a plane carrying him, Treasury Secretary Robert Anderson, Mrs. Anderson, and four others to Washington from a Memorial Day weekend in Texas.

Without trying to be adversarial in my questions to Rayburn, I referred to an old charge Republicans leveled at Democrats about being "big spenders."

Rayburn glared at me. Then he huffed, "I don't have time for this!" He turned abruptly and walked away. While I attempted to keep up, Rayburn hurried toward the airport's Dobbs House restaurant.

I fell into step beside him and kept talking. I knew that as a congressman in the 1930s he had helped President Franklin D. Roosevelt win establishment of the Securities and Exchange Commission, the Federal Communications Commission, and other New Deal legislation. I also remembered that historians called him "the most effective House Speaker in history."

I do not remember what I said in that fast walk that caught his interest, but he slowed down and began to answer me. He expressed satisfaction at a recent Democratic victory in the House of Representatives involving passage of a $2.1 billion housing bill.

Referring to a report that minority Republican congressmen asserted they lost the housing bill battle but not the war, Rayburn said, "All the Republicans have got left to do is talk. They haven't won a battle in so long a time." Then he returned to the subject of big spending.

"We've cut below the President's request in all appropriations bills we've passed. They can't say we're spendthrifts." As we parted, we shook hands, and he headed for a chicken lunch.

TEXANS IN TOWN—House Speaker Sam Rayburn (center), Secretary of Treasury Robert B. Anderson and Mrs. Anderson returned to their plane yesterday after stopping for a meal of Southern fried chicken at Municipal Airport. They were headed back to Washington after spending the Memorial Day week end in Texas.
—Photo by Lou Lowry

Gilleland provokes House Speaker Sam Rayburn to lose his temper in Memphis Airport.

Rayburn Fires Barbs At GOP In Visit Here

By LARUE GILLELAND

House Speaker Sam Rayburn, refreshed and spunky after a holiday in Texas, tongue-lashed Republicans yesterday for dubbing Democrats "big spenders."

Mr. Rayburn, flying back to Washington for more congressional budget fights, stopped briefly at Municipal Airport with a few other prominent Texans, including Secretary of Treasury Robert B. Anderson.

Cut Below 'Ike's' Figures

"We've cut below the President's request in all appropriations bills we've passed," said Mr. Rayburn, waving his straw hat. "They can't say we're spendthrifts."

He mentioned his recent House victory in passage of a $2,100,000,000 housing bill.

Referring to a report that Republican congressmen now say they may have lost the housing bill battle, but not the "war," Mr. Rayburn said:

"All the Republicans have got left to do is talk. They haven't won a battle in so long a time."

Also aboard the Coast Guard Martin 404 plane, which arrived here from Houston, were Texas Democratic Representatives Albert Thomas, Omar Burleson and W. R. Poage. Mrs. Poage and Mrs. Anderson also were in the party.

Here For About An Hour

They ate Southern fried chicken in the Dobbs House Restaurant at the Airport and left in the plane at 3:30 p.m. They were here about an hour.

Secretary Anderson said he and his wife were returning from Houston where he had delivered the commencement address at the University of Houston. He was born and reared in Texas.

Mr. Rayburn, whose home town is Bonham, Texas, and the other congressmen had been home for the Memorial Day week end.

An incident occurred about this time at *The Commercial Appeal* that made me proud to be working for Editor-in-Chief Frank Ahlgren. While Ahlgren was out of town one afternoon, his teenage son, Gibson, driving around with friends in his father's car without permission, violated the city's strict anti-noise law. Gibson blew a loud siren at the wrong man.

At a stop light on Poplar Avenue, a major thoroughfare, Gibson pointed a hand-held siren out the car window and blasted away at a nearby waiting car -- with a criminal court judge at the wheel. The judge said he rebuked the boys, and "they told me where to get off."

The judge telephoned the license plate number of the car to police, who stopped it several blocks away. Later that day, I happened to be sitting nearby when Malcolm Adams, the city editor, called Ahlgren, vacationing in San Francisco, to ask what should be done with the story about Ahlgren's son.

The city editor quoted Ahlgren as saying, "Play it prominently, of course. Put it on the front page -- or main local -- above the fold, depending on the day's news." The story appeared the next morning at the top of the main local page. Later, Ahlgren's son publicly apologized, and the judge withdrew his complaint.

I don't know how, or if, Frank Ahlgren disciplined his son Gibson. But I do know the editor-in-chief could be stern. He fired a Memphis reporter about the same time who failed to inform the newspaper about his outside publicity work. The reporter received pay for turning out press releases for a Louisiana firm that tried to revive Hadacol, a patent medicine. Its twelve percent alcohol content may have been its most effective ingredient.

As a professor years later, I often told my students in reporting and journalism ethics classes about Frank Ahlgren.

On a reporting assignment in Texas about 1957 for *The Commercial Appeal,* I visited the Houston Press Club. Few people were there that evening. I sat at a table with three other newsmen when comedian Bob Hope entered. A local reporter accompanied him. They joined our table. Hope then was in his mid 50s.

The conversation bounced from Texas to national topics and to Hope himself. Although sometimes witty, Hope did not put on his comedian hat, and no one encouraged him to do so.

One reporter asked Hope about his early effort to become a professional boxer in Ohio. Hope said that as a young man he boxed under the name "Packy East." For the first time that evening, he uttered a funny line, "I was on more canvasses than Picasso."

As the evening grew late, one after another of our group departed, leaving Bob Hope and me with our drinks.

"Where are you staying?" he asked.

I named the hotel, several blocks away. "My hotel is only a short distance beyond yours, and I'm going to walk. Does a walk interest you?" he asked.

I said yes. We finished our drinks and left.

Outside, searching for a conversation starter, I said, "I've heard that comedy and tragedy require the same talent -- that any good comedian can play serious roles."

He agreed with that premise, but added a twist. "All good comedians can perform dramatic roles, but not every dramatic actor has the timing necessary for comedy. Comedy, in my opinion, is more difficult."

I had apparently struck a responsive chord, for Bob Hope spent the duration of our stroll, nearly a half hour, elaborating on it.

He said, "The doctrine that theater should never mix comedy and tragedy in the same play has a long history. It goes back further than the Elizabethan era. But I don't agree with it.

"Ancient Greeks and Romans and even French classicists generally kept humor and pathos separate. When Shakespeare combined them, many considered it disgraceful. But life does not separate them. Shakespeare knew that humor can sharpen tragedy's edge. Events that make us laugh and cry occur in everybody's life, often in the same day.

"A playwright should be able to put comedy and tragedy into a single scene, if necessary. And a great actor should be able to bring that scene to life. I'm confident I could do that."

He said, "I might have played serious, even tragic roles, if commitments to comedy had not absorbed all my time."

In front of my hotel we shook hands, and Bob Hope disappeared into the night. "Thanks for the memory," I thought.

13

Religion Beat

I had covered police and courts about two years when Managing Editor Gordon Hanna called me into his office one morning. This was after a later night than usual for me at the Memphis Press Club.

Hanna said, "As you probably know, Phil Thomas, our religion editor, has taken a job at the Washington *Evening Star*. He'll be leaving in two weeks. We need a replacement. I and other editors think it should be you."

"Why me?"

"Because we think you need it the most," he smiled, adding a barb about my "bachelor life style."

"Seriously, I think it's a job you'd like," he said. "I've heard through the Press Club grapevine that you sometimes read philosophers and theologians -- like Paul Tillich and Martin Buber. The job would only take about three days a week. You'd be on general assignment the rest of the time."

He asked me to think about it over the weekend. On Monday morning, I told him I'd take the assignment.

Far different from the police beat, the new duty turned out to be more interesting than I expected.

I soon spent most of a day with Martin Luther King Jr. He and baseball star Jackie Robinson came to Memphis for a speaking engagement promoted by local black clergy, shortly after the 1955 Montgomery, Alabama, bus boycott. I went to hear him and Robinson address a large crowd in the auditorium of a black south Memphis church. I was the only white person among hundreds there. The Montgomery bus boycott was still a major topic.

Robinson spoke first. He had just retired after an outstanding decade with the Brooklyn Dodgers and a World Series victory. Robinson said he coped with big league racism by repeatedly "turning the other cheek." Racial threats, he said, began in the late 1940s as soon as he started playing for a Dodgers' farm team from Montreal. The affronts forced him, among other things, to cut short a stay in Sanford, Florida, during one of his early baseball road trips.

Robinson, in his speech, praised his wife for steadfast courage and thanked baseball's leaders who helped him in his career, especially Dodgers' manager Blanch Rickey.

Martin Luther King's talk followed. He said Robinson's acceptance as the "first Negro" in the major leagues had been "the mere start of a glorious new era." (The terms "black" or "African-American" would not come into widespread use until later.) King lamented discrimination still faced by many seeking jobs or buying homes, the latter an oblique reference, I thought, to an incident of being rebuffed when Robinson and his wife were looking for a house to buy in Connecticut.

After the speeches, Robinson departed the auditorium with friends. Several people lined up in front of me to talk to King. He surveyed the line, and his eyes paused momentarily when he spotted me.

He glanced quickly from me to the big auditorium, as if to confirm that I had probably been seated there. After waiting my turn, I introduced myself to King. He genially answered my questions, without haste. It was, I thought, as if he did not want me, the only white person in the building, to feel uncomfortable.

He described leading the Montgomery bus boycott after Rosa Parks, a seamstress, was arrested for refusing to give up her bus seat to a white man and move to the rear. King spoke of the detailed effort that went into organizing car pools that took blacks to work for more than a year. The boycott touched off the national civil rights movement that brought King to public attention.

As King and I stood talking, Benjamin Hooks joined us. He was a Memphis lawyer and Baptist minister. He and King invited me to join them for coffee at Hooks' house. Hooks drove us there in his car. Soon, two more black men arrived. Hooks walked around his living room turning on lights and closing window shades. I assumed he wanted to avoid attention from any passersby who might see one white man sitting amid blacks. I realized later Hooks probably feared for King's safety.

Over coffee, King and Hooks exchanged stories. Hooks mentioned his humiliation in World War II when barred from eating in the same American restaurants where the army occasionally assigned him to guard Italian prisoners at meal times. King said that when he was a boy, white parents sometimes forbade his playing with their children.

He also told of being ordered to stand with other black students on the bus carrying them and white students home from a neighboring town where he had just won a high school oratory contest.

King spoke of his admiration for Mahatma Gandhi in India and of President Benjamin Mays of Atlanta's Morehouse College, where King studied as an undergraduate. After majoring in sociology at Morehouse, King was encouraged by Mays to enter the ministry. King did so, following in the footsteps of his father and grandfather. They preceded him as ministers of Ebenezer Baptist Church in Atlanta. When he was a boy, his father changed their first names, Michael, to Martin Luther in honor of the Sixteenth Century German Protestant reformer.

The son earned a doctorate in theology from Boston University shortly before his visit to Memphis. About this time, he influenced author Margaret Mitchell to establish scholarships for black medical students.

When someone in the room mentioned hearing a rumor that the Federal Bureau of Investigation, headed by J. Edgar Hoover, was paying special attention to civil rights groups, King acted unconcerned. He said civil rights leaders he knew, including himself, did not plan to break any federal laws.

King said his own non-violent approach to civil rights had been influenced by a biography of Gandhi's life in South Africa and India written by E. Stanley Jones, white Methodist missionary. Jones had known Gandhi for years and observed his work with India's untouchables. King said he hoped soon to visit India.

No one in the room that night, except perhaps King, would have guessed that within Hooks' lifetime (he died in 2010) a black man would win election as president of the United States -- and live in the White House, built by former slaves.

When the evening ended, I thanked King and Hooks for inviting me to socialize with them. They drove me a few miles to my parked car.

Hooks later served as the first black judge of a Southern trial court since Reconstruction and as board member of the Federal Communications Commission.

Like most of the country, I watch on TV in 1965 as Martin Luther King led three civil rights marches fifty-four miles from Selma, Alabama to the state capitol in Montgomery. They sought equal voting rights for blacks. Beaten to death during one march was a young Unitarian-Universalist clergyman, James Reeb, visiting from Boston.

In 1968, an assassin killed King with a rifle shot as he stood on a motel balcony during a visit to Memphis.

In 1977, Hooks became executive director of the National Association for the Advancement of Colored People. George W. Bush presented him the Presidential Medal of Freedom in 2007.

A few weeks after my visit with Hooks and King, E. Stanley Jones, the 75-year-old missionary, came to Memphis. Remembering King's admiration of him, I covered his speech to an overflow crowd of about 1,500 in white Union Avenue Methodist Church. The missionary predicted that the South would be racially integrated in ten years, words seldom heard before.

"And when it's all over, our democracy will be sounder and our consciences clearer," Jones said.

Jones' prediction came close to the mark, even within the segregated newsroom of

The Commercial Appeal. Before long, Editor-in-Chief Frank Ahlgren and Managing Editor Gordon Hanna took increasingly active roles in local civic organizations to improve race relations. They worked with Protestant, Catholic and Jewish groups, both black and white.

The Commercial Appeal hired its first city room black reporters and copy editors. It ceased always identifying minority newsmakers by race, especially when involved in crime. When the newspaper did mention race, it finally substituted "black" for "Negro."

The newspaper withdrew Calvin Alley's syndicated cartoon, "Hambone's Meditations" because some readers considered its portrayal of a witty black street philosopher to be racially insensitive. Hambone's thoughts were usually wise, even though he spoke in dialect. For example, Hambone said one day, "Mos' folks, dey loses at de mouf whut dey taks in at de ears."

After Hambone disappeared from syndication, Alley continued drawing "The Ryatts," an amusing strip about a white family, until he died in 1970.

While *The Commercial Appeal's* editors and I tried to give equal treatment to Roman Catholic, Jewish, mainline Protestant, and fundamentalist congregations, we overlooked Islam, I realized later. Few, if any, Muslims lived in the Memphis area at that time, or so we thought.

I, like many journalists, failed to foresee that Islam's global numbers would equal, if not surpass, Roman Catholics and Protestants by century's end.

Memphis would eventually have hundreds, if not thousands, of Muslim residents. We didn't yet recognize that Islam's impact on Zionism, both Jewish and Christian, also provided an adequate news peg for writing about it.

A group of Christian Zionists became active in the city, led by a Memphis couple, Susan and James Dean. Fundamentalist and mainline Protestant laymen and ministers returned from visits to the Near East to tell their congregations that rebuilding Israel fulfilled biblical prophecy. A typical sermon topic: "God is again choosing the chosen people."

Although not a member of the Christian Zionist movement, I tried to cover its activities accurately and fairly. After some of these stories appeared, Baron Hirsch Synagogue, the city's largest Orthodox Jewish congregation, invited me to speak at a forum it sponsored.

I described to the congregation the Christian Zionists' joy at Israel's success in turning desert into farms and defeating Arab armies that invaded on the day of Israel's birth in 1948.

I pointed out that Christian Zionists liked to quote the Prophet Isaiah: "Israel . . . fear thee not, for I am with thee. . . they that war against thee shall be as nothing." After my talk, the Orthodox congregation gave me an elegant Jewish Bible that I treasure today.

Baron Hirsch Congregation
March 2, 1959

May we tell you again how much we enjoyed your presentation last Friday night. I wonder if it would be possible for you to send us a copy of your remarks. Thanking you again.

Herman Lazarov, Forum Chairman

Christian Zionist advocates came from many denominations, such as Southern Baptist, Adventist, Assembly of God, Nazarene, and Church of God, among others. They included fundamentalists, evangelicals, and charismatics.

While mainline faiths -- such as Episcopal, Presbyterian, Southern Baptist, Methodist, and Lutheran -- dominated public discourse in this era, my newspaper did not hesitate to give significant space to a national meeting in Memphis of the fundamentalist Church of God, attended by hundreds of delegates.

Church of God teenagers, I found, provided an open window on their denomination. So, I focused on them. These young people showed no distress about never dancing or wearing makeup or class rings -- things most their age took for granted.

"I never go to movie theaters. And I never wear shorts or lipstick or jewelry," Barbara Yates, an 18-year-old New Yorker, told me. "But I'm happy and feel I'm just as popular as any average American girl."

A minister's daughter, Barbara said she felt comfortable with a doctrine that encouraged willing acquiescence by women to leadership of men in marriage and church.

Blue-eyed, brunette, and attractive, she said she normally dated only young men from her church. I asked her what she did when someone outside her denomination asked to take her out, perhaps to a movie.

"I explain that my church has a party or hay ride planned and ask him to come with me. I've never been refused." Only once did she recall taking an outsider to a Church of God service where members regularly shout, clap hands, and speak in unknown tongues.

"He was from a denomination that is very formal. I prayed that everything would go just right. Before the service was over, I think he was scared. But a month later he joined the Church of God. Then I was ashamed of feeling as I had during that service."

She said she first spoke in tongues when she was 9. "Speaking in tongues is evidence that the Holy Ghost is in our hearts and that we are not alone. It is a way for us to talk to God and for God to talk to us. It's the power which occurred on the day of Pentecost as described in Acts."

The moral, she said, is this: "A young person doesn't have to compromise his or her convictions to get along in this world. I've found that people respect you for living up to your beliefs."

Another group of females living up to their beliefs was the Poor Clares, cloistered Roman Catholic nuns in the Memphis suburb of Frayser. I telephoned Mother Superior Mary Annetta at the Monastery of Saint Clare, and she agreed to talk to me -- through a curtained grill.

I drove to the monastery and entered its empty parlor. One wall contained the grill. I walked to it and said "hello" through the cloth. "I've been waiting for you," a soft voice replied.

From the hidden mother superior I learned the Poor Clares never saw their families again after going behind the monastery's walls. The nuns pledged themselves to lives of chastity, prayer and manual labor. They were anonymous foot commandos in a vast Vatican army ready to face travails throughout the world.

The nuns began their day at 5 a.m. They rose, worshipped together, attended Mass at 6:30. Then they ate a meager breakfast of coffee and bread, and prayed again. They even got up during the night, shortly before midnight, to pray for an hour and a half. Other duties included sewing, reading, raising flowers and shrubs, and baking altar bread used by ninety-eight churches in three states.

The nuns ate sparingly at all meals, and never touched meat. "Each of us prays nine hours a day," the mother superior said. "We pray for betterment of the world."

My story, with a photograph of the monastery taken from a low-flying plane by the newspaper's top photographer, Robert Williams, told how some of the nuns had not left its seven acres since it opened twenty-five years earlier. They came from many states and Canada, England and Portugal. Their ages ranged from 18 to 70.

The mother superior described their dress. They wore sandals and long, hooded, ash-colored garbs -- tied around them with white cords. The habit was the same as worn by Saint Clare, the young woman who founded the order in 1212 A.D. as an affiliate of the better-known Franciscans. The daughter of an Italian nobleman, Saint Clare renounced wealth for poverty and self-sacrifice.

Four nuns called "externs" conducted monastery business outside the monastery. Only externs received permission to travel to "meet the world." The mother superior was not one of them.

A young woman planning to devote her life to the monastery underwent a trial period of five years. She could leave at any time she expressed unhappiness. After that, she took a vow to remain until death. Only two non-externs had ever been permitted outside the walls, and that was for emergency hospital treatment.

I put the above facts in my story. My lead:

This is a love story. It's taking place now behind a high brick wall. It's about 22 secluded women in love with the same man -- Jesus.

To complete the story I asked a Catholic bishop what he thought the nuns accomplished. He replied, "In the dead of the night, when sin and iniquity stalk the city, and even when the good are enjoying their rest, these nuns are keeping vigil with their Lord in the chapel, begging Him to look on their poor acts of love and devotion and forgive the sins of the world."

Monastery of Saint Clare
August 18, 1957

Dear Mr. Gilleland,
This is just a little note to tell you how pleased we are with the article and picture in The Commercial Appeal last Saturday.

Every day we receive a number of telephone calls or visits from friends and benefactors telling us how pleased they were to see the article, and commenting most favorably on it. The calls began on Saturday, and have continued every day since then.

Very gratefully,
Mother Mary Annetta

Memphis
Aug. 22, 1957

Thank you for your article on the Poor Clares. Apart from it being very well written, it gave so much information that is little known.

Gladys Smith

In 1958, I called Samuel Cardinal Stritch, Chicago's Roman Catholic archbishop. Many expected him eventually to become America's first pope.
Pope Pius XII had just appointed him pro-prefect of the Congregation for Propagation of the Faith and member of the Roman Curia, the body of cardinals in Rome who helped the pope administer the Church. The office of Congregation for Propagation

of the Faith supervised missionary work throughout the world. Cardinal Stritch had been a priest in Memphis and bishop of Toledo, Ohio, before his appointment to head the Chicago archdiocese, the nation's largest, in 1940.

On the phone, he expressed surprise at his appointment. "Never before in history has an American prelate been called to such an important office," Cardinal Stritch said in answer to my questions. After my conversation with him, he departed for the Vatican and assumed his new duties. He died there two months later at the age of 70.   Any possibility of a North American pope in the foreseeable future died with him.

It would be from the office of Congregation for Propagation of the Faith (renamed Congregation for Evangelization) that German cleric Joseph Cardinal Ratzinger would be elected Pope Benedict XVI in 2005.

The Church hierarchy honored Cardinal Stritch by naming for him Loyola University's College of Medicine in Chicago and a private university in Madison, Wisconsin.

First Unitarian Church, the most liberal congregation in Memphis, became divided when its minister, Paul Carnes, exchanged pulpits occasionally with black clergy and invited minorities to join some of his church's youth activities.

My newspaper's interest in Carnes increased when he and some clergy from other denominations began working together to encourage integration while avoiding the level of discord in Little Rock.

Carnes told me in his church office that an organization being formed would tentatively be called the Memphis Council on Human Relations. He was pleased that many leading Protestant, Catholic, and Jewish clergy had expressed interest.

"I am saddened, but not surprised, that some clergy and church laymen are critical of our efforts. They assert they will have nothing to do with us," Carnes said. "But our belief in the inherent worth of each man and woman will enable us to prevail."

His soft-spoken self-confidence (and strong chin) impressed me. A graduate of the University of Indiana, Carnes served as an army Second Lieutenant in World War II until being captured in 1942 in North Africa by German troops. He spent the remainder of the war as a prisoner of war.

I could not resist asking if in the prison camp he had met Harold Clotworthy, the POW from Eldon, my home town. Carnes said he had not crossed paths with Clotworthy.

After the war Carnes graduated from Harvard Divinity School and served as a Unitarian minister in Youngstown, Ohio, until coming to the Memphis Church in 1954.

Barnes moved to Buffalo, New York, in 1958, and eventually became president of the national Unitarian Universalist Association. While holding that position, he died of leukemia in 1979.

His race relations organization came into existence before he left Memphis and metamorphed through the years into the Memphis Committee on Community Relations (MCCR) and Metropolitan Interfaith Association. In 1968, during the Memphis sanitation workers' strike, the MCCR ran a full-page advertisement in *The Commercial Appeal* headed "Appeal to Conscience." The ad said in part, "Anyone who loves God must also love his brother. . ." Two weeks later, Martin Luther King was assassinated in front of a Memphis motel.

I'd been covering religion several months when I received a call from Phil Thomas in Washington. He said he liked his new job with the *Evening Star* covering city government and politics. Then he asked, "Would you like to work here?" While I stammered for a non-committal reply, Phil continued. "The *Star* wants to hire a couple of new reporters. My boss asked me if I could recommend someone, and I told him about your work. He told me to make this call."

I answered that the possibility "appealed to me," but I needed to establish some longevity before my next move. I had jumped from job to job too often, I thought.

Phil said his boss would be disappointed by my reply. We agreed to stay in touch. I never heard from him again. *The Evening Star* printed its final edition in 1981, a harbinger of rough times ahead for many daily newspapers.

Although a journalist's job is to report the news, not create it, I came close to violating the rule while covering Norman Vincent Peale on January 27, 1958. I listened to him address a businessmen's luncheon at the Peabody Hotel and concluded he'd said nothing not found in his books, *The Power of Positive Thinking* and *Art of Living*. His speech and books stressed suppressing negativity and planting good thoughts in one's mind, both conscious and sub-conscious.

When his speech ended, I wondered how I could write a newsworthy story. Because he'd made a passing reference to juvenile delinquency in his talk, I asked him later if he thought Memphis, with its churches of many denominations, could be a place where parents might effectively work together to do something about the problem. He apparently liked my question. He elaborated on his affirmative answer.

My story the next day began:

Dr. Norman Vincent Peale challenged Memphis parents yesterday to start a program to cure the nation's juvenile delinquency problem.

"Here in Memphis -- where devotion to churches is so pronounced and where loyalty to Christian faith is so real -- is the place to work out a pattern for the entire country," the New York preacher and author said.

I listed in my story the steps he suggested parents could take, such as reading aloud from the Bible, daily prayers in the home, and setting good examples for children through action and positive thinking.

I came away admiring his quick mind and convinced he deserved his wide reputation. During a career that ended with his death at 90 in 1993, Dr. Peale, like Billy Graham, visited every U.S. president in office.

Brooks Hays reappeared on my radar at the national Southern Baptist Convention in Louisville in 1959. I reported a stormy debate he had with a North Carolina preacher that led to the preacher's forcible ouster from the speaker's platform.

The Reverend James J. Bulman of East Spencer, North Carolina, had delivered a blistering attack on the Baptists' most historic theological seminary. Bulman charged that some faculty members at Louisville Baptist Theological Seminary taught ideas contrary to church doctrine. Among these, he said, were assertions that the virgin birth and resurrection of Jesus were myths. Hays, convention president and outgoing Arkansas congressman, told Bulman he was out of order because time allotted for discussing the seminary matter had expired.

"No, no," shouted the nearly 15,000 delegates (called "messengers") when Hays asked if Bulman's time should be extended.

When Bulman refused to leave the platform, Franklin Owen, convention business chairman, placed an arm around Bulman's shoulders and half pulled, half led the reluctant preacher from the podium.

The story I sent to *The Commercial Appeal* that night turned out to be a national exclusive, for I was the only reporter to witness the incident. It occurred late in the day when the twenty or more reporters for wire services and other newspapers had left the convention floor.

East Spencer, N.C.
July 30, 1959

My attention has been called to an article that you wrote concerning my being removed from the platform of the Southern Baptist Convention.   I think that you were quite correct in so emphasizing that incident.

James M. Bulman, Minister

Before the convention, Brooks Hays lost his seat in the U.S. Congress after sixteen years because he invited federal troops to intercede in the Little Rock school integration dispute. As an Arkansas representative, he had given major support to the congressional effort that inserted "under God" in the Pledge of Allegiance in 1954 and placed "In God We Trust" on national currency in 1955. After leaving Congress, Hays served as special assistant to President Kennedy and taught at Rutgers and University of Massachusetts before dying at 83 in 1981.

I interviewed an elderly retired clergyman who made a long sled-dog journey through Alaska to save lives -- a quarter-century prior to the famous Iditarod run. He was 95-year-old Loyal Lincoln Wirt. Before talking to me, he addressed a couple of Memphis church congregations as part of his visit from the West Coast. He appeared agile, alert, and eager to tell his story.

Wirt's Alaska adventure began when he was a Congregational missionary stationed near Nome in 1899. He volunteered to seek assistance for hundreds of sick gold miners, many down with typhoid, in a snow-bound camp close to the Bering Strait. To inform the outside world of their plight, the 37-year-old Wirt volunteered to mush more than a dozen dogs over a thousand miles. With a sled loaded with supplies, he endured sub-freezing temperatures and frequent delays from storms. He cut through forests, crossed frozen streams, and passed isolated native villages. He reached a small port on Shelikof Strait in about a month. It resulted in help being sent to the trapped miners, and nearly all survived.

Wirt made his trip alone. Because he carried a message rather than medicine, his trek received less world attention than the famous run that later inspired the Iditarod races. That's when twenty mushers in 1925 worked in relays to carry antitoxin serum 674 miles from a rail terminal to diptheria-stricken Nome. To commemorate their trek, the annual Iditarod races began in 1973 -- after Wirt's death. Fifty or more sled-dog teams and mushers enter the Iditarod each year. It approximates the longer length of Wirt's trip rather than the original serum run to Nome.

After leaving Alaska, Wirt held pastorates in Brisbane, Australia; Harrow, England; and Oakland, California.

As we parted that day in Memphis, I asked Wirt the secret of his long, vigorous life. He said, "Have a hobby, trust in God, and drink at least six big glasses of water every day."

14

Blind Date

One day in 1958 Paul Vanderwood, a Memphis *Press Scimitar* reporter, fixed me up with a blind date. Her name was Betsy (Elizabeth). She was a close friend of the woman he dated, Penny McClure, whom I had met.

Paul described Betsy as "witty, pretty, and the mother of two small daughters." She had been divorced about two years. Paul planned a party for several friends at his apartment on Saturday before a night football game between Memphis State (now University of Memphis) and the University of Mississippi.

After leaving the newspaper, I arrived as the party reached its peak. Paul's friends debated in small groups and danced to recorded music. Betsy and Penny sat side by side on a sofa opposite the entrance. I approached and Penny introduced me. I noticed Betsy's easy smile and sense of humor. We hit it off immediately.

Our conversation began at the party and continued through the football game. Looking back, I only remember the opening kickoff. After the game, we returned to Paul's apartment for nighrtcaps.

After a month, I called Betsy for a date. When she came to the phone, I said, "Hello, this is LaRue." She said, "LaRue, Who?" I apologized for not calling sooner, and she accepted the date.

When I arrived to pick her up, I met her daughters, Louise, 5, and Virginia, more than a year younger. They seemed at ease with me. Betsy and I saw each other often over the next two years, and kept in touch after I left the newspaper to return to the University of Missouri in Columbia for graduate work. Vanderwood later earned his Ph.D. in history and became a professor at San Diego State (later University of San Diego) and wrote books on Latin America.

While completing a master's degree in journalism, I was hired as a graduate assistant to teach a beginning newswriting course for undergraduates and help editors of the daily *Missourian* process student-reporter news copy.

In the group of graduate students with whom I socialized and drank beer at nearby pubs was Mary Jane Rawlings, niece of author Marjorie Rawlings. Mary Jane looked like a younger version of her aunt when photographed in 1939 on winning the Pulitzer Prize in Literature for her novel, *The Yearling*.

A couple of my friends dated Mary Jane at different times, and everyone in our circle considered her brilliant. Like Helen Watson, she maintained a straight-A average with little apparent effort. I got to know Mary Jane even better when we both ended up in a General Semantics course taught by School of Journalism Dean Earl English.

Dean English stressed linguistic pitfalls that journalists should avoid. He taught that structure of language can lead to misleading unconscious assumptions. He often repeated semanticist Alfred Korzybski's mantra, "The map is not the territory."

I thought the class relatively easy at first. I had encountered similar ideas in a philosophy course dealing with Ludwig Wittgenstein and logical empiricists called the "Vienna Circle." Mary Jane did well because she found any academic subject easy.

Noting my enthusiasm for General Semantics, Mary Jane one day teasingly bet a beer that she would earn a higher final exam grade than I. After agreeing to the bet, I used the Helen Watson method overtime for weeks preparing for the final, although I knew Mary Jane probably wouldn't need to put in such effort.

We both received 98 percent on Dean English's final exam, the highest in class. Afterward, we bought each other a beer at the Shack, one of the oldest watering holes near campus.

When I last heard of her, Mary Jane Rawlings worked for a major advertising agency in Chicago.

As part of my graduate study, I researched laws affecting the press at the Freedom of Information Center at the School of Journalism. The center was, and is, a reference library promoting access to meetings and government documents the public has a right to see.

Paul Fisher, FOI center director, asked me to do a study for graduate credit on the enduring controversy over what degree, if any, obscene literature endangers public morality.

I researched works as far back as the 1610 Chinese classic, *The Golden Lotus*. I presented arguments of historians, sociologists, psychologists, and legal scholars. Their conclusions, I wrote, depended mostly on the assumptions they started with. I said the question needed scientific, clinical study. The FOI Center published my report under the title, "Obscenity -- Anybody's Guess."

I celebrated finishing the paper by driving to Kansas City to hear blues-jazz guitarist B. B. King of Memphis perform in a large auditorium. An incident on stage demonstrated how adversity sometimes provides reward. As B. B. King pounded notes from "Lucille" -- the name he gave his guitar -- his upper E-string broke. Without missing more than a beat, he adjusted his fingering to finish the long tune with a flourish, receiving the evening's loudest ovation.

One of my grade school teachers, Alice Irene Fitzgerald, had become a professor in the University of Missouri's College of Education. After leaving Eldon, she gained recognition as an authority in children's literature. In my conversations with her around campus, sometimes over coffee, she described her research, and I listened politely.

Years later, when she was deceased and I had retired, I finally read one of her favorite children's books, *Le Petit Prince* by Antoine de Saint-Exupery. Lines from this French classic that impressed me: "Language is the source of misunderstanding . . . . One sees correctly only with the heart. What is essential is invisible to the eyes." ("Le langage est source de malentendus"…."On ne voit bien qu'avec la coeur. L'essential est invisible pour les yeux.")

On closing the book, I wished I could converse once more with my old teacher. *Le Petit Prince* had prepared me to share her excitement.

The Missouri Historical Society established an Alice Irene Fitzgerald Collection of Literature for Children and Youth.

After obtaining my master's degree, I stayed on to complete most of the course work toward a Ph.D. in philosophy. I considered a dissertation topic on the influence of the Seventeenth Century's Baruch Spinoza on modern thought. I also hoped to apply concepts in philosophy to daily journalism. Another professor, Elliot D. Cohen, beat me into print with his book, *Philosophical Issues in Journalism*.

On some holidays, I visited Betsy, and she came to Columbia, Missouri, a couple of times. At Betsy's house in Memphis one day, her daughter, Virginia, then about 7, greeted me at the front door. With a frown on her face and fists on her hips, she demanded, "When are you going to marry my mom?"

I was flabbergasted. I stammered some incoherent, embarrassed reply and whisked Betsy away from the kids -- and her mother, Mrs. Marie Ross.

Betsy's father had died about twenty years earlier. He was John Ross, the Memphis businessman and philanthropist who befriended blues composer W. C. Handy by lending him money to start a sheet music company. When Betsy was a little girl, local civic or flag celebrations sometimes invited her to take part as "Betsy Ross."

Back at the Missouri University that spring, Dr. Bryce Rucker, one of my professors, said, "There's a job at Arkansas State College in Jonesboro in the fall that might interest you." He told me it was teaching English.

"But my degrees are in journalism," I said.

"It might not make any difference," he answered. "Why don't you drive down to Jonesboro and talk to them." I did, and Arkansas State College (now Arkansas State University) offered me an instructor's job. I needed the money, and I figured I could finish my Ph.D. dissertation later. So, I signed a year's contract.

Hired at the same time was a young man who'd just received his Ph.D. in English from Yale. The college assigned us different sections of the same freshman and sophomore courses.

I next asked Betsy to marry me. She accepted, concluding, I suppose, that she already had daughter Virginia's approval. We married in June of 1962 and moved with the kids to a rented house in Jonesboro, Arkansas.

I found my first semester of full-time college teaching exhilarating for two reasons -- challenging courses and the Cuban Missile Crisis. The crisis occurred about six weeks after classes began.

My students and I, like other Americans, heard President Kennedy's startling television announcement on October 22, 1962 that an American U-2 plane had photographed Soviet missiles on the island of Cuba. Government officials feared missiles armed with nuclear warheads could reach most of North America and as far south as Lima, Peru. Cuba's Fidel Castro said he needed the missiles to prevent the United States from attempting to repeat the failed 1961 Bay of Pigs invasion. Cuban exiles in the United States warned that Fidel Castro planned to use the missiles as leverage for subversion of Latin America.

For a week, classes continued while faculty and students moved about campus more somber and subdued than normal. We hurried home to watch television accounts of a U.S. blockade of Cuba, a military alert around the globe, and progress of a Soviet fleet heading toward the island. Everyone believed nuclear war hung in the balance.

When students insisted on talking about the crisis in class, I let them do so -- to release tensions -- before gently guiding them back to the assigned subject. The crisis ended on October 28 when the Soviet Union's Nikita Khrushchev announced he would dismantle the missiles if the United States would promise never to invade Cuba. President Kennedy agreed. What the world did not know for weeks was that Kennedy also agreed to dismantle U.S. missiles in Turkey aimed at the USSR.

I taught multiple-sections of Freshman English Composition and a two-semester course in World Literature required of every sophomore regardless of major. Assigning and grading dozens of English Composition essays presented no problem. But staying a step ahead of students in the world literature course required late-night hours.

I liked the sophomore literature requirement. I thought every university should adopt it. The course started in the fall with selections from the Confucian *Analects*, the Hindu *Mahabharata*, and the *Old Testament*. It proceeded through Homer, parts of the *Koran*, the *Nibelungenlied*, various French and English writers, and ended in the spring with works by Walt Whitman, Emily Dickinson, Thomas Mann, and T. S. Eliott.

The academic year came to a close, and Arkansas State invited me to remain on the faculty. Although I liked my job and believed a second year teaching literature would be much easier than the first, I took a journalism position at the University of Nevada, Reno, paying about thirty percent more than I received in Arkansas.

Arkansas State, I was told, did not offer to renew the contract of the young Ph.D. from Yale.

15

Biggest Little City

The University of Nevada, Reno (UNR) made national news a decade before my arrival when its president and faculty clashed over admissions standards and academic freedom. *Time* magazine, the New York *Times*, and other media played the story prominently. Some key figures in the dispute still held campus positions when I got there.

I arrived in Reno more than a week ahead of Betsy and the children. I immediately reported to A. L. Higginbotham, Journalism Department chairman. He told me the courses I'd teach when the semester began the next month. We had a pleasant conversation.

Because of a couple of business conventions in the city, every hotel and motel I passed on leaving Higginbotham's office displayed a "no vacancy" sign. I headed toward Carson City, about thirty miles away, hoping to find a room.

As I drove, I heard on the car radio a Reno disc jockey play the music of a new British rock group called the Beatles. The disc jockey, Jack Cafferty, I learned later, led most of the country in recognizing the Beatles' talents and introducing their records. He had been a student at UNR before dropping out. Cafferty years later would work as CNN commentator, criticizing Democrats, Republicans, and the U. S. invasion of Iraq.

En route to Carson City I saw a sign, "Whitney Ranch -- Guests Welcome," with an arrow pointing down a narrow road. I drove to a sprawling ranch house with a view of the Sierra Mountains, walked in, and obtained a room.

After I signed the guest book, the female desk clerk surprised me with the comment, "Free cocktails will be served at 5 o'clock at pool side."

Not later than 5:05 I approached a large swimming pool around which stood several women, all well dressed. Holding a martini, I felt better when I saw another man approach. He obtained his drink and introduced himself as "Shanti Gupta from India." He was about five years older than I.

His name and demeanor, I thought, suggested one of India's upper castes. After we exchanged a few words, I asked, "Who are all these women?" He said, "Don't you know where you are?" I replied, "The sign on the highway says Whitney Ranch."

"This is a divorce ranch," he said. "These women are here to satisfy a six-week residency requirement in order to obtain a quick Nevada divorce. I'm here for the same reason."

He explained, with no accent, that he grew up in India where his parents arranged his marriage years earlier. It had been an unhappy match. His wife, among other things, refused to follow him to America when he came to earn his Ph.D. at the University of North Carolina.

I asked him his field, and he said he chaired the mathematics and statistics department at Purdue University. I explained I had just taken a job teaching journalism at UNR. As two academics, we found common ground for conversation.

He said, "Tonight at the top of the Mapes Hotel, an outstanding Egyptian belly dancer will perform. I've seen her before. Do you want to come along?"

I went, and the dancer lived up to his description. Her performance was voluptuous without being vulgar. The house band did a respectable job accompanying her with atonal Middle Eastern music.

She wore a full-length skirt, slit at the sides. In front, from bra to hips, a filmy see-through gauze enhanced her belly. For part of her performance she attached brass finger cymbals ("sagat") to counterpoint the rhythm.

"Dancers like this start very young in Egypt and in my country, where the style is only slightly different" Shanti said.

"Unfortunately, she might not be able to get a job in Egypt right now. Every decade or two, fundamentalists who consider belly dancing too revealing pressure the government to suppress it. But later, demand from wealthy Arabs visiting Cairo from other parts of the Middle East brings the dancers back."

Shanti said, "Because belly dancers in the Orient perform at wedding parties, partly to stimulate the groom and partly educate the bride, most people in the West associate their performers only with sex. But a great belly dancer expresses life, happiness, sorrow -- and dignity. And often these dancers are highly educated. Some speak several languages."

I have long forgotten the performer's name that night at the Mapes, but she looked much like a picture of Cairo dancer Soheir Zaki I saw years later in a magazine.

A couple of days after watching the belly dance, Shanti offered another invitation. "I have to make a one-day business trip to Palo Alto in California. For most of the day I'll be tied up in a meeting. If you've nothing better to do, you can ride over with me, stroll the Stanford campus and inspect the Hoover Institute. I'll pick you up at 5 in front of the institute and take you to the best Indian restaurant in the San Francisco area." I immediately agreed.

I spent a day inspecting Stanford and browsing periodicals in the Hoover Institute.

The Indian restaurant did not disappoint. After dinner, he picked up the check and said, "I got paid today, so I'm buying."

As his car climbed the interstate highway over the Sierra Mountains back to Reno, I asked what kind of job had led him to buy my dinner.

He said the San Francisco 49ers football team hired him a few months earlier to design a computer program it could use in recruiting. His design included data about positions prospective recruits played, their high school and college records, height, weight, bench-press strength, and 100-yard dash speed, among many other things. That day, he said, he had one of his final meetings with 49ers' management. He made it clear they paid him big money -- at least from a Nevada assistant professor's perspective.

Another Shanti remark I remember came when we walked through a Reno casino. Knowing nothing about gambling, I dropped a couple a quarters in a slot machine while he watched action at a blackjack table. I conjectured that he probably could do well at the games since his expertise in math and statistics probably gave him an edge over others. His reply, "My expertise has taught me that the only way to win at gambling is to own the casino. The bettor is sure to lose, especially if he keeps returning."

Betsy and the kids arrived from Arkansas. I left Whitney Ranch, and Betsy and I made down payment on the house in which we would live for the next eighteen years. I adopted Louise and Virginia, and we eventually had two more children, Michelle, who was born in Arkansas shortly before we moved to Reno, and Ross who was born two years later.

Shortly after arriving in Reno in late August 1963, we watched the TV broadcast of Martin Luther King's "I have a dream" speech during the Civil Rights march on Washington, D.C.

About three months into my new job, while I worked in my office one day, another professor looked in and said, "President Kennedy has just been shot in Dallas."

I hurried toward the United Press International machine in our lobby. Students, including Sig Rogich, an upperclassman, crowded around it, staring at emerging wire copy. The early reports indicated the president and Texas Governor Tom Connelly, also wounded, had been whisked to a hospital from the plaza near Texas School Book Depository Building. Conversation among the students became increasingly excited. A young woman had tears in her eyes.

Journalism chairman Higginbotham walked by and said to me, in an aside, "Students today get so emotional."

The pronouncement that the president had died came about thirty minutes later. To gather my thoughts, I walked out of the building and stood on the front step. Sig Rogich joined me. We stood there speculating on whether the gunman might be a "lone nut" or part of some conspiracy, perhaps involving Cuba or the Soviet Union.

More students walked up. It was Rogich, as I remember, who observed that

Dallas security must have been especially high since Adlai Stevenson, the U.S. ambassador to the United Nations, had been jostled, spat upon and struck with a sign during a visit to Dallas only a month earlier. I went home and watched a report on television about Lyndon Johnson being sworn in as president.

After graduating, Sig Rogich built Nevada's largest advertising and public relations firm in Las Vegas. His clients included Frank Sinatra and Donald Trump. Rogich served as consultant to presidents Ronald Reagan and George H. W. Bush, and he received appointment as U.S. ambassador to Iceland, his birthplace.

Another two years went by during which Betsy and I joined a faculty "gourmet club." About ten couples, representing different academic disciplines, took turns hosting a dinner once a month. As we sat around a long dining table one night, I told my story about meeting the Purdue professor, Shanti Gupta.

A Nevada mathematics professor at the far end asked, "What was his last name again?" When I told him, he said, "Shanti Gupta is among the top three or four probability mathematicians in the world. He founded Purdue's statistics department. He's an expert in statistical reliability, and he's probably published more than a hundred academic papers and books."

The University of Nevada, in my opinion, was a far better institution than most Nevadans realized. Its School of Engineering was a leader in recruiting women to a once all-male field. The Psychology Department opened a new field of scientific inquiry when two of its professors taught the first chimpanzee to communicate in American Sign Language. The English Department's reputation was enhanced by such scholars of national stature as Walter Van Tilburg Clark, author of *The Ox-Bow Incident,* and Charlton Laird, compiler of Webster's *Thesaurus.* Robert Laxalt, author of *Sweet Promised Land,* headed the University Press.

The School of Medicine, emphasizing family practice, offered career opportunities to many young people from nearby Western states that provided no medical education. The Journalism Department, formed in 1946, produced several Pulitzer Prize winners.

A campus controversy that received national media attention in the previous decade before I arrived had been between University President Minard Stout and a disgruntled faculty group led by Frank Richardson, Biology Department chairman. Richardson and a half dozen other faculty professors voiced objections to Stout's plan to lower admission standards. President Stout sent them letters of dismissal.

Rollan Melton, a sophomore journalism major and staff member of the student newspaper, the *Sagebrush,* wrote a column saying Stout violated traditional academic freedom. President Stout called young Melton into his office and warned him his future on campus was in "jeopardy." Melton, remembering lectures on freedom of speech and press by Professor Higginbotham, defended Richardson in another column.

121

Four Reno lawyers offered Richardson pro bono support. When the lawyers and others urged Melton to write more columns backing Richardson, Melton thought he had said enough and sought his professor's counsel. Higginbotham invited Melton to his home. He praised Melton for a courageous stand but agreed he should now remain silent.

The Board of Regents held public hearings on whether Stout's termination of Richardson should be upheld. Higginbotham was one of the first witnesses. Responding to questions from the regents' attorney, Higginbotham made it clear he was a strong pro-Stout man. That statement shocked Melton, seated in the audience. Higginbotham pulled out a notebook and recited from it. He said Melton had come to his home and professed "shame" for his role in the controversy. Melton felt betrayed, he told me later.

The Regents voted unanimously to terminate Richardson. In protest, author Walter Tilburg Clark resigned from the English Department. The next year the Nevada Supreme court reviewed the case and ordered Richardson reinstated.

A subsequent study showed that Higginbotham and several more Stout advocates had received unusually high salary increases during the controversy, while incomes of Richardson supporters remained frozen. In 1957, the Board of Regents fired President Stout.

I had read about the firing and reinstatement of Richardson but knew nothing when I arrived on campus about the involvement of Higginbotham or Melton.

Rollan Melton grew up in Idaho, Oregon and the Nevada town of Fallon. His divorced mother worked as a restaurant waitress. As a boy he did odd jobs for a Fallon printer. He attended UNR on football and Harolds Club Casino scholarships, the latter awarded in those days to one student from each Nevada high school.

He played center on the university football team. He married, graduated with a major in journalism, and served a stint in the army. He worked as reporter and sports editor with the Reno *Evening Gazette* for several years. With two or three children and desperate for money, he crossed a union picket line during a Newspaper Guild strike that had lasted several weeks. He served first as the newspaper's wire editor and later as promotions director.

I met Rollan in the fall of 1963 when, as promotions director, he conducted a tour of the newspaper for about twenty students from my introductory journalism class. The attention he gave these young people impressed me. While guiding them through the newspaper building, he questioned them in turn about their career ambitions. It was obvious he listened to each, for he often posed relevant follow-up questions.

I wrote him a thank-you letter, and we became friends for nearly forty years -- until his death. He taught me lessons about succeeding in the news business that I tried to pass along to students.

A few weeks after my class's visit, the newspaper announced that Rollan had been transferred back to the newsroom -- as editor in chief. Higginbotham, I learned, immediately telephoned the newspaper's top management to tell them they had made a

122

mistake. Management ignored his call.

Three years later Melton became publisher of Reno Newspapers, which included the afternoon *Gazette* and the morning *Nevada State Journal.* They were owned by the Speidel Company, a group of twelve newspapers in locations from Visalia, California, to Poughkeepsie, New York.

On becoming publisher, Rollan received stock options, which he first exercised with a loan. In 1972, Speidel named him its president. In 1977, Gannett, the nation's largest newspaper at the time with about sixty publications, merged with Speidel -- with stockholders receiving eight Gannett shares to every ten Speidel shares. Gannett expanded rapidly to surpass Scripps-Howard and all other chains to become the country's largest. It acquired about ninety newspapers and twenty television stations in this country and several newspapers in Great Britain.

Rollan became Gannett senior vice president and board member. Gannett stock split more than once, and Rollan found himself a multi-millionaire. One day I asked Rollan the secret of his success. He answered, "I work long hours, and I ask questions." He explained that at appropriate moments, say, over coffee in an office or over beer in a bar, he would politely ask an associate with specialized knowledge how some issue in the past had been resolved or how a plan was progressing.

Rollan would then focus his questions on budget, methods, and staffing in ways that made the responder feel good about himself and his job. Meanwhile, Rollan listened closely and committed answers to memory. Over months and years, Rollan's knowledge expanded, and word circulated among top management that he asked pertinent questions and had a genuine interest in the business.

Rollan also collected information from people in lower ranks. I remember waiting with him for an elevator in a newspaper lobby late one afternoon when a janitor came by cleaning the floor. Rollan introduced himself and asked the man how long he'd worked for the firm. Then Rollan asked the man where he lived, the hardest part of his job, how much of the building he had responsibility for, and what he liked least about it. He did this in a friendly, low-key fashion that hardly interfered with the man's duties. Rollan appeared genuinely interested in the answers. The attention obviously pleased the janitor.

Only once did I question Rollan's interrogation methods. It was in Reno in 1974 when Nevada's Democratic Lieutenant Governor Harry Reid spoke to a meeting of the Society of Professional Journalists. This was years before he became majority leader of the U.S. Senate.

Reid, a Mormon about 35 years old, first campaigned for the United States Senate against Paul Laxalt, former governor.

Several newspaper and broadcast journalists at the meeting interrogated Reid about his campaign plans and about Nevada-related issues to be addressed in Washington. Reid was soft-spoken and deferential.

Rollan, a Republican, spoke up. "How's your health?" Reid appeared a little surprised. But he readily answered. The question appeared to be a normal in a political campaign. Then Rollan persisted. "What was your last serious illness?" "When was that?" "When did you have your last physical exam?" Reid stiffened a little, set his jaw, and answered. Rollan persisted. "What were the results?" "Have you made an appointment for your next exam?" "Why have you waited so long?"

With each response, Reid appeared less comfortable.

After the Reno meeting, I asked Rollan about his motive. "Did you have some inside information about Reid or his health that the rest of us in the room didn't have?"

"No," he said. "I just think knowing the health of a future senator is important." I reluctantly dropped the matter.

Although Reid lost the 1974 election to Laxalt, he succeeded in winning a U. S. Senate seat several years later. His low-key firmness as U. S. Senate majority leader during early 21st Century crises over gun control, debt ceiling, sequestration, and filibuster rule change was reminiscent to me of the Reno meeting. Rollan, a Republican, may have contributed unintentionally in a small way that night to young Democrat Harry Reid's political toughness.

On Rollan's recommendation, Betsy and I dug into our modest faculty savings to purchase a small amount ($2,000) of Gannett stock. Then Rollan invited us to accompany him and his wife Marilyn to a Gannett stockholders meeting in San Francisco. We dined with Gannett board members and met Al Neuharth, company president and chairman. Neuharth treated Betsy and me courteously, although he must have realized we were probably the smallest stock holders ever to mix with that entourage.

Rollan could laugh at his mistakes. After joining the Gannett board of directors, he told me about being invited to Neuharth's home in Cocoa Beach, Florida. I mentally pictured the two newspaper executives conversing over drinks on Neuharth's back porch overlooking the ocean. They had much in common. Neuharth grew up in rural South Dakota, and Melton in rural Nevada. Both graduated from their respective state universities. Their Depression-era mothers had reared them while working in restaurants for minimum wages and tips. Al's mother washed dishes. Rollan's mother waited tables.

Rollan and Al started as reporters and became multi-millionaires in the newspaper business, a rare feat.

Neuharth asked Rollan to react to Neuharth's idea of someday publishing a national, general-circulation newspaper to be called "USA Today." Rollan answered he didn't think the idea would work. He cited printing and distribution difficulties.

Rollan told me how Neuharth smiled, thanked Rollan for his input -- and ignored it.

Neuharth's proposal got a similar back-porch reaction from George Steinbrenner. When the New York Yankees owner died in 2010, Neuharth recalled in his *USA Today* column that Steinbrenner said, "You're crazy. . . All you would do is lose a helluva lot of money."

Rollan eventually joined other Gannett board members in voting yes to Neuharth's plan for a national newspaper, molded during a 1980-81 recession.

Gannett launched *USA Today* in 1982. It broke even in seven years and quickly sold more than two million copies a day, surpassing the *Wall Street Journal* as the nation's largest circulation newspaper. Besides *USA Today*, Gannett entered the 21st Century owning more than eighty newspapers and twenty TV stations in the United States, digital operations, and several TV stations in Britain.

Rollan returned enthusiastic from his first encampment with many of the world's most powerful persons at Bohemian Grove, an hour's drive north of San Francisco. He described as "worthwhile" talks he heard on world issues amid acres of redwood trees.

In answer to my question, he expressed doubt that the discussions affected such weighty issues as world prices and selection of future government leaders. He said he heard only casual mention of a "Trilateral Commission" or "Bilderbergers," whose memberships, although smaller, overlapped that of Bohemian Grove. Members of the exclusive club included heads of state, defense contractors, bankers, oil company CEO's, and some other media executives. Among invited guests were Henry Kissinger, Prince Philip of Great Britain, and Walter Cronkite, to name a few.

I listened more than once to Rollan's account of how Higginbotham, my boss, had disappointed him in the Stout-Richardson case. I noticed with amusement that Higginbotham posted newspaper articles about himself on journalism hallway bulletin boards with "Congratulations, Prof" scrawled with felt pen in his own handwriting. Higginbotham died in a few years, and Theodore Conover replaced him as chairman.

Because I had some broadcast experience in Columbia, Missouri, and Tulsa, Oklahoma, I was assigned radio-TV news courses to teach on the Nevada campus. Exceptional broadcast students included Dave Cooper, Ed Pearce, and Doug Bruckner, among others.

After graduating, Dave Cooper went to work for KORK-TV in Las Vegas. Ed Pearce spent more than thirty years with Reno's ABC affiliate, KOLO-TV, as reporter and anchor. Doug Bruckner, while still in his junior year, won a national Society of Professional Journalists (Sigma Delta Chi) award for radio script writing and broadcasting.

When *Quill* magazine and *Editor & Publisher* ran stories about Doug's award, announced in Pittsburgh in 1966, they identified me as his professor. Frank Ahlgren, my former Memphis boss, and Earl English, my former J-School dean, saw the stories.

The Commercial Appeal, Memphis
November 10, 1966

I want to congratulate you. You have made your mark pretty quickly in the world of journalism education. Of course, we will want to take some notice of it here and identify Professor Gilleland as an alumnus of this newspaper.

Frank Ahlgren, Editor

Nov. 14, 1966

Congratulations on your fine Sigma Delta Chi award. I should be glad to place the news release in your file. I'm sorry I did not get to the Pittsburgh convention. As you probably know, we have 600 students enrolled here at this time, a fact that makes it increasingly difficult to leave the scene. I hope all goes well with you. I heard fine reports about your work on the Nevada faculty.

Dean Earl English
School of Journalism
University of Missouri

Doug Bruckner later worked for KNBC-TV in Los Angeles and became investigative reporter for "Hard Copy" and other syndicated TV magazines. He won Emmy, Golden Mike, and Associated Press awards, among others.

In 1968, at the height of the Vietnam War's Tet Offensive, a gunman assassinated Martin Luther King in Memphis. It was three years after President Johnson signed the National Voting Rights Act that removed racial barriers from polling booths. Warren Lerude, Reno *Evening Gazette* editor, asked me to write a sidebar recalling my meeting with King in the previous decade. I did so and *Quill* magazine reprinted it.

Dr. King, a year older than I, consented to give me some time after his address. He spoke of Rosa Parks, the seamstress arrested when she refused to give up her seat to a white man and move to the back of a Montgomery bus. Dr. King explained how he, an obscure Montgomery pastor, met the next night with fifty black leaders of the city to discuss the case.

The decision they made was momentous, although, he told me, it didn't seem so at the time. The whole black community of Montgomery would boycott the buses in mass protest. It was from the boycott that Dr. King became a major spokesman for black aspirations through "non-violence."

As we talked in the crowded Memphis auditorium that night years ago, the young black minister put me at ease with a ready smile and the quiet, friendly way he answered questions. It was as if Dr. King did not want a stranger to feel uncomfortable amid a multitude whose skin was of different color.

Professor Recalls King Interview

EDITOR'S NOTE: A meeting with Dr. Martin Luther King, long before he had reached his summit of world attention, is recalled by LaRue Gilleland, associate professor of journalism at the University of Nevada. Prof. Gilleland is a former staff writer for the Commercial Appeal in Memphis. He wrote this account for the Reno (Nev.) Evening Gazette.

MARTIN LUTHER KING, boyish and rather short, stood tall that night in the eyes of his people.

His own modest self-confidence reflected in their black faces. It was near the beginning of his career — almost a dozen years ago in Memphis.

Only 27 then, the Negro minister had brought his new crusade for racial equality for the first time to the city in which he was destined to die.

The hot South Memphis auditorium was crowded with hundreds of Negro men, women and children waiting for a message of hope.

I was the only white man and the only news reporter present. Dr. King, despite his part in the 1955-56 Montgomery, Ala., bus boycott, was not yet recognized as a major news maker.

I probably would not have gone to the meeting at all if the program had not included Jackie Robinson. The Negro baseball player had come to town with Dr. King.

Though I went mainly to see the Dodger star, I gave my attention to the Baptist preacher.

Already a commanding orator, Dr. King appeared to induce happiness as he spoke. To the multitude that night he was like some young Mohandas Gandhi, a symbol of power and beauty beyond their individual lives.

He was poised, handsome, and well-educated with his recently acquired doctorate from Boston.

He told his listeners that acceptance of the first Negro in major league baseball had been "the mere start of a glorious new era for our race."

"There will be Jackie Robinsons in politics, in business, in theater, and in every occupation and profession in this great land" he said.

Dr. King found time to talk with me before and after his speech. I was only a year younger than he. But I discerned at once his far greater strength. I was white. He was black. He was the superior man.

He spoke to me of Rosa Parks, the seamstress who was arrested after she refused to give up her seat to a white man and move to the back of a Montgomery bus.

Dr. King explained how he, an obscure Montgomery pastor, met the night after Mrs. Parks' arrest with 50 Negro leaders of the city to discuss the case.

The decision they made was momentous, although, he told me, it didn't seem so at the time. The whole Negro community of Montgomery would boycott the buses in mass protest.

Out of that unfolded all the Negro protests and demonstrations since, including the march which Dr. King — before he was killed by a sniper on April 4 — had returned to Memphis to lead on behalf of striking sanitation workers.

It also was out of the Montgomery boycott that Dr. King became the spokesman for Negro aspirations through "nonviolence."

As we talked in the crowded Memphis auditorium that night years ago, the sensitive young Negro minister put me at ease with a ready smile and the quiet, friendly way he answered questions.

It was as if Dr. King did not want a stranger to feel uncomfortable amid a multitude whose skin was of different color. ■

Black protests and demonstrations later would include the march in Memphis that Dr. King returned to lead on behalf of striking sanitation workers -- before a sniper killed him.

I learned later that my Martin Luther King story played a role, although minor, in the resignation of a *Gazette* editor. On the day of King's assassination, editorial page editor John Sanford refused to write an editorial extolling King's career.

"I have no respect for Martin Luther King, and I will not write one good word about him," he told Editor Lerude, Publisher Melton, and Speidel President Charles Stout. I heard Sanford also was miffed that Lerude had asked me to do a story about King. Sanford figured my story probably would be favorable to King.

Then Sanford changed his mind. He said he'd do the editorial, "but it will be the last thing I ever write for the *Gazette*, because effective this afternoon, I resign." Sanford had served as the newspaper's editor-in-chief for years before being moved to the editorial page.

The Nevada campus was surprisingly conservative to be located in a city of gambling casinos. Some of my graduate and upperclass students worked in casinos as dealers. They liked the jobs because they paid well and provided frequent 20-minute breaks during which the students could study undisturbed in employee lounges. Casinos provided the breaks because they believed tired, un-alert dealers could cause them to lose money.

While Nevada had its share of women lending their voices to the nation's feminist movement, it missed most of the unrest about racial issues and the war in Vietnam that hit Kent State, Columbia, Berkeley, San Francisco State, and other universities. About the only anti-war sentiment heard on the Nevada campus was directed at ROTC.

Some students and faculty thought ROTC should have no place at the university. I disagreed. I supported the ROTC's officer-training program at the same time I doubted the "domino theory" that led America into the Vietnam War. The theory held that if the United States lost in Vietnam, all Asia would fall to communism. I went out of my way to let ROTC faculty and students know the journalism program and I welcomed them on campus.

The Reno campus also remained relatively isolated from the Haight-Asbury anti-war Hippie culture in nearby San Francisco, where Allen Ginzburg's poem "Howl" and illicit drugs turned on young people. The Nevada campus hardly noticed when the shotgun used in slaying a San Rafael Superior Court judge was traced to Angela Davis, a dismissed "black and beautiful" UCLA philosophy teacher.

I received permission to teach press law because my court reporting and work at the University of Missouri's Freedom of Information Center gave me more legal background than most of my Nevada colleagues.

In addition to studying many past and present libel and invasion of privacy cases, my students watched progress of Pentagon Papers and Watergate cases in the early 1970s. They also studied prior restraint cases dating back to early England.

My journalism history students dug into France's colonial expansion into Indo China in the 1800s and news coverage of President Truman's aid to France as it tried to regain control there after World War II. They reviewed the Vietnamese ouster of France in 1954 at Dien Bien Phu and U. S. military buildup in the region under Presidents Eisenhower, Kennedy, Johnson and Nixon. President Ford pulled out all U. S. troops in 1975.

To hear student discussions of this and other legal issues affecting the press, Warren Lerude and Rollan Melton audited some of my class sessions. With more attentiveness and smiles than usual, class members indicated apparent pride that a course required of them held interest for two local professionals.

Lerude led a team of three that won the 1977 Pulitzer Prize in Editorial Writing. They exposed the influence on Nevada politics of Joe Conforte, owner of Mustang Ranch, one of the state's most famous brothels. A federal court eventually seized control of the ranch after Conforte failed to pay a tax bill. I met Conforte when he accepted an invitation to speak to a local chapter of the Sigma Delta Chi, Society of Professional Journalists.

One day, as forty press law students and I talked about excessive punitive damages in libel cases, someone in class mentioned an exorbitant award in a recent medical case involving an accusation of botched hemorrhoid surgery. A young woman, Susan Forrest, about 21, raised her hand and innocently asked, "What's a hemorrhoid?"

As the class of young adults roared with laughter, my mind fumbled for a professional reply. Fortunately, another young woman, majoring in both nursing and journalism, articulated a sober, clinical answer.

After graduation, Susan Forrest went to work for the Lawrence (Massachusetts) *Eagle-Tribune.* There she helped win the 1988 Pulitzer Prize in General News Reporting.

I frequently gave talks at programs sponsored by such organizations as the Nevada Press Association, the Society of Professional Journalists, the Stanford Editors Conference, and the National College of the State Judiciary (later called National Judicial College).

At the Stanford Editors Conference, sponsored by the California Newspaper Publishers Association, I told participants that it was in their best interest to get involved in -- and help support -- the programs of journalism schools and departments near them.

Reno Evening Gazette
June 26, 1973

Thanks again for your participation in the Stanford Editors Conference program. I'm sure some editors will, in fact, go to a campus because of your urgings and insights. And we will be the better off for it.

Warren Lerude, Executive Editor

Press-Enterprise
Riverside, California
June 28, 1973

Jack Craemer of the San Rafael Independent Journal, when I arrived late at the Stanford Editors Conference, said that you had made a very interesting presentation during the panel on journalism education. He thought that you could supply me with a text of your remarks and, if you can, I would appreciate it.

Howard H. (Tim) Hays Jr., Editor & Publisher
Temple University
June 29, 1973

. . . It was an excellent speech; I am circulating it among our faculty so that they may get the benefit of your thinking.

Bruce Underwood, Chairman, Journalism

Stanford University
September 8, 1973

I returned from a trip just in time to serve on a panel at the Stanford Editors Conference. Unfortunately, I missed your presentation, which was scheduled just before my panel. I heard from several who attended that your presentation was excellent.

Bill Rivers, Professor

Appearing on the same Stanford Editors program at Rickey's Hyatt Hotel in Palo Alto was Frank McCulloch, a UNR graduate who had covered the Vietnam War for Time-Life. He also conducted the last known interview with industrialist-movie mogul Howard Hughes in 1958, before Hughes went into years of seclusion.

His editors at *Time* asked McCulloch to do a story on Hughes' plan to buy the first jets for his airline, TWA. Hughes returned a call in the middle of the night to tell McCulloch to park his car and wait at a major Los Angeles intersection. From there a chauffeur for Hughes took McCulloch to a remote part of Los Angeles International Airport, where Hughes ushered him into a new Boeing 707. Also aboard were a co-pilot and Hughes' wife, Jean Peters. Hughes took the controls and flew the plane over parts of Mexico, Arizona, and Nevada, returning for a bumpy landing four hours later. McCulloch wrote a story and filed away his notes. They later would play a role in a controversial court case.

When McCulloch joined the Sacramento *Bee* as its managing editor, Nevada faculty, students and I benefited from his occasional campus visits.

At the Stanford Editors Conference, Betsy Gilleland laughs at Time-Life's Frank McCulloch's account of his last interview with industrialist Howard Hughs.

About 1966, three Nevada faculty members and I came away from a meeting in Las Vegas believing we had watched an unusual casino show in the presence of the mysterious Hughes. He had just bought the Desert Inn Hotel-Casino. He lived on the ninth floor and housed his aides on the eighth.

I joined faculty colleagues for a drink at the hotel after attending a day-long Nevada Press Association meeting. While rock and pop musicians entertained in the hotel's main showroom, a small lounge near the front lobby advertised chamber music by a women's string quartet. We professors stopped at a hallway advertisement to marvel that a Las Vegas casino would feature classical music in one of its showrooms. A hotel employee told us that Hughes, the new owner, had booked the quartet for an extended engagement. We decided to see for ourselves.

We entered a nearly empty lounge. We took a table at the back. All tables were vacant except for one near the stage. There sat two men in business suits watching four talented young women in long gowns play stringed instruments.

We sipped our drinks and listened to several well-performed numbers. Then one of our group – Professor Kieste Janulis, who had covered portions of Europe during World War II for the Chicago *Tribune* before going into teaching – said he thought the taller occupant at the other table looked like Howard Hughes. The others at our table agreed. If they were correct, we were among the last few people to see Hughes in public.

We became more convinced when the tall man and his companion left through a door near the stage, an exit to upper floors not used by tourists.

In a few weeks, news stories began appearing about Hughes' new self-imposed, ninth-floor isolation. The stories described him as addicted to prescription painkillers. They said he refused to cut his hair, beard and fingernails.

Without appearing in public, Hughes bought other Las Vegas hotels. He also acquired the city's KLAS-TV, so that it would present movies he wanted to watch at the times he preferred.

A controversial event occurred in 1967 when Melvin Dummar, a service station owner, said he rescued a disheveled man from beside a desert highway near Cotton Tail Ranch, a brothel, and returned him to Las Vegas, one-hundred-fifty miles south. Dummar said he did not know the man's identity at the time.

After Hughes' death in 1976, a hand-written will surfaced that named Dummar as beneficiary to one-sixteenth of Hughes' estate. Among others named were the University of Nevada, Boy Scouts of America, employees, ex-wives Jean Peters and Ella Rice, and the Church of Latter-Day Saints (Mormon), to which several of his aides belonged. Officials in Hughes' company challenged the will, and a court ruled it invalid. Later, the pilot of a small plane claimed he was hired by Hughes to fly him to a landing strip adjacent to Cotton Tail Ranch. This was a day or so before Dummar found the man he later believed to be Hughes.

The National College of the State Judiciary, founded on the University of Nevada campus by the American Bar Association, sought to improve performance of state court judges. It sponsored seminars on legal issues, from victims' rights to prison overcrowding, and how to deal with news media. Judicial College programs brought hundreds of trial judges and other court personnel from all over the country to UNR each year. I received these letters:

National College of the State Judiciary
August 4, 1975

Let me extend to you the thanks of the National College for your assistance as a panelist. Your contribution to the continuing education of the judiciary is invaluable. I know that those in attendance appreciated your efforts as much as I did. You may justly take pride in your contribution to this most worthwhile movement.

Dean Ernst John Watts

National College of the State Judiciary
August 9, 1975

My sincere appreciation for your having taken the time from your busy schedule to participate in the sentencing program at the National College of the State Judiciary. Your involvement was of great benefit to the judges attending the College.

Joseph Mattina

My Nevada colleague Bill Ward suggested to the editorial board of an academic journal that the publication be transferred to the Nevada campus on retirement of its editor. The quarterly, *Journalism Educator* (JE), helped university teachers prepare young men and women for productive media-related careers. The American Society of Journalism School Administrators (ASJSA) published it. JE showed concern for small, developing programs working toward accreditation and those large and well established.

The journal transferred to UNR from the University of Long Island. Bill Ward and I became its co-editors and Theodore Conover its business manager. After the first year, Ward accepted a job at Southern Illinois University-Edwardsville, and I became the sole editor. I performed the job for seven years.

In the journal, educators offered teaching tips and shared their classroom successes and failures. *Journalism Educator* and ASJSA also took these editorial stands:

1) Students should acquire writing, editing, interviewing, and other professional skills, not just theory. They should learn to work under deadline pressure. Journalism courses should not exceed one-fourth of a student's undergraduate work.

2) Most of an undergraduate's courses should be in history, literature, philosophy, economics, math, science, and fine arts, among others.

3) Public relations courses for practitioners should stress accurate research, prompt response, and truth. On most days about half of all news stories begin with PR material submitted to media, which generally develop them further.

4) Future publishers, in addition to studying writing, editing and press law courses, benefit from a course or two in advertising -- on which their publications will depend.

5) Media executives should realize they have a vital stake in the quality of university journalism programs and take active interest in them.

6) University journalism teachers, along with graduate work, should have completed at least five years of full-time media experience.

JE and ASJSA expressed concern that hiring university faculty with little or no journalism experience paralleled a similar development in media ranks: appointing corporate officers and directors who could run real estate or other empires, but knew nothing about the news business.

West Virginia U. School of Journalism
June 2, 1970

The current issue of **Journalism Educator** *pleases me a great deal.*

I like the fact that you are including editorial comments, and I like especially what you say. Your articles are of superior grade.

Perley Isaac Reed, Director Emeritus

California State-Hayward
July 28, 1971

You have done a great job with the JE, and I hope the new arrangement makes it possible for a much larger readership to appreciate what a fine and valuable journal JE really is.

Reuben Mehling, ASJSA Secretary-Treasurer

Kent State University
February 3, 1972

My compliments. Journalism Educator is a real magazine.
Keep up the good work.

Harold Van Winkle Professor

The faculty and I often attended conventions of the Association for Education in Journalism and Mass Communication (AEJMC); the Society of Professional Journalists; Kappa Tau Alpha, journalism honor society; and other media-related organizations. Meetings took place in Minneapolis, Atlanta, San Diego, Boston, Chicago, Pittsburgh, and San Francisco. Guest speakers included editors, such as Norman Cousins and John Seigenthaler; writers, such as Thomas Wolfe; and scientists, such as Edward Teller.

Edward Teller provided copy for a story and an anecdote that I used later in my classes. I listened to the conclusion of the Hungarian-born, German-educated physicist's speech on America's need for strong nuclear deterrent. After he spoke, I left the lecture hall to take in some sunshine on an outside bench during the lunch hour. A young female television reporter, who'd asked Teller for an interview, stopped with him and a cameraman at another bench within earshot.

They sat down, and I heard her ask, "How old were you when you invented the atomic bomb?" Teller stiffened. He stood up and said angrily, "You're wasting my time. You have done no preparation for this interview!"

He walked off. The reporter sat several moments in disbelief before she and the cameraman departed.

Although I'd had a news source or two get mad at me, I told my students later that Teller's pique at slipshod interviewing by the TV reporter was probably justified. The reporter could have learned with only a little research that Teller did not invent the A-bomb. His main contribution came later with the hydrogen bomb. It was Teller who argued successfully that heat from atomic fission could start hydrogen-bomb fusion.

Teller in those days worried about more than pesky reporters and H-bombs. He warned that a possible asteroid strike is a greater threat to Earth than any bomb. Governments, he said, should put resources into preparing defenses in space to avoid a catastrophic strike similar that which destroyed dinosaurs and nearly all of life millions of years ago.

16

GOSS Formula

In *Journalism Educator* in 1971, I published a simple formula I developed to help reporting students ask effective interview questions. It was intended to supplement, not replace, the traditional Who? What? When? Where? Why? and How? that reporters traditionally put to news sources.

I based the formula on the premise that nearly any individual or organization making news has a purpose and has confronted, or will confront, some obstacle; that the newsmaker has found -- or is looking for -- a solution to the obstacle, or a way around it; and that the goal sought originated with someone's idea.

My students dubbed it "Gilleland's GOSS formula" because the acronym GOSS -- Goal, Obstacle, Solution, Start -- provided a memory aiding device. It reminded the reporter, after jotting down preliminary information, to ask:

GOAL revealing questions, such as "What are you trying to accomplish?" or "What's the objective of your organization?"

OBSTACLE revealing questions, such as "What challenges did you face?" or "What are your concerns now?

SOLUTION revealing questions, such as "What plan do you have for dealing with the problem?" or "How did you solve the conflict?"

START revealing questions, such as "When did the program have its beginning?" or "Whose idea was it?"

Former students sent testimonials. Hampton Young, a Reno *Evening Gazette* reporter, said, "I have found the GOSS technique is excellent when I have a story to do about a subject for which I have no background.

"Always before, without background information, I found myself groping for 'feeler' questions, and often there would be that one question I would forget to ask. With the GOSS technique, everything just falls right into place. There is no need to reach for questions. I know what I'm going to ask. When I'm through I have all the information I need for a story. No pain or mental anguish is involved."

Virginia Heck, a reporting intern, said, "It's so simple. When I first had interviews to do, I was often upset. So I started using your GOSS symbol. It brought questions to mind and I started to relax. I also began listening more closely to what the person I was interviewing was saying, because I no longer was worried about my next question." *Editor & Publisher* magazine published GOSS on September 18, 1971. My Nevada faculty colleague, Bill Metz, a former Honolulu *Star Bulletin* news editor, put the formula in his 1972 textbook, *Newswriting: From Lead to '30'* (Prentice-Hall).

Among other textbooks including it during that decade were *Basic News Reporting* by Michael Ryan and James Tankard (Mayfield Publishing Co.), *Research Guide in Journalism* by Paul J. Anderson (General Learning Press), and *Creative Interviewing* by Ken Metzler (Prentice Hall). The formula also appeared in journalism books in Germany and China.

GOSS helped me move to full professor rank.

Years later during a trip to Mysore University in India, where a colleague and I spoke about benefits of cooperation between media and academic leaders, an Indian student in the audience surprised me with the unrelated question, "How did you come up with GOSS?"

I replied that I got the idea from reading philosophers Schopenhauer and Nietzsche. "I applied to interviewing their notions of inevitable struggle in nature and their concepts of 'Will to Live,' and 'Will to Power.' "

The Province, Vancouver, B. C.
October 15, 1971

I was impressed by your GOSS formula...

Gordon Purver, City Editor

The Spectator, Hamilton, Ontario
September 23, 1971

... I plan to tell our staff about it.

Larry Perks, Editorial Training Director

Edwards Air Force Base, California
August 23, 1974

I am happy to report that my journalism students have really benefited from your GOSS formula for interviews. I've been using it ever since your article appeared in the 1971 summer issue of Journalism Educator, *and I've always experienced highly successful results. So, many thanks from one teacher who has appreciated your helpful teaching tip.*

Nanci Knopf Dawdy

Northeastern University
October 22, 1975

I've been using your GOSS formula to teach students how to interview since I read about it in Editor & Publisher *a few years ago. It's very effective.*

Bill Kirtz, Associate Professor

University of Oregon
February 1, 1979

We've never met, but I feel as if I know you -- having taught the Gilleland GOSS formula through many years of reporting, writing, and interviewing classes. The more I teach and write, the more I'm convinced that the formula is philosophically sound.

Ken Metzler, Professor

Boston, Massachusetts
May 12, 1985

GOSS is a good idea. . . . . I plan to give you credit when I pass it along to others.

Michael Short
Chief of Bureau, Associated Press

If I were drafting the formula again, I would lengthen it to add an assumption. The assumption is that most belief systems -- political, religious, economic, and even mathematical – are constructed on postulates, i.e., assumptions taken for granted without proof.

I would lengthen the acronym to GOSS-A. The hyphen would indicate to the reporter that postulate detection may not be needed in every interview situation.

Journalistic interviews provide news sources opportunity to explain ideas in depth and offer specifics. But news sources seldom reveal their postulates unless prodded by the interviewer.

Conservative, liberal and moderate politicians, and leaders in various spheres, probably act on numerous postulates. If more postulates were revealed, some of the world's most serious conflicts might be reduced.

A Marxist politician might hold the assumption that equal distribution of wealth could be accomplished and maintained despite vast differences in the interests, talents, and needs of individuals.

A laissez faire politician might hold the assumption that a few people could accumulate unrestricted wealth without a widening gap between haves and have-nots eventually causing major social instability.

Euclid based his geometry on postulates. Modern scholars have pointed out that some of Euclid's "axioms," accepted as self-evidently true, began as postulates, or assumptions.

17

Academic Life

My university acquaintances included a female ape. The chimpanzee's name was Washoe. The chimp and I often met getting on or off an elevator in Mack Social Science Building, where journalism offices and classrooms occupied the ground floor in those days. The four-foot female, born in West Africa, received international attention by learning to communicate in American Sign Language.

Nevada psychologists Beatrice and Allen Gardner taught Washoe sign language after adopting her when she was several months old. Washoe lived at their Reno home. The Gardners, usng the elevator, often brought her to their offices on a floor above the Journalism Department.

The chimp's first hand sign, without immediate prompting, was "bird." The Gardners said she gave this sign one day on seeing a swan swimming in Manzanita Lake in the middle of campus. Washoe learned to combine hand signs to make phrases. An early phrase she mastered was "time to eat." After that her vocabulary grew to nearly two-hundred signs, including pronouns "I," "my," "you." On finding a tiny doll in her favorite cup, Washoe signed, "Baby in my drink."

The Gardners did not want me or anyone to speak to Washoe, for they thought hearing spoken language would interfere with her instruction in signs. At the elevator, I simply smiled at the barefoot chimp, and she usually stared at my feet.

She would look closely at my shoes and sign "brown" or "black" for the colors I wore. She liked to inspect everybody's shoes.

After about three years with the Gardners, Washoe moved with a graduate student, Roger Fouts, to Central Washington University in Ellensberg. There Washoe's vocabulary increased even more. She taught another chimp, her foster son, some sign language. She died at age 42 in 2007. The chimp's name came from the Nevada county in which Reno was located. Elsewhere in later years a number of chimps would surpass Washoe's language proficiency.

I observed the beneficial impact one student could have on others. An advisee showed me a couple of assignments from a beginning news writing class on which his professor had placed low grades and many red ink corrections. The student, Martin Bibb, said he felt discouraged, although still determined. As I looked at his many grammatical errors, it appeared to me that he at least grasped most of the story-structure principles his teacher wanted.

With Martin in mind, I suggested an experiment to the department chairman and other faculty. They agreed. They designated a half dozen of their worst writing students, mostly freshmen, willing to meet with me a few hours each week on a voluntary basis. Most had more problems than did Martin. All frequently misspelled words, and one even often started sentences with lower case letters.

Although I fussed a lot with the students about incorrect spelling for the next few weeks, I avoided as much as possible talking about such mechanics as verb conjugations and noun declensions, which had scared them since high school. Instead, I emphasized the difference between independent and subordinate clauses and the various kinds of punctuation and conjunctions needed to put clauses together in clear sentences. Then I had the students add phrases that did not dangle. The writing problems of most of the students diminished by the time we got around to discussing subject-verb and pronoun-antecedent agreement.

Most of the improvement came from the personal example set by Martin Bibb. His enthusiasm affected other students. He made it clear in class that he knew acquiring good writing skills would be important to his career. All six students eventually graduated, and Martin ranked near the top of his entire senior class.

Nevada Department of Motor Vehicles
December 9, 1971

Again thanks for all your help . . . In the shuffle one knows as college, it is nearly essential that the student feels what he has to say is listened by his instructors in more than a casual manner.

You listened and showed that you cared. While not every single student may have said this to you, I know a number of Nevada J-students who felt the same way about you, Prof.

Martin Bibb, Public Relations Director

In addition to teaching duties, I received a five-year assignment outside the Journalism Department that quickly stretched my academic horizons. Arts and Sciences Dean Harold Kirkpatrick appointed me to chair the college's Courses and Curricula Committee.

The committee studied proposals from every college discipline -- natural sciences, mathematics, social sciences, humanities, and fine arts -- that wanted to add or delete a course or change a graduation requirement. When necessary, the committee invited pertinent faculty to answer questions on why modification was needed and how it might impact other disciplines. An abolished math course, for example, could affect natural science requirements.

Sometimes a department objected that a proposed change, usually a course or program to be added, threatened its turf. The six-member committee and I took our work seriously. Our recommendations generally received college and university approval.

John D. Mott of Northern Illinois University informed me in 1972 he was putting together a book, *The Journalist's Prayerbook*, for the Augsburg Publishing House of Minneapolis. His co-editor was Alfred Klausler, a commentator for Westinghouse Broadcasting Company.

They already had received contributions -- religious prayers and poems from Clifton Daniel of the New York *Times*, Walter Cronkite of CBS, Martin E. Marty of *Christian Century*, Louis Cassels of United Press International, and Billy Graham, who regularly wrote a nationally syndicated column.

When I heard the laudable news that their book would contain Walter Williams' "Journalist's Creed," I submitted a free-verse poem that I titled, "For a Good-Evil World."

Mott and Klausler published it in their volume. The verse:

God, whatever is Ultimate,
few will conclude from today's news
that the world is all good;
but deliver us
from the debilitating thought
that it is essentially evil.

If it is your will,
comfort us who are paid
to observe and write
with the understanding
that we see the world one way or another
largely by the frame of reference
in which you place us.

Comfort us with the understanding
that even with your omnipotence,
creation and perfection of a universe
in time and space may, by necessity,
take a moment in time.

From our prospect
on a tiny particle of the vast cosmos,
that moment -- in which imperfection, disease,
pain, controversy, war occupy
our working lives -- may appear
to be very long.

But from your perspective,
that moment may be
infinitesimally brief.

Help us to comprehend
that seeing the world as fundamentally evil
is seeing it from the position of suffering man;
that seeing it as fundamentally good
may posit the point of view of God.

If both views are real, the world
is temporarily good-evil.
Help us to observe
and write effectively
in a good-evil world.

When *The Journalist's Prayer Book* appeared, the Reno Evening *Gazette* and *Nevada State Journal* reprinted my verse. A few days later I received a telephone call from musician Gregory Stone, who recently moved to town to organize the Reno Philharmonic Orchestra.

He had two proposals. He said he'd like to set my verse to music, and he invited me to join the philharmonic's board of directors. I agreed to both.

Gregory was about 72. Born in the Ukraine, he had come to this country in the 1920s. He made a name for himself as a successful composer in New York and Hollywood. In 1935, he co-wrote "Let's Dance," popularized by Benny Goodman. Stone and collaborator Morris Stoloff received an Oscar nomination three years later for their musical score for a movie, "Girls' School."

Gregory succeeded in organizing the Reno Philharmonic, and he directed it in well-attended performances. He assured me I would soon hear the music he was composing for my poem. He died before its completion. After his death, the orchestra continued to grow under other directors.

Betsy and I flew to the Soviet Union in August 1969, a month after the successful U. S. Apollo 11 mission to the Moon. We did the usual sightseeing in St. Petersburg (then called Leningrad) by visiting the Hermitage, the Mariinsky (Kirov) Theater, the Yusupov Palace, the Peterhof, and Tsarskoe Selo.

In an era when American currency ranked among the world's strongest, our trip cost relatively little. We paid in advance for a guide, car and driver to take us wherever we wanted six hours a day in each Russian city we visited. We were free to move about on our own the rest of the day.

We assumed our daytime escorts periodically reported our activities to Intourist, the KGB, or some other government agency.

In our hotel rooms, Betsy and I sometimes joked loudly about being overheard by hidden microphones. I answered the phone one day to hear a male voice rapidly speaking Russian. When I said I did not understand, the caller persisted. His tone had an overly friendly lilt, as if he were telling a funny story. When it occurred to me the call might be a connivance merely to determine if I spoke or comprehended Russian, I hung up.

A couple of experiences reinforced stories we'd heard about a bent by some Russians for heavy tippling and short tempers. Walking down a St. Petersburg street one evening, Betsy and I passed a hotel from which lively music emerged. We entered the hotel's nightclub, ignoring an official caution given us earlier to patronize only hotels and restaurants designated for tourists. The Soviet government at the time didn't like visitors getting too friendly with its citizens.

We made our way aross a crowded dance floor and found an empty table. We ordered drinks as a small combo that included a three-stringed balalaika played Russian and Western tunes. While Betsy listened, I decided to look at a local tour book I carried. I would have to tell our guide-interpreter early the next morning what we wanted to see that day.

While music played and I flipped the book's pages, a tall Russian man approached our table. He stopped in front of me and made it known by gestures he would like to ask Betsy to dance. I indicated he could ask her. She decided to dance with him.

The band struck up a fast waltz, and Betsy and the Russian began to whirl around the floor. When I saw him stumble, I realized he might be intoxicated. On the opposite side of the room, he released Betsy, lost his balance and fell backward across a table.

With a loud crash, table legs broke and glasses splattered across the floor. Fearing Betsy and I might be jailed for contributing to disturbance in a forbidden club, I jumped up, grabbed her arm, and we hurried out the door to the street -- and to our hotel.

A couple of days later we boarded a plane from St. Petersburg to Moscow. The Aeroflot stewardess directed us to two seats from which she removed a pair of sunglasses and a bouquet of pink and white carnations. She placed them in the third seat from the aisle.

A young Russian man arrived who grew angry when he saw Betsy and me in seats he had been saving for two companions. He shook the flowers first at me, then at Betsy, and gave us a piece of his mind in violent spurts of Russian. We were helpless to explain. We appeared to be the only Americans on board. A female airline employee quieted the young man and told him to take the third seat. She also directed his two buddies to seats in the next row.

In the air I asked if anyone nearby spoke English. One of the angry man's companions behind me said, "Yes . . . a little."

So I asked him to tell his aggrieved friend next to me that my wife and I had not chosen to sit where we were. With that the frown faded from the young man with the flowers. I confirmed, in response to his question, that we came from the United States.

His name was Mikhail. He asked through his friend, our mutual interpreter, which state we were from. We told him. He then wanted to know our names, my occupation, the exact location of Reno (I drew a crude U.S. map), how far I drove to work, what kind of housing we had, how much we paid for it, and how much money I earned.

By now his two friends stood in the aisle of the plane to hear better. The translator passed along our replies to other passengers. Betsy and I tried to give straightforward answers.

The Russians showed surprise that Americans could afford four children. Most Russian families, they said, had no more than two. The Russians appeared impressed that we lived in a seven-room house rather than a small apartment, as did the typical urban Soviet family.

The three men, all about 30 or younger, were mechanical engineers heading to a Black Sea vacation. Mikhail, who had the flowers, had been born in Leningrad during its 900-day German siege in World War II. He sucked in his cheeks to indicate hunger experienced during the ordeal.

The talk grew increasingly animated for about an hour until we prepared to land in Moscow. The engineer-translator said, "This has been EEN-ter-ES-ting conversation. Thank you."

When the plane came to a stop, Mikhail stood up, turned to Betsy, and handed her the flowers. His smile and manner left no doubt that he offered the flowers in sincere friendliness. Betsy was delighted.

We checked into Moscow's huge Rossiya Hotel near Red Square. Inside the first hotel elevator we entered hung a large poster of American astronauts Buzz Aldrin, Michael Collins and Neil Armstrong, who had made the first walk on the Moon a month earlier. The elevator operator turned to us and asked, "Americans?" When we said yes, he pointed to the poster with broad smile and approving nod.

We visited the Bolshoi Theater and rode the city's excellent subway. We viewed the Kremlin's few remaining enameled Faberge Imperial Eggs and admired the Tretyakov Art Gallery's icons. At Moscow State University on Sparrow Hills, I fantasized about someday being connected with a student exchange program established there for Americans.

While Betsy browsed nearby Children's World Department Store, I walked outside and through Moscow's Dzerzhinsky Square, within view of KGB Headquarters a block away. I stopped beneath the three-story high statue of Felix Dzerzhinsky, secret police founder. As I studied the ruthless Bolshevik's bronze face, a well-dressed young man confronted me. Speaking English with thick Russian accent, he wanted to exchange Soviet for U. S. currency at a very tempting rate. Such transactions were a crime for which foreigners from time to time went to prison. I said, "no thanks." He persisted. I turned and walked away.

I wondered if the KGB recognized the irony of attempting entrapment under Dzerzhinky's statue. Betsy and I together refused a similar offer on a different street the next day. (With the Soviet era's end in 1991, Moscow authorities removed the Dzerzhinsky statue.)

Betsy and I had fun eating Chicken Kiev in Kiev. The only official reluctance to showing us everything we wanted to see occurred in Kiev. Each day we asked our guide there to visit Babi Yar, the ravine in the city's northwest where in 1941 Nazis, helped by collaborators, executed more than a hundred-thousand Ukranians, Gypsies, and Jews. The number murdered in two days set a Holocaust record. I had read Yevgeny Yevtushenko's sad poem about Babi Yar, set to music by Shostakovich in his Symphony No. 13.

Because we persisted, our guide finally drove us to Babi Yar. Atop the ravine, filled in by Nazis before they retreated and later overgrown with grass, we found a fresh bouquet of flowers. We learned on returning to America that the Soviet government ordered flowers placed there just before any persistent tourists arrived. Years later, Babi Yar became a commonplace tourist stop.

Back in Reno, I engaged in friendly debate with a UNR engineering professor about Russian character. It took place after dinner on the patio of Eugene Kosso, whose parents had emigrated from the Ukraine after the 1917 revolution. We compared recent trips to the Soviet Union. I commented that I had encountered a number of "boorish" Russians.

"You don't understand their character," Gene said. "Russians are impulsive and blunt. It's not rudeness to them."

I told him the story of our encounter on an airplane with the young engineer holding flowers. "You just made my point," Gene said.

Hot type and letterpress began to disappear in the 1960s from newspaper production departments, replaced by "cold type" photocomposition and offset printing. Computerization reduced manpower and other expenses. Video display terminals (VDTs) made typewriters obsolete in newsrooms.

The Nevada journalism department proudly acquired its first computerized VDT about this time. We could afford only one at first. The faculty member with the most expertise would show an entire editing class such mysteries as how to insert words into copy and transpose paragraphs with a few keystrokes. Each student could reserve time on the VDT to practice alone.

After all students started using computers, Ted Conover, who taught a typography course, required every print media major to set a small page of text the old fashioned way -- by hand -- and print at least one copy on a small press. The exercise would have looked familiar to Johann Gutenberg. The students performed it in a room of "job cases," or cabinets containing drawers filled with type fonts of different sizes. The assignment turned out to be one of the department's most effective history lessons.

A few universities producing print and electronic journalists adopted the term "mass communication." It was an improvement, I thought, on "communication" or "communication arts." I don't recall back then seeing precise definition of these terms, but "communication" and "communications arts" too often included instruction in speech, theater, creative writing, or movie making. The older term, "journalism," and the newer "mass communication" in academe connoted preparation for careers in newspapers, radio-television news, advertising and public relations.

18

Home Front

Nevada life appealed to Betsy, the children, and me. Our family made excursions to Lake Tahoe and other spots in the high Sierras and picnicked on the Paiute Indian reservation in the lower desert beside Pyramid Lake. We visited old ghost towns and dined in Virginia City. Like many faculty members and other Nevada men, I often adopted comfortable cowboy boots and string bolo ties for everyday wear.

At 4,400 feet above sea level, Reno snuggled close to the high Sierras. Summers remained relatively cool despite nearly three hundred days of annual sunshine. A blanket felt good on July nights with open bedroom windows. A typical winter snowfall left only two or three inches in Reno, while dumping several feet in mountains clearly visible above the city.

Betsy and I went to the casinos only for dinner and floorshows. We almost always saw Liberace and Louis Armstrong perform when they came to town. We attended a great Armstrong performance at Harrah's in 1965 for the cost of two $5 prime-rib dinners and a couple of drinks. No faculty members we knew gambled at the casinos, except when entertaining out-of-town guests.

Betsy's sense of humor became well known on campus. When a colleague called me one day, Betsy answered the phone. Trying to be amusing, he asked, "May I talk to that intelligent man you sleep with?" "No," Betsy answered, "but LaRue's here."

We usually owned a dog or two. If asked what breed either dog was, Betsy would say, "It's a 'Hushutt." Confronted with the questioner's blank expression, she would add that Hushutt meant "Humane Shelter mutt."

The dogs often slept on our bed. Once when Betsy and I shopped for a new mattress, she, with tongue in cheek, tested the sales clerk's risibility, "May we bring in our dogs to see if they like it?"

She became active in the Faculty Wives' Club and served a year as its president. At

148

a Faculty Wives' bridge party one night, someone asked, "How did your husband get the name LaRue? Is he French?"

Betsy, arranging her cards, answered, "No, he has no French blood that I know of. But his mother, on her honeymoon in Paris, started feeling birth pains while walking down the Champs Elysees. Because he was born in la rue, right there in the street, she called him LaRue."

Since I had not grown up with any brothers or sisters, I often found myself dismayed by the normal bickering between sisters Louise and Virginia. On one occasion, Virginia, then 12, said to Louise, 14, "Let's talk. You never talk to me." Louise replied, "Okay. But it'll cost you a quarter every fifteen minutes." Later, when Louise said, "That's all. Time's up!" they squabbled over how much time had elapsed.

But I found most of the kids' antics amusing.

Michelle, 6, after answering the phone, told Betsy, "The mother of a girl in my class wants to talk to you. She sounds as if she wears glasses."

From his bed, Ross, nearly 5, called to Virginia in the next room. "Virginia, I know how you can get a boy friend."

"Oh, how?"

"First, give him lots of presents. Second, you've got to like him, and third, don't go to his house too much."

Ross asked Michelle one day, "Can we go to that church where the bell's ringing?" "No," Michelle said. "That's a Republican church."

Later, after the kids expressed interest in a nearby Episcopal Church, we started attending. We explained to Michelle that "it has Republican, Democratic and Independent members."

Michelle announced excitedly on the next Easter that Ross told her he'd heard the Easter Bunny during the night shout, "Ho, Ho, Ho."

A week or two later Michelle said, "I don't know if I can go through another day like yesterday. My mouse Scruffy dying and me getting called down by the safety patrol in one day is too much!"

Ross, now 6, invited to dinner at a friend's house, said to the friend's father, the university ski coach, "Mr. Magney, may I have some more milk? But don't give it to me yet. I didn't say please."

Ross came home from first grade one day and said, "Daddy, I got two gold stars today in school. One for knowing my letters and the other for not biting on my pencil."

Among other memories:

Ross, 6, said, "Every time I say 'I love you' to mommy she gets happy and reaches over and hugs me."

Third-grader Michelle entered my den as I worked one evening, put her arms around me, and said, "I need a daddy."

Betsy gave me the same Valentine's Day card five straight times. She carefully put it away each year until I finally recognized that I'd read it before.

The Reno Police Department sponsored a boxing program for boys called the Mitey Mites. Ross entered it about the age of 8. He stayed with it several years, winning most of his bouts against opponents from other clubs.

The police officers in charge had a way of designing the program so that it gradually gave shy boys confidence and brought schoolyard bullies down a notch or two.

Washoe County provided ski instruction for children every weekend during winter months. All of our children took part, and all became good skiers. Betsy and I also learned to ski. She became proficient enough to volunteer as a ski program instructor. Ross, after a few years, joined the Nevada Ski Patrol.

Our four children graduated from Reno High School, which we felt had good teachers. Except for Louise, our oldest, the children graduated from universities. To our disappointment, Louise dropped out in her freshman college year and worked at odd jobs until her twenty-first birthday when she started dealing blackjack at Reno's Circus Circus Casino. She did well at dealing, learned other table games, and became a Las Vegas casino floor manager.

Virginia graduated from the University of Utah with a degree in nursing. She spent a year working at a hospital in the United Arab Emirates. The Abu Dhabi emir built and maintained a hospital for his country's residents. For any member of his family who became ill, he also set aside a suite. At the hospital, Virginia became acquainted with the king's brother, Sheikh Shakhbut, the previous ruler. She accepted his invitation to visit his family at his home.

On her return from the Middle East, Virginia earned a master's degree at Columbia University in New York. She served as a psychiatric nurse practitioner at Veterans hospitals in Virginia and Louisiana.

When Michelle, who had a knack for mathematics, was about 13, Betsy and I invited UNR Engineering Dean James Anderson and his wife to dinner so that Michelle could hear him describe benefits of engineering as a career for women.

Five years later she entered the University of Massachusetts at Amherst, where she graduated in civil engineering. She helped in the designing of nuclear-powered submarines for General Dynamics before joining Bechtel Corp. on the infamous Central Artery/Tunnel Project, "Big Dig" project in Boston. The project, the largest transportation project in the U.S. at the time, relocated a six-lane elevated highway into a new tunnel beneath the city and built a new tunnel under the Boston Harbor to Logan International Airport.

"Those tunnel leaks you read about didn't occur in my segment," she once told me. Later, she joined the Federal Highway Administration as an Area Engineer, working on the Big Dig and other highway and bridge projects in Massachusetts.

Something in Dean Anderson's presentation to Michelle apparently appealed to

Ross, who was about two years younger. He also decided to major in civil engineering, with a focus on environmental engineering. He earned his degree at Northeastern University, Boston. After graduation, he served in the Coast Guard Reserve as a Boatswains Mate on search and rescue boats operating out of harbors in Massachusetts.

The U.S. Environmental Protection Agency hired him as a Remedial Project Manager overseeing the cleanup of abandoned contaminated sites in New England. Several years later he became an EPA computer guru solving problems in storage and retrieval of the agency's extensive records. He also was elected chairman of his town's school committee in Norfolk, Massachusetts.

19

New Duties

In 1975 the Nevada journalism faculty elected me department chairman. The department had seven full-time and several part-time faculty members, about 250 undergraduate majors, and 15 master's degree students.

The following editorial appeared in the Reno Evening *Gazette* on April 30, 1975:

A Fine Choice

Excellence in journalism education at the University of Nevada is assured with the election of LaRue Gilleland as chairman of the department in coming years.

Gilleland has been selected by his colleagues in a departmental vote, a salute of respect by professional peers to his experience, knowledge, judgment and devotion to hard work.

Gilleland will succeed Ted Conover next year and become the third person to chair the department which has established a national reputation for turning out good journalists. The first was A. L. Higginbotham . . . .

LaRue Gilleland is the kind of person journalism education needs in this country. He has academic stature and the gift of teaching ability. But more important, he has professional knowledge. He's a newspaperman's kind of practical journalist.

A veteran newspaperman who is also expert in broadcast journalism, Gilleland serves his profession nationally as editor of The Journalism Educator and as executive director of the American Society of Journalism School Administrators.

More importantly, he has served Nevada's young people well since joining the faculty in 1963. Said one of his former students, Sheila Caudle, now city editor of the Gazette, "Gilleland is a man with deep dedication in the principles of this profession -- accuracy, fairness, integrity, and humanness."

That says it all.

Nevada's journalism program, started six decades ago, distinguished through the years internationally, continues on a course that will inspire greater excellence.

✻   ✻   ✻

March 13, 1975

Professor Gilleland is an outstanding educator and has proven his ability both in the classroom and in public forum. He is a fine teacher of reporting and editing and is particularly knowledgeable in the areas of press law and the ethics of reporting. Perhaps most important, he has consistently shown an ability to develop a fine rapport with his students.

Mike O'Callaghan, Governor of Nevada

May 26, 1975

Dear Professor Gilleland:
Congratulations on being named department chairman. I'm sure the faculty made a wise decision. As you know, you were among a handful of highly qualified persons who were being considered for the deanship here.

William Francois, Search Committee Chair
School of Journalism
Drake University
Des Moines, Iowa

May 28, 1975

To follow "Higgie" and Ted Conover is not easy but I am confident the knowledge and experience you bring to the position will be a credit to the

University. I hope that I shall have the opportunity to visit with you on one of my trips to Reno.

Howard Cannon, United States Senate

Shortly after I occupied the department chair, I received a visit from Frank McCulloch, with whom I had shared a speaking assignment a decade earlier at the Stanford Editors Conference. He had just been hired as managing editor of the Sacramento *Bee*, the McClatchy Company's flagship newspaper.

McCulloch's name surfaced in 1972 in the plagiarism case of writer Clifford Irving. Irving came close to pulling off a major publishing sham with a fake "authorized" biography of the reclusive Howard Hughes. Irving did so after apparently deceiving McCulloch and others with stolen documents.

McGraw-Hill, the book publisher, and Time-Life finally concluded that Irving or someone associated with him forged letters from Hughes. The forger apparently gained access to notes from McCulloch's old interview with Howard Hughes on file in the Time-Life Building in New York. The Irving manuscript also included reference to a "loan" from Howard Hughes to President Richard Nixon. That may have motivated Nixon, some say, to approve the break-in at Watergate.

McCulloch came to my office not to talk about Howard Hughes or Watergate, but about his son-in-law, Mike Parman. Mike, also a Nevada graduate, had been one of my advisees, both as undergraduate and graduate student. He went to work for the Sacramento *Bee*, first as copy editor and later as sports editor, before McClatchy hired his father-in-law, McCulloch.

McCulloch, sitting in my office, said he felt conflicted. He made it clear he wanted the best for his son-in-law and daughter, whom I knew as "Dee Dee." But McCulloch did not want his new executive position at McClatchy to be perceived as an opportunity to engineer breaks for Mike that he might not deserve. McCulloch asked me for my assessment of Mike, since I had known him as long or longer than McCulloch had.

I told McCulloch that Mike, after a slow start in a course or two as a freshman, developed into one of the department's best students. Orphaned at 14 in Reno, Mike had almost raised himself. He lived alone and cooked his own meals while in high school. On weekends an out-of-town aunt and a rancher uncle, who lived in different parts of the state, took turns driving to Reno to check on him. Mike made good grades, played basketball, and led the Reno High School wrestling team before enrolling in the university.

I reminded McCulloch that I chaired Mike's graduate committee when he wrote a splendid master's thesis. It focused on the Virginia City's *Territorial Enterprise* and the writing that a young Samuel Clemens did for it in the early 1860s. Mike's research dug up a number of little known historical facts from that era.

I said I thought Mike had so much talent that McCulloch did not need to worry about him. "Mike will open doors for himself, and your associates will know it," I said. "My advice is show confidence in him, praise him when he does good work, and be prepared, if he ever asks for it, to write a good letter of recommendation to another newspaper."

When in the mid-1980s McCulloch took over editorship of the San Francisco *Examiner*, he got the opportunity to write Mike's reference letter. Mike became executive editor of the Santa Rosa (California) *Press-Democrat*, owned by the New York *Times*. Mike did so well that in 1991 the Times company named him *Press-Democrat* publisher.

When Mike died of pancreatic cancer in 2006 at the age of 61, his newspaper said he had served with "decency, conviction and compassion." Arthur Sulzberger, New York *Times* publisher, wrote: "Among Mike's great strengths were his commitment to his craft, his dedication to his colleagues, and his devotion to his community."

Another outstanding student, Barbara Henry, rose rapidly in Gannett ranks. After serving as publisher of the Des Moines *Register*, she became president and publisher of Gannett's Indianapolis *Star* and senior president of Gannett's Interstate Newspaper Group.

A UNR journalism graduate, E. W. "Ted" Scripps II, was grandson of the founder of the Scripps-Howard League. It owned United Press International, TV stations, and such newspapers as the Cleveland *Press*, the Rocky Mountain *News* in Denver, and *The Commercial Appeal* in Memphis.

A Scripps-Howard board member, Ted and his wife maintained a large home near Reno. They invited Betsy and me to dinner on a couple of occasions, and they often attended Journalism Department functions.

One of my students was E. W. Scripps' great grandson, called "Ted Jr." I always felt "the damned old crank" would have been proud of him, although Ted was anything but cranky. A polite, demure young man, he worked hard.

He contributed often to class discussions, while keeping quiet when his great-grandfather or other Scripps-Howard executive was mentioned. Colleagues knew well his family lineage because all had to pass a journalism history course that included details of the family history. They appeared proud to have a Scripps descendant sweating through the same requirements they had to take.

When Ted graduated from the university with a journalism degree, he joined Scripps-Howard. Other faculty members and I believed he would be groomed for management ranks someday.

His father, Nevada graduate Ted Scripps II, arranged campus visits by Helen Thomas, UPI reporter recognized as "dean of the White House Press Corps."

She was the first female president of the White House Correspondents Association. She usually asked the first question as press conferences and closed the meetings with "Thank you, Mr. President."

She and Frank McCulloch became two of most popular guest lecturers to Nevada journalism classes. Both warned of dire consequences for the nation if reporters ever cease putting tough questions to political leaders because of political party affiliation, or for any other reason.

Helen Thomas told students she was born in Kentucky and grew up in Detroit as daughter of Christian Lebanese immigrants. Her father operated a grocery store. She majored in English at Detroit's Wayne State U., she said, because it had no journalism major.

Her first newspaper job was with the Washington *Daily News* as copy girl. She became a beginning reporter for United Press, and after years of hard work was promoted to UP's White House bureau chief.

Any mention I heard her make about conflict between Israel and Arab countries was balanced.

She told students they could find inspiration in journalism's pioneers, such as John Peter Zenger, editor of the New York *Weekly Journal,* who won court recognition in 1735 that truth cannot be libelous. She urged students to be cautious about too freely voicing opinions of stories they cover.

In her 50s, she married AP reporter Douglas Cornell. He died a few years later. Thomas' many awards included thirty honorary degrees and the Freedom Forum's Al Neuharth Award for Excellence.

In 2000, she resigned from UPI when News World Communications, owned by Sun Myung Moon's Unification Church, bought the wire service to add to its media collection, which included the Washington *Times.*

She became a columnist for Hearst. Ten years later she resigned from Hearst at age 89 after making the controversial statement, "Jews should get the hell out of Palestine." She apparently forgot the restraint she had urged on my students many years earlier.

My administrative duties included supervising the department budget, conducting faculty meetings, appointing faculty committees, preparing for periodic accreditation visits, making suggestions about undergraduate and graduate curricula revisions, and overseeing faculty hiring, promotions and merit pay. I also taught some courses, although fewer than in the past.

One such course, Journalistic Evaluation, required of all graduate students, focused on research methods and statistical analysis. Studying statistics enabled graduate students to perform research, read technical publications, and spot questionable statistical methods in fields they would cover as journalists. Some seniors took the course as an elective.

Among graduate students who stood out in my course were Al Pacciorini, Sandy Macias, and Celia Scully. Al, easy-going and quick to grasp difficult concepts, went to work for the Palo Alto *Times* in California after obtaining his master's degree from the University of Nevada, Reno.

Palo Alto Times, California
Dec. 8, 1978

Three years out of college, and the most worthwhile class I took was J-485/985, the evaluation or statistics class you taught. At the Palo Alto Times, we've worked with a variety of surveys on our coverage and planning. Were it not for the exposure I had in the evaluation class, "levels of confidence," "random samples," "errors" would mean nothing.

Because of this exposure, I've been way ahead of most of the other staffers. We've dealt with several studies, including those conducted by Copley International, Market Opinion Research and Yankelovitch, Skelly and Company.

I think the evaluation class should be required of all students. And I can't stress enough the value of having such a class taught by a journalist, rather than a mathematician. That way, the statistician's abstract thought can be translated for the working journalist.

Thanks for the class.

Al Pacciorini

Sandy Macias, I soon learned, was the niece of Governor Samuel King of Hawaii, whose office I had covered as a reporter. She descended from Hawaii's prominent Castle family that settled in the islands as missionaries. Sandy spent her childhood on Oahu, including the World War II years, and graduated with an English major from the University of Nevada, Reno.

After marriage and teaching high school for sixteen years, Sandy enrolled in the journalism graduate program upon deciding she wanted to be a newspaper reporter. She and I occasionally compared thoughts about her uncle, whom we both remembered fondly. Sandy demonstrated thoroughness in research and care in writing. After getting her master's degree, she took a reporting job with Reno Newspapers.

Celia, bright, hard-working and imaginative, was wife of Thomas J. Scully, dean of the Nevada School of Medical Sciences. She expected no favors because her husband was a university dean, and she received none. She volunteered to be my research assistant in a lengthy study of how the department could help fulfill manpower and continuing education needs of Nevada print and broadcast media. The study, as far as we could determine, was the first of its kind in the country.

The Frank E. Gannett Newspaper Foundation in Rochester, New York, funded the study in 1978, and work began. The result was a 318-page report, *Nevada News Media Needs*, co-authored by Celia and me. The Gannett Foundation published it.

The study collected responses from most of the state's media executives about their hiring needs; from department graduates of the past thirty-five years about strengths and weaknesses in their college preparation, and from current journalism students regarding what they liked and disliked about the program. We also interviewed a selected list of news media executives and journalism school administrators in other parts of the country for critiques of the study.

Writing skills, journalism ethics, interviewing techniques, knowledge of government, research methods, and press law, in that order, were the top needs listed by media executives for hiring future graduates. Nearly all executives said they would recommend UNR to someone planning to study journalism. The replies of graduates already working in the field correlated closely with those of the executives.

Of a dozen required courses, the graduates considered journalism history the least important, although most liked it and thought it should be required. More than eighty percent of respondents said they would major in journalism again. Forty percent indicated interest in taking mid-career graduate or undergraduate courses.

After receiving her master's degree, Celia and her husband, Thomas Scully, the medical school dean, co-wrote *Making Medical Decisions* and other books. He became professor of pediatrics after giving up the deanship.

The Scullys' son, Thomas A. Scully, an attorney, became administrator of Medicare and Medicaid during President George W. Bush's administration. The younger Scully played a key role in the passage of the "Medicare Reform Act" of 2003.

While serving as journalism chairman, I held a part-time paid assignment as executive director of the American Society of Journalism School Administrators, an organization representing 125 universities. The administrators ranged in professional diversity from T. Joseph Scanlon of Carlton University, Ottawa, to Tony Hillerman of the University of New Mexico. Scanlon had reported for the Toronto *Star* and Canadian Broadcasting Corporation. Hillerman worked for United Press International and edited Santa Fe's newspaper, the *New Mexican*, before writing mystery novels set among Navajo, Hopi and Zuni cultures in the American Southwest.

ASJSA administrators elected me president of the organization in 1980-81. At its business meeting that year on the campus of Boston University, I broke precedent by recommending that membership be extended to the Defense Information School, Fort Benjamin Harrison, Indiana. Although not a four-year degree granting institution, the school provided effective journalism training for armed services personnel. ASJSA members accepted my recommendation and invited the Defense Information School to be a non-voting member.

The ASJSA later merged with the Association of Schools of Journalism and Mass Communication. Journalism at the University of Nevada, Reno continued to prosper after I left. Its department became the Donald W. Reynolds School of Journalism under a succession of good leaders.

The *Evening Gazette* and *Nevada State Journal* became one newspaper, the Reno *Gazette-Journal.* Warren Lerude, publisher, eventually left the company and joined the UNR journalism faculty. He took over my press law class, probably improving it.

20

Bean Town

After eighteen years in Nevada, I received a job offer from Northeastern University in Boston. That was in 1979. George Speers, who had headed the Journalism Department since founding it fifteen years earlier, planned to retire because of illness.

I flew to Boston to be interviewed by Northeastern's Journalism Search Committee. It was chaired by Bob Miller, in charge of placing journalism students in media jobs for the university's Cooperative Education Division. Serving with Miller on the committee were two faculty members and several alumni, including Walter Robinson, Boston *Globe* investigative reporter.

I declined Northeastern's initial offer because of illness of my daughter Michelle, just entering high school. She fully recovered by late summer of 1980. That was when Miller called to ask if I again would be interested. I said yes.

Because I had just signed another year's contract at Nevada, I could not move until the start of the 1981 academic year. So, during 1980-81, I continued to head the Nevada program while responding to frequent phone calls from Northeastern about departmental problems there -- problems that would still be relevant when I arrived. I may have been the only journalism administrator making decisions about two programs at opposite ends of the country.

Betsy and I arrived in Massachusetts in the summer of 1981 to look for a house. We bought in Scituate, a coastal community about thirty miles south of Boston.

Northeastern's Cooperative Education Program and location of the university campus appealed to me. The university was on Huntington Avenue near the Museum of Fine Arts and Symphony Hall. It also was within walking distance of Fenway Park, home of the Red Sox.

Co-op students alternated quarters in the classroom, including summers, with paid jobs related to their majors. A typical young man or woman at Northeastern completed as many classroom hours as at any university by graduating in five years instead of the usual four. But along with a bachelor's degree, the Co-op student accumulated up to two years of paid, full-time experience in his or her field. Pay usually increased with each Co-op assignment. Upon receiving a degree, the Northeastern graduate often held a competitive edge in the job market.

Gilleland opens a seminar with Northeastern University students.

Northeastern's many Co-op graduates included John S. Driscoll, Boston *Globe* editor-in-chief; Walter E. Mattson, New York *Times* president; Andrew Gully, Boston *Herald* managing editor; George Merry, *Christian Science Monitor* political columnist; Nat Hentoff, jazz expert and contributor on many topics to the *Village Voice*, the *New Yorker*, and Washington *Times*.

New York Times president Walter Mattson (right), a Northeastern University graduate, compares notes with Gilleland about recent interns hired by the Times. They conferred at a 1986 Northeastern alumni dinner in Boston.

Driscoll, in the wake of court-ordered integration of south Boston schools, organized his reporters for coverage so balanced that it angered many whites. They broke Globe windows, stoned school buses, and threw eggs at Senator Ted Kennedy. Driscoll's coverage won the 1975 Pulitzer Gold Medal for Public Service.

Despite the Northeastern journalism department's success, its two-hundred majors worked on antiquated classroom equipment in cramped quarters when I arrived. The university promised me it would add faculty, equipment, and space.

The department's payroll listed only two full-time professors, Bill Kirtz and Patricia Hastings (later Patricia Kelly). A new Search Committee and I soon recommended the hiring of Charles Fountain, Jim Ross, Nancy Gallinger, and Jim Willis, all in print media; Jane Bick, advertising; Louis Conrad, radio-TV news; and Roy Harris, public relations.

Part-time instructors included the Boston *Herald's* Andrew Gully and Mary Helen Gillespie. For courses in the evening division, I hired Peter Woloschuk, a Boston PR practitioner assigned by the Vatican to help coordinate a papal visit to America, and John Brodeur, one of my former University of Nevada students who had just started his own Boston-area PR firm. We hired other faculty members later, including Bill Coulter, editor and co-publisher of the *Daily Item* in Clinton, Massachusetts. The newspaper had been owned by his family for four generations, going back to the Civil War. One of Coulter's favorite staff members was Thomas P. Farragher. Farragher later joined the Boston *Globe* "Spotlight" team. He worked with Walter Robinson in the Pulitzer Prize-winning exposure of sexual abuse of boys by some Roman Catholic clergy.

In addition to the Co-op program and good teachers, the presence on campus of the New England Press Association (NEPA) enhanced the Northeastern journalism department's prestige among regional news media. Years earlier, George Speers had invited NEPA to move its headquarters to the department. The press association represented about 350 community daily and weekly newspapers in six states. NEPA invited me to serve on its board of directors, which I did for more than a decade.

A faculty committee and I set to work revising the curriculum. We established a required professional core and four concentrations -- print media news, television-radio news, advertising, and public relations. All students completed two print-media newswriting courses to acquire fact gathering, story-structure and grammatical skills. The discipline also improved the conversational writing style that broadcast and advertising students needed later in their own concentrations.

The faculty and I added rigorous Arts and Science requirements to the journalism degree. Among them were courses in history, government, literature, logic, and science. Our majors took more science than any department on campus required, except the sciences.

While journalism may have had a "trade school" image for many academics, the faculty and I knew our majors graduated more well-rounded than students in a lot of other disciplines. Journalism majors wrote and gathered information better than most of their contemporaries, an important indication of sound, liberal arts education.

By the 1980s, we joined other journalism schools and departments in updating writing labs with computers.

Linda Levin, chair of the University of Rhode Island Department of Journalism, invited me to speak to her students and faculty in 1983 about concerns I'd expressed in print about journalism education and news media. On the phone, she said one of her star graduates, a young woman who had just gone to work for CNN, would be in town that day and would be invited to attend.

On the Rhode Island campus, I told students that I feared increasing numbers of media owners -- although not all -- lacked the historical, legal and ethical concepts taught in journalism courses. I said a parallel problem in academe was that some university administrators associated journalism more with speech or theater than with the social sciences.

After my talk, several students came to the lectern to ask questions. A young, black-haired woman with a no-nonsense demeanor wanted to know more specifically why I gave so much importance to the issue. She was the recent graduate Linda Levin told me about earlier – Christiane Amanpour.

I said I thought categorizing journalism as a social science emphasizes its fact-gathering function over entertainment or opinion. Ms. Amanpour asked a few more questions, said "thank you" with a perceptible smile, and walked away. A URI faculty member standing nearby described her as an excellent student with an Iranian father and British mother.

Over the next twenty-five years, Ms. Amanpour covered major hot spots in the world for CNN with distinction. She joined Helen Thomas and a few other journalists in criticizing newspapers and cable TV for sloppy, erroneous reporting of the federal administration's claim that Saddam Hussein maintained weapons of mass destruction and secret ties to Al Qaeda prior to the 2003 invasion of Iraq.

When the Challenger space shuttle disintegrated over the Atlantic shortly after launch on January 28, 1986, the Northeastern campus mourned. Gregory Jarvis, recipient of a 1969 Northeastern M.S. electrical engineering degree, died in the accident with six others, including Christa McAuliffe, the first school teacher in space. The accident occurred at 11:40 a.m., 73 seconds after launch. Freezing temperatures caused a leak in a solid rocket booster.

Jarvis became Air Force captain and astronaut after graduating from high school in Mohawk, New York, and Buffalo University and completing graduate work at Northeastern U. He posthumously received the Congressional Medal of Honor.

By the late 1980s, the number of Northeastern journalism majors grew to more than five hundred. The department faculty and I began a campaign to become a school of journalism. We felt the change would help us compete with the country's largest academic programs in our field. We submitted a proposal to the University administration and

Faculty Senate. Alumni and the New England Press Association, representing large and small newspapers in six states, backed us.

The J-school project became a regular agenda item at the evening meetings I held once a month in my office with Journalism Alumni Association officers. The association, among other activities, helped sponsor a dinner each spring when top students received awards and scholarships for outstanding work in classroom and Co-op jobs.

Los Angeles
May 8, 1986

I have learned through the Northeastern Alumni Association that the Journalism Department has petitioned to become a school. Please accept this letter in wholehearted support behind the effort. As a 1985 graduate of the journalism program, I witnessed the major restructuring of the program by Chairman LaRue Gilleland. In one word -- Outstanding.

His efforts have transformed the department into one of the premier education centers for journalists on the East Coast. I believe it won't be long before Northeastern's national reputation for producing outstanding professionals surpasses those of schools that have been at it much longer. I sincerely hope the Senate will give every consideration to the Journalism Department's petition. It's a splendid idea.

Art Hagopian, Financial Writer
Investor's Daily

The Faculty Senate, after hearing presentations by journalism alumni, media representatives and me, voted to recommend our proposal. The university president and Board of Trustees approved it. The new School of Journalism emerged officially in 1987. I became the school's first director.

A number of phone calls offering congratulations for the new J-school came to my office. One was from Susan Forrest, a Nevada graduate working for the Lawrence (Massachussetts) *Eagle-Tribune*. She sounded happy and upbeat. She talked about the "old days" in Nevada. She recalled with laughter the incident in my class when she amused other students by not knowing what "hemorrhoids" meant. I remarked that the Nevada faculty had taught her well that good reporters never hesitate to ask questions out of fear of sounding silly.

I next heard about Susan when she played a significant role in outcome of the 1988 national presidential election. She wrote a story pointing out that convicted felon

Willie Horton raped a woman and stabbed her husband after being furloughed during the governorship of Governor Michael Dukakis of Massachusetts, the Democratic Party presidential candidate.

The Lawrence newspaper hit hard in scores of follow-up stories and editorials emphasizing that Horton, after twelve years behind bars, should not have been released on a weekend pass from which he did not return.

The Horton story, distributed nationally, inspired election attack ads against Dukakis produced by the Las Vegas advertising-PR firm of UNR graduate Sig Rogich. Rogich and I had shared a UPI wire machine in Reno on the day President Kennedy was assassinated.

One of Rogich's TV spots portrayed Massachusetts inmates going in and out a revolving prison door during Governor Dukakis' administration. Another segment showed Dukakis, looking less than presidential, riding in an army tank. The *Eagle-Tribune* stories and Rogich's TV ads, distributed nationally, helped George H. W. Bush defeat Dukakis for president. It also won a Pulitzer Prize in general news reporting.

Commenting later on the Pulitzer announcement, Susan Forrest sent shock waves through media circles by criticizing her bosses. After her original story, she said, the Lawrence *Eagle-Tribune* encouraged shoddy research by failing to scrutinize old court records during its editorial campaign. The newspaper said Horton years earlier had murdered his first victim, a teenage service station attendant, during a robbery. But Horton had been convicted only of being an accomplice. The newspaper quoted a state legislator as saying Horton cut off the slain teenager's genitals. Susan pointed out that court records contained no account of any bodily mutilation.

She refused to attend the newspaper's Pulitzer victory party, saying she felt "ashamed." Susan later went to work for New York *Newsday* and New York *Daily News*. She earned a reputation there as a determined, accurate reporter, covering such sensational stories as 17-year-old Amy Fisher's 1992 shooting of Mary Jo Buttafuoco, the wife of Amy's lover. Mary Jo survived, and Amy became known as the "Long Island Lolita."

At 42, Susan Forrest died in her sleep, apparently of sleeping pill overdose. No note was found.

Betsy and I felt at home watching Boston sporting events. The first baseball World Series was played in 1904 in a Huntington Avenue stadium that became part of the Northeastern campus. We saw the Red Sox win exciting games at nearby Fenway Park despite the "curse of the Bambino." The curse had lingered since 1911 when a Red Sox owner sold Babe Ruth to the New York Yankees to pay for his investment in a Broadway play. It became the musical, "No, No, Nanette."

We watched Larry Bird lead the Celtics by frequently hitting 50 percent of baskets from the floor and 90 percent from the free throw line. We saw Jim Calhoun coach Reggie Lewis and Northeastern basketball to its all-time best winning streak -- before Calhoun moved to the University of Connecticut. We thrilled to Northeastern men's Beanpot hockey victories over Harvard, Boston University, and Boston College in 1984, 1987 and 1988. Watching the Northeastern women's hockey team, we decided women's rules improved the game.

About this time news broke that the KGB in Moscow had arrested journalist Nicholas Danilof. Danilof, an Oxford and Harvard-educated American of Russian ancestry, accumulated a distinguished career covering the Soviet Union for United Press International in the 1960s and *U. S. News and World Report* in the 1980s.

Soviet watchers in America speculated that the espionage charge against Danilof must be trumped up. The charge appeared to conflict with Communist Party Secretary Gorbachev's new policies of "glasnost" (openness), "perestroika" (market restructuring), and reduced military armament.

Danilof's arrest, a major story, would eventually prove relevant to Northeastern and me.

I often relied on Bill Kirtz, the School of Journalism's senior professor, for historical and background information on the university. Kirtz had worked for the Quincy (Mass.) *Patriot Ledger* and published the Marblehead (Mass.) *Messenger* before joining the Northeastern faculty during George Speers' chairmanship. Kirtz also served as acting director while I made three professional trips to India.

Kirtz taught such courses as reporting, editing and journalism ethics. He may have been the fastest reader I ever met. He could absorb information almost as fast as he could turn book pages, or so it seemed to me, a relatively slow reader.

Dean Richard Astro of the College of Arts and Sciences was instrumental in establishing the Center for the Study of Sport in Society on the Northeastern campus headed by Richard Lapchick. The center worked to raise graduation rates among athletes and promote racial and gender fairness in college and professional sports. It also sought to reduce gambling and drug use in sports. As the center gained national recognition, the School of Journalism benefited.

Lapchick brought top athletes to Northeastern to recognize their help in achieving the center's goals. He also invited leading sports journalists, such as Robert Lipsyte of the New York *Times* and Howard Cossell of ABC network. They gave generously of their time in speaking to journalism classes. Richard's father was Joe Lapchick, former Boston Celtic center and New York Knicks coach. Richard held a doctorate in political science. He left Northeastern to direct the Devos Sports Management Program at the University of Central Florida, where years later he tried to dampen a public feud between golfers Tiger Woods and Sergio Garcia.

Another guest speaker Northeastern students liked had no connection to sports. She was Kay Fanning, editor of the *Christian Science Monitor*. In her youth as an elegant and poised debutant, she married Marshal Field of the Chicago mercantile and publishing family. She divorced Field, reportedly with no alimony settlement, and moved to Alaska with three children. There she worked her way up from librarian to editor of the Anchorage *Daily News*. She and her second husband bought the newspaper for a fire-sale price (reportedly less than a half-million dollars). She became the first woman president of the American Society of Newspaper Editors.

Fanning described to Northeastern students how the *Daily News* under her direction won the 1976 Pulitzer Gold Medal for disclosing Teamster Union influence on Alaska's oil pipeline and politics. She told our female students, "You can expect to confront less of a glass ceiling in newspapers than almost any other industry."

After her second husband died of a heart attack, she sold the Anchorage newspaper to the McClatchy company in 1983 and moved to Boston as *Monitor* editor. She twice invited me to speak at *Monitor*-sponsored conferences on media problems and ethics. The fourteen-acre plaza containing the Christian Science headquarters and publishing center, designed by I. M. Pei, was a short walk down Huntington Avenue from my office on the Northeastern campus.

Fanning died in Boston in the year 2000 at the age of 73. I agreed with a description of her by Allan Frank, one of her Anchorage reporters. He said: "Kay Fanning was, in life, the character Katherine Hepburn and Grace Kelly tried to be in the movies."

The *Monitor* switched from print to on-line editions in 2008.

I made recommendations that contributed, at least in part, to Northeastern University's granting honorary doctorates to *Patriot-Ledger* publisher Prescott Low, network broadcaster Irving R. Levine, public relations founder Edward Bernays, and actor Ed Asner.

Asner's daughter Liza enrolled in the Northeastern J-School in the mid-1980s. I served as her adviser. She wanted to pursue a public relations career. She proved to be a talented, hard-working student. When Liza completed her degree in 1989, I submitted her father's name as possible commencement speaker. The university administration agreed.

Although Asner had never been a newsman, his TV portrayal of fictional newspaper editor "Lou Grant" earned high marks from professional journalists. They liked the effort of the character he played to deal realistically with ethical issues that journalists frequently encounter. Most journalists I knew even admitted enjoying his earlier light-hearted, less accurate portrayal of a TV newsman on the "Mary Tyler Moore" show in the 1970s.

Asner, past president of the Screen Actors Guild, accepted the university's invitation to deliver the commencement address. I also invited him to talk to journalism students. He arrived in Boston a couple of days in advance of Liza's graduation.

Asner, who grew up in Kansas City, Missouri, recognized my Osage Valley accent when I introduced him to an assembly of journalism students and faculty. He amused students by poking innocent fun at me. He pointed out that I pronounced "born" like "barn." I responded that the student body and I envied the superb enunciation he had acquired in theater work on leaving Kansas City.

After speaking to journalism classes, Asner made an excellent commencement speech in Boston Garden. He addressed thousands of parents and graduates of the university's many academic disciplines, and he proudly watched his daughter receive her journalism degree. I last heard that she was doing public relations work in Portland, Oregon.

Actor Ed Asner gets chummy after speaking to Gilleland's students at Northeastern University, Boston. His daughter was one of Gilleland's students.

I enjoyed introducing journalism students to Edward Bernays. Some textbooks listed Bernays as a public relations "pioneer." Others said he was "the "father of public relations." Bernays began accepting invitations to speak to Northeastern classes when he was in his late 90s. Students liked Bernays, older than most of their grandfathers.

Rather short with a ready smile, he walked without a cane. He appeared nimble, except, on rare occasions when his administrative assistant, Joan Vondra, helped him step up or down a curb.

When a young Northeastern coed asked, "How did you get into public relations," Bernays smiled and replied, "I didn't. Public relations did not exist then. I created it."

Then he told the rest of his story. He was born of Jewish parents in Vienna, Austria. His uncle was psychoanalyst Sigmund Freud. His parents brought him to this country at the age of one. He graduated from Cornell and began editing a small medical journal.

In 1913 the producer of a new Broadway play asked Bernays how to avoid censure by Anthony Comstock's New York Society for the Suppression of Vice. The plot of the play, "Damaged Goods," contained a venereal disease theme, forbidden in those days. Bernays came up with the idea of connecting the play with a fund promoting public health. The idea worked. The play opened on schedule and had a successful New York run.

While serving with Walter Lippmann on the U. S. Committee on Public Information in World War I, Bernays helped convince the government to sell the American public on the idea that the war was being fought "to bring democracy to Europe." After the war, he opened a New York office to provide what he called "counsel on public relations," thus popularizing, if not coining, the term.

Among Bernays' early clients were singer Enrico Caruso and the Russian Diaghileff Ballet. Not all of his early PR tasks were glamorous, he said. In the middle of a night, tenor Caruso convinced Bernays he needed sixteen extra pillows in a New York hotel to block a draft the singer feared would affect his voice. Bernays alerted the front desk and roamed the hotel in the middle of the night to find extra pillows.

Vaslav Nijinsky, the famous dancer, declined to meet New York reporters until Bernays convinced him he'd have no audience unless he did.

When one of my students asked Bernays if he had been influenced by his uncle, psychoanalyst Sigmund Freud, Bernays answered, "Yes. I was able to apply psychotherapy techniques to help troubled companies. In an effort to influence public opinion, I also manipulated the unconscious – of large groups of people."

He advocated to a new government of India in the late 1940s that it would gain American backing faster by putting such phrases as "bill of rights," "freedom of the press" and "freedom of religion" into its laws.

Among Bernays' early clients were General Motors, Dodge Motors, AT&T, Henry Ford, President Coolidge, President Hoover, and Eleanor Roosevelt.

My students threw a party for Bernays on campus in 1991 in recognition of his 100th birthday. Because he had made it clear in advance he wanted no gifts, most students gave him cards. A few girls presented him flowers. When he said he was writing a biography titled "My First Hundred Years," they applauded.

A student asked, "How does it feel to be 100?" Bernays answered, "Like 18." Then he got serious. He told the students, "Set a goal. Most people don't. Then pick out a dozen role models and write to them and ask what steps to take."

A student asked Bernays about Ivy Lee, his contemporary who advised the Pennsylvania Railroad and Chilean mining firms before World War I. A few historians had mentioned Ivy Lee as "a PR founder." Bernays dismissed him as a "publicist."

Bernays also contrasted Lee's relationship with Nazi Germany before World War II to his own. Ivy Lee, Bernays said, received money from a subsidiary of I. G. Farben, the German chemical conglomerate, to disseminate pro-Nazi propaganda in this country. Bernays turned down a lucrative PR job offer from Adolph Hitler about the same time, he said. Nevertheless, Hitler's propaganda chief, Joseph Goebbels, kept on his desk a copy of the 1923 book, *Crystallizing Public Opinion*, which Bernays wrote with his wife, Doris Fleischman, a newspaper reporter. She died in 1977.

Bernays said a big disappointment in his life came on learning that Goebbels had used Bernays' book in the Nazi's destructive campaign against European Jews.

Students saw in Bernays not the past, it seemed to me, but what was possible in their own careers. He told students he had made mistakes, and they could expect to do the same. But, he said, their mistakes should lead to professional growth.

He illustrated his point by admitting he earned money from tobacco companies before he and most people realized smoking was dangerous to health. He engineered a campaign in the 1920s to overcome social taboos against women smoking in public.

He made another "mistake" in the early 1920s when recent Yale graduates Henry Luce and Briton Hadden proposed to him a new publishing idea. Bernays, as usual, researched the matter before giving an answer. When his investigation showed nearly two thousand English language daily newspapers and ten thousand weeklies publishing in America at the time, he told Luce and Hadden that starting a weekly newsmagazine would be a financial disaster. They ignored his advice and started *Time*.

I remembered Rollan Melton's similar story about Al Neuharth ignoring Melton's advice not to start *USA Today*.

Bernays told the Northeastern journalism students they must stay informed about domestic and world events. He said he tried to read a number of newspapers every day, and he advised students to do the same.

He also said, "While you may expect a logical progression of events, you also must be prepared for the illogical."

Life magazine, *Time's* sister publication, named Bernays one of the hundred most influential Americans of the Twentieth Century. The magazine said major clients in the 1990s still paid him $1,000 an hour for his advice.

Bernays invited Betsy and me to dinner twice at his Victorian home near Cambridge's Harvard Square. As we approached his home, I remembered years earlier fantasizing as a graduate philosophy student in the Midwest about attending one of the famous "evenings at the Whiteheads" in Cambridge. The famous philosopher Alfred North Whitehead had died in 1947 while I was still in high school, but I had wondered what it would have been like to take part in his salon for students and older adults.

Although Bernays was not Whitehead, he had put his mark on journalism and public relations. Courteous, efficient Joan Vondra, his administrative assistant, acted as hostess. Some of Bernays' acquaintances described her as his much younger "intimate friend."

The first dinner included several officers of the Northeastern University chapter of the Public Relations Student Society of America. At the second were just Betsy and me, our daughter Michelle, and son-in-law Dave Daigle.

Dave, who majored in hotel management and had been in the restaurant business, asked what advice Bernays would give to someone considering opening a restaurant. Bernays immediately suggested studying U. S. Census reports on nationalities living within a 30-mile radius of the restaurant site. "Then," he said, "prepare menu items to appeal to them."

At his dinner Bernays said public relations professionals should be licensed because, as he put it, "any nitwit can call himself or herself a public relations practitioner." He later expanded this proposal in a public announcement covered by newspapers across the country. He said licensing criteria should be based on education, character, and knowledge of research methods. He wanted to put PR on a professional level "approaching that of physicians and lawyers."

"Press agentry begins with writing press releases, but public relations begins with market research," he said. On his behalf, a Massachusetts legislator submitted a public relations licensing bill. It got nowhere. Among the many PR practitioners opposing the bill was John Brodeur, one of my former students from Nevada. He had created a highly successful Boston-area PR firm, John Brodeur & Associates.

A bitter dispute between Bernays' daughters and Joan Vondra marred the final months before he died at age 103 in 1995. The daughters, novelist Ann Bernays and Doris Held, challenged Vondra over their father's estate and power of attorney.

Ms. Vondra asked me to write a letter on her behalf to her attorney to be submitted to the court. I wrote the letter. It described her competent, thoughtful relationship with Bernays as I observed it. But I made no judgment about the daughters or their lawsuit. Bernays' daughters won their case and were named joint conservators of his estate.

On his 100th birthday in 1991, Ed Bernays (right), nephew of Sigmund Freud, lectures Gilleland on the history of public relations, which some say Bernays invented.

As the Northeastern journalism program grew, the faculty and I puzzled over why we attracted increasing numbers of students from foreign countries but few blacks from the inner city where Northeastern was located. Members of the faculty, especially Jim Ross, Nancy Gallinger and Charles Fountain, visited predominantly black Boston-area high schools to convince guidance counselors and students to consider journalism careers and Northeastern.

We enrolled some black students, although fewer than we hoped. One, Rhondella Richardson, recruited in the late 1980s, was among the first to make us proud. After graduating, she worked for the New York *Times* before becoming news anchor for Boston's WCVB-TV.

I often took noon walks in the neighborhood around Northeastern -- past dormitories, Symphony Hall, the Museum of Fine Arts and the Isabella Stewart Gardner

Museum. On a morning after such a walk in 1990, the city awoke to news that the largest art heist in history had occurred during the night at the Gardner Museum. Two burglars disguised as police stole thirteen masterpieces valued at half a billion dollars. They included Vermeer's painting, "The Concert"; three Rembrandts, including "Storm on Sea of Galilee"; a Manet landscape, and five drawings by Degas.

The crime still had not been solved more than twenty years after I retired.

Billy Graham came to Northeastern University in the year of the Gardner Museum theft to speak to a large audience of students and Boston residents. I went to hear him. After his talk, a number of people crowded around him. When they thinned out, I introduced myself to the evangelist as a former reporter who had interviewed him in Honolulu nearly forty years before.

I asked if he remembered the incident. He surprised me by saying, "Yes, I do." Then he recalled details I had forgotten and some I never knew. He told me what he had done during the day prior to our meeting at the Royal Hawaiian Hotel and where he went in Honolulu the next day.

If his memory is that good, I thought, he probably remembers my newspaper story about him. I apologized that editors had cut the story so much that it emphasized an angle he wanted to avoid. I did not repeat the concern he expressed to me that night on the Honolulu hotel lanai about being photographed with hula dancers. He appeared to know what I meant.

21

Academic Pot Holes

Like all administrators, I dealt with some touchy personnel problems during the sixteen years I headed journalism programs at the University of Nevada and Northeastern. Although most were similar to those any administrator encountered, they occasionally proved especially difficult. Among them:

- A disappointed job applicant whose case led to a legal hearing. The job called for teaching editing, which requires a knack for accurate detail. The legal hearing ended when I pointed out under questioning that the applicant's résumé contained several spelling and grammatical errors, including spelling Johns Hopkins University as "John Hopkins." It was the institution from which the applicant claimed to have received a Ph.D.   The applicant lost the case.
- A tenured professor who missed classes often, regularly marked "A" on term papers he had not read and scheduled movies to be shown to students during his absence. One was an irrelevant film few in his class could understand because it was in a foreign language. My complaint led to a university hearing at which his attorney represented him. After the hearing, the professor resigned.
- An assistant professor who received leave to cover the 1991 Gulf War on assignment for a national news organization. The faculty member promised the university and me to return in time to start the fall academic term. When September courses began without him -- and we learned he resided comfortably in Amman, Jordan, not the war zone -- the university told me to begin proceedings to fire the professor. I did so. I had to scramble to fill his courses with part-time instructors.

A different kind of problem that arose at Northeastern involved an effort to combine journalism with speech communication. The journalism faculty and I opposed the idea. We saw it as part of a national trend that blurred the distinction between fact gathering and entertainment.

Some speech professors and a couple of university administrators believed journalism and speech had enough in common that they could be called "communication" and placed under one administrator. A benefit, they said, would be saving money. After all, they argued, both programs trained students for television and radio careers in labs using the same equipment.

One university administrator hinted that I might be named to head the combined program. Even the theater department received occasional mention on campus as a possible partner in this arrangement.

I often recommended that a journalism student take a speech or drama course for one reason or another. But I vigorously resisted any administrative change. I maintained that journalism should be considered a social science. I said we could lose credibility with news media employers who hired our graduates if the programs were combined. To wit:

MEMORANDUM

TO: *Richard Daynard, Chair, Senate Agenda Committee*
FROM: *LaRue Gilleland, Director, School of Journalism*
SUBJECT: *Your January 14, 1992 letter*

I find it hard to believe that the University administration, in a period of declining enrollments, would consider tampering with a successful journalism program that has nearly doubled in majors in the past four years. The School of Journalism, one of the university's largest academic units, with about 600 graduate and undergraduate majors, maintains high respect among leaders in news media and related agencies that hire its graduates at a rate far exceeding the national average. It receives support from an active Journalism Alumni Association, whose members leave high professional marks with daily and weekly newspapers, magazines, broadcast news departments, advertising agencies, and public relations firms throughout the world.

It brings 600-800 of the best and brightest high school juniors and seniors from all six New England states to the Northeastern campus for the annual conference of Yankee PEN (Press Education Network). It is engaged in one of the most active minority outreach programs to Boston inner city schools of any academic unit at Northeastern. It is recognized widely for academic quality, having one of the College of Arts and Sciences' highest percentages of honors students and Ell Scholars.

The School of Journalism -- which emphasizes writing, editing, and research skills -- and the Department of Speech Communication are far more different as academic disciplines than they are similar. It would make about as much sense to combine these two programs as it would to merge Biology and Geology based on the argument that both are natural sciences.

Perhaps a source of the idea that Journalism and Speech Communication might be combined comes from the fact that Speech Communication and one of Journalism's four concentrations use television equipment, although for different purposes. A logical extension of the notion that equipment should determine administrative structure would be to merge all of the university's academic units, since all use computers.

The School of Journalism has grown dramatically and has become a center of excellence. This has occurred because it has a dedicated faculty and because it adheres to the philosophy and academic standards of the oldest and most respected journalism schools in the country -- the University of Missouri School of Journalism, founded in 1908, and Columbia University Graduate School of Journalism in New York, founded in 1912. The School of Journalism at Northeastern University will continue to grow and demonstrate academic excellence, in my opinion, as long as it continues to be identified with the Missouri and Columbia models.

The public becomes confused when media blur the line between information and entertainment. Today, the journalism schools on which the Northeastern program is modeled stress that they have a responsibility to keep that line clear and distinct in their curricula. Although there are respectable places in academe for teaching non-journalistic forms of communication -- such as fiction, fantasy, and effective oral communication -- one of those places, as most English, speech, and theater departments would agree, is not the journalism school. The educational philosophy of the Northeastern J-School emphasizes the best of professional and liberal arts education and maintains that the gathering and dissemination of news is a public trust. It stresses careful investigation and research; clear, concise, accurate writing; and familiarity with legal and ethical principles applicable to print and broadcast media. The best journalism schools hold that an important distinction must exist between news and entertainment, between fact and fiction, between information dissemination and communication performance technique.

The School of Journalism's healthy number of majors has a beneficial impact throughout the university because, among other things, the school limits its students to about one-fourth of their courses in their major. Thus, three-fourths of our students' courses, one of the highest percentages on campus, are taken elsewhere in the Arts and Sciences and the University. To dilute a vigorous Northeastern School of Journalism by merging it with Speech Communication would, in my opinion, result in loss of credibility with the news media leaders the J-School deals with and a decline in the large number of students attracted to Northeastern because of its well-respected journalism program.

The School of Journalism at Northeastern University should not be altered; it should be emulated.

22

Foreign Affairs

Nicholas Danilof, safely home for two years after release from Moscow's Lefortovo prison, lived in Chester, Vermont. It was convenient driving distance to Northeastern University. His arrest in 1986 had turned out to be KGB retaliation for the FBI's placing an espionage charge against a Russian employee at the United Nations.

Danilof's highly publicized fourteen-day incarceration ended when the Reagan Administration traded a Russian U. N. employee for him. After returning home, Danilof wrote his autobiographical book, *Two Lives, One Russia*. In it, he compared his Moscow arrest with his great-grandfather's exile to Siberia for minor involvement in the 1825 "Decembrists" uprising against Russia's tsar.

J-School faculty members sometimes invited Danilof to speak to their classes. The Search Committee and I courted him as a prospective faculty member. On realizing we were serious, he not only expressed interest, but also asked me one day if he could attend faculty meetings. That impressed me. Even our faculty didn't much look forward to those frequent meetings. For weeks Danilof quietly observed our discussions and our votes on mundane academic matters. When the first journalism faculty position opened, the search committee and I recommended that the university hire him. It did.

Danilof plunged into Northeastern academic life. He soon mixed writing and teaching at Northeastern with organizing a student exchange program in Moscow, where he was again welcome, and working to raise standards at a journalism school in Tashkent, Uzbekistan. Uzbekistan was one of the former Soviet states that perestroika and glasnost helped gain independence.

The Northeastern graduate program included students from India, China, and other parts of the world. In early June 1989, two worried Chinese students, a young man and woman, came to my office during the Tiananmen Square "Massacre" in Beijing. Far from home, they needed to talk to someone sympathetic to their concerns about the pro-democracy demonstrations in their homeland.

The two sat in my office for a long time telling their versions of the Chinese student protests reported from Beijing by print and TV media throughout the world. They worried that their friends back home faced injury or death.

The confrontation in China started in mid-May when a few hundred young people gathered to voice opposition to a purge two years earlier of former Secretary General Hu Yaobang, considered an advocate of democracy. The media reported some students had been killed, although numbers varied.

The young people sitting in my office said they thought they recognized the photograph of a man refusing to move from in front of a line of Chinese tanks. A report said he climbed atop the lead tank and said to the driver, "Why are you here?" Then he returned to his position in front of the tank until onlookers dragged him away, apparently afraid the tank would crush him.

My graduate students called him "Wang Ai-min." They spoke highly of him. The young Chinese woman in my office choked up. "I'm worried," she said.

I tried to comfort her and her companion by saying the situation might not be as bad as it appeared on television, although I doubted my own words. I invited them to come back whenever they again wanted to talk. They left my office after more than an hour. They returned several days later to give me a t-shirt printed with a photo of the man and the tank. The shirt contained the words: "You stand for freedom. We stand with you."

Over the next few days, media reports of the number of Chinese killed ranged from as low as three-hundred to as high as five-thousand. Later, a Canadian journalist reported that Wai Ai-min had been arrested and executed. The Chinese government denied the report.

A few years later, Betsy and I made a visit to Tiananmen Square and other parts of China. We found the 1989 confrontation to be a forbidden topic everywhere we went, much like any mention of Falun Gong or the independence movements in Taiwan or Tibet. Ordinary citizens of China we met had never seen the famous photo of a young man challenging the tanks. Chinese schoolbooks, we were told, omitted the Tiananmen Square incident.

China introduced me to acupuncture. A mysterious pain that began in my right leg shortly after we arrived by plane in Beijing increased daily. Walking atop China's Great Wall proved difficult, especially going downhill.

After visiting Shanghai and Wuhan, I felt grateful when Betsy and I boarded a riverboat for a five-day Yangtze River trip to Chongqing. But I still had to walk up and down stairs between three or four decks to get from stateroom to dining room. I dragged my right leg one step at a time. On the second day aboard, I made an appointment with the riverboat's staff physician.

The name on his door on the lowest deck said "Dr. George Zhang." He claimed to have been trained in Western and Chinese medicine. In his office, he asked me a lot of questions in fluent English. After saying something about my "imbalance in Qi (Ch'i) energy flow," he told me to remove most of my clothes and lie on a table. He inserted three or four long needles in my right leg that I barely felt. He also put a couple of needles in my left leg and chest.

During the hour I lay there, he returned to the room periodically to adjust the needles by twisting them. Finally, he removed them. I stood up, dressed, walked out of his office. Without pain for the first time in days, I climbed the steps to our stateroom on the top deck. I later walked with ease around the busy cities of Wushan, Wanxian, Chongqing, Xian, Guilin and Hong Kong.

The United States Information Service and other agencies sent me to India as part of a two-man team to help improve that country's higher education in journalism/mass communication. The other team member was Dr. Walter Bunge, director of the Ohio State School of Journalism. We made three trips to India between 1989 and 1991.

Walter represented American public universities and I represented private universities. In addition to the USIS, our sponsors included the Indo-U.S. Sub-Commission on Education and Culture, the Smithsonian Institution, and the Indian government. The New England Press Association recommended us.

The long air flight Walter and I made to India on the first trip was delayed twice for hours in New York and Frankfort, Germany. This occurred because a passenger, different at each airport, was discovered to be missing after everyone else boarded the plane. For security reasons, all suitcases had to be removed, identified, and replaced on the Boeing 747. The task took hours each time.

When we got off the overdue flight in Delhi, groggy from time-zone changes and little sleep, we were informed to our surprise that the Indian Institute of Mass Communication had scheduled us to make talks at the institute in three hours. To this day, I have only a vague notion of what either of us said to that audience of university and media representatives.

We arrived in India during a nationwide military alert. The government put it into effect after executing two Sikh assassins of Prime Minister Indira Gandhi. The men, her bodyguards, shot her in retaliation for her decision to send troops to storm the holiest Sikh shrine, the Golden Temple in Amritsar. She ordered the attack because Sikh separatists had resorted to violence in an effort to establish an independent state in the Punjab. The assault Indira ordered killed more than four hundred resisters.

We learned that Sikhism, founded in early 1500s by a Hindu guru, Nanak, hoped originally to erase the caste system, raise the status of women, and end antagonism between Hindus and Muslims. Conflict had begun when Muslims invaded India from Afghanistan and

Iran. Nanak said "Hari," Sanskrit word for God, referred both to Allah and Brahma. Sikh men left their hair uncut and carried a dagger. All adopted Singh as their last name. The Sikh separatist movement began in the 1970s.

Indira Gandhi's son, Rajiv, succeeded his mother. He held office as prime minister when we arrived. To prevent rioting, he stationed military police at the airport, key points throughout Delhi, and outside our hotel.

After a sound night's sleep in deluxe hotel rooms provided by our sponsors, Walter and I began our three-week escorted tour of thirteen universities and training centers in India's northern cities.

Problems similar to those facing Indian J-education had been debated for most of the Twentieth Century in America: How beneficial are college degrees in journalism? What should be the percentage of specialized skills courses versus general education courses? Who should teach journalism -- academics with theoretical backgrounds or ex-professionals hired from the media? If there's a place for both, what should be the proportion?

At the universities we visited, we found inadequate facilities and too many faculty members lacking both formal training and practical experience. We documented this in a report.

Much in India impressed us, including its colorful history and diverse cultures. Prevalence in Delhi shops of little statues of comely Lakshmi, Hindu goddess of prosperity, brought to my mind India's industrious graduate students I'd known at Northeastern. The goddess, usually portrayed with four arms, remind devotees that she dislikes laziness. Many Jains and Buddhists also respect her, especially on the night of Diwali, India's autumn festival of lights.

I wrote in *Northeastern* magazine on returning home in 1989 that Lakshmi might one day symbolize a promising economic future for India after centuries of privation for most of her people.

A short time later, Sikh separatists in the Punjab shot a number of Hindus. Also, Kashmiri Muslims, with Pakistani support, revolted against Indian control. Rajiv Gandhi tried to respond to both problems with harsh crackdowns.

In January 1990, Walter and I flew back to India on our second three-week visit. This time we focused on the country's southern half. Our guide on each visit was Kosru Korah of the Indian Press Information Office in New Delhi. He led us through rural villages, temples, cities and universities.

We inspected nine university journalism and mass communication programs. Some performed well, but most did not. In addition to inadequate equipment and lack of practical experience on the part of many faculty members, we found dissatisfied students who said their instructors emphasized theory over hands-on writing and editing experience. Media professionals we visited expressed reluctance to consider teaching as a career, mainly because of low pay.

India's newspapers published in fifteen major languages and scores of minor ones. Walter and I toured more than twenty newspapers. Among them were *The Hindu*, published in the Hindi language, and *Indian Express* and *Times* of India, both published in English. Hindi newspapers had India's largest readerships. The smaller *Express* and *Times* circulated one million and three million daily copies respectively.

A regional newspaper we visited in the southernmost tropical state of Kerala was the influential *Malayala Manorama*. It published in the Malayalam language. The Kandathil family owned the newspaper, which descended from its 1890 founder, Varghese Mappillai.

In Trivandrum, Walter and I met with K. M. Mathew, *Malayala Manorama* editor. His newspaper's daily circulation exceeded 700,000, he said. Although it also published in English, its editions in regional Malayalam had faster rising circulations. It distributed in Trivandrum and nearby cities of Kottayam, Calicut, and Cochin. Those cities had seventy per cent literacy rates, twice that of the rest of India.

Before I realized Mathew belonged to the Kandathil family, I asked if the newspaper's owners ever interfered in editors' decisions. He graciously answered, "No, they don't interfere." From his viewpoint, the question may have been reasonable. His answer may have meant that family members not directly involved in running the newspaper do not try to dictate to those devoting their working lives to it.

Kandathil family members belonged to a branch of the Syrian Christian Church that had been influential in shaping Kerala culturally and educationally. Tradition says Christianity came to Kerala when St. Thomas visited in the First Century A. D. The first Jews arrived about thousand years earlier when King Solomon's trading ships landed at the Kerala port of Poovar.

The report Walter and I wrote suggested visits by Indian educators to selected U.S. university journalism/mass communication programs. We also recommended that solutions to problems we found be discussed at a meeting in India of university, government, and media representatives. Both ideas were accepted.

We made our third trip in November 1991 to observe a two-day media conference in New Delhi, prompted by our reports. The conference gave each of us time to present our observations at the end.

We complimented participants and emphasized for their consideration American accreditation standards. We recognized that India's press faced different problems from those in the United States. Foremost among them: Most of India's graduates must be prepared to write in two or more languages.

After the conference, Walter, Kosru and I traveled to Kolkata (Calcutta). We stayed in the Tata Company's luxury Taj Hotel near the city center. Resting in my comfortable room, I imagined how rich Rajas of a bygone era must have felt in their elegant palaces surrounded by crowded poverty.

We left the Taj to visit Mother Teresa's House of the Pure Heart, a sanctuary for dying street people in the city's southeast. It stood within a block of the city's largest prostitution district and in view of Kalighat Kali Hindu temple. The temple was dedicated to the Hindu red-eyed goddess of death. Some say Kali also represents time and change and dispels fear of death.

Inside Mother Teresa's nearby sanctuary, people dying of malnutrition, pneumonia, venereal disease and traffic accidents lay side by side on low, narrow cots. Only a few had strength to sit up. Male patients filled one very large room, and female patients filled another. A busy mortuary occupied the building's rear.

Sister Nirmala Joshi showed us around, because Mother Teresa had left on a trip to Mexico, where she had a heart attack and received a pace maker. Meanwhile, her order's nearly four-thousand nuns continued to run scores of orphanages, homes for the poor, and hospices in several countries.

When I met her, Nirmala, soon to be Mother Theresa's successor, looked in her mid fifties. She wore a white robe trimmed in blue. The daughter of an army officer of the Hindu Brahmin class, she studied law for a while and saw Hindus and Muslims slaughter each other when India partitioned itself in 1947. She said she converted to Catholicism upon meeting Mother Teresa.

"I joined her Missionaries of Charity because of the order's compassion for the poor," Sister Nirmala said.

While we stood talking to her, a middle-aged couple, appearing relatively well to do, interrupted. They tried to leave a dying female servant in the sanctuary. Sister Nirmala scolded the couple.

"This is a sanctuary for the homeless," she said, "not a haven for the wealthy who want to shirk responsibilities." She told the couple to take the servant to a hospital.

Several years later, when Mother Teresa died, Sister Nirmala succeeded her as Superior General of the Missionaries of Charity, including the House of the Pure Heart.

I felt a bit subdued when Walter and I left Mother Teresa's home for the dying and its shabby neighborhood to return to the Taj Hotel. It was one of several elegant hotels built throughout India by the Tata family. The Tatas, members of the Parsi religion tracing its traditions to ancient Persia's Zoroaster, got wealthy in the cotton business.

The Tatas prospered when the American Civil War interrupted much of the world's textile trade in the mid-1800s. Later, the Tatas added dozens of other companies, including tea, chemicals, truck manufacturing, hotels and information technology, to become one of the richest families in Asia. By 2008, the Tata Company announced a plan to begin manufacturing inexpensive small cars for its domestic market. To compete globally, Tata also bought the Jaquar and Land Rover brands from Ford.

Walter and I found time to visit many historical sites connected with Mahatma Gandhi's life. Among them was the Mumbai (Bombay) house where he lived for nearly two decades as a young attorney after returning from South Africa where he resisted racial discrimination for years.

The house on Mumbai's Laburnam Road, now a museum, held an added attraction for me. Martin Luther King spent a night there shortly after I met him on his visit to Memphis. King insisted on sleeping on the floor mat where Gandhi spent many nights. The female curator of the museum showed me large and small spinning wheels Gandhi used. She also let me inspect samples of cloth he made from cotton and wool. Spinning was part of his campaign to encourage the poor of India to free itself from expensive foreign textiles.

I also visited Gandhi's Ahmadabad ashram from which he led a 240-mile march to the sea in 1930 to protest a burdensome British salt tax. I recalled both King and E. Stanley Jones describing Gandhi's impact on their lives.

I visited the garden at the rear of a New Delhi home where a Hindu fanatic assassinated Gandhi in 1948 for advocating concessions to Muslims.

The Yamuna River flows through Delhi. A spot along its route is sacred to Hindus. It's where devotees cremated Gandhi's body. The river, which is pristine as melted ice when it flows from the Himalayas, becomes highly polluted before reaching the cremation site. Pollution is a growing problem for the millions of people who live along the river's banks.

At a picnic to which we had been invited near the river, I met Indian entrepreneurs involved in "micro-lending" or "micro-finance." They were terms I had not heard before. Our hosts explained that they lent small amounts of money, often less than a hundred dollars, at minimum rates to the poor, especially women, to encourage them to start small businesses, improve their homes or farms, and educate their children. The hosts were enthusiastic about the success of their efforts. They bragged about high rates of repayment.

A high point of our visit was getting to know an "untouchable" who rose to become mayor of Mumbai (Bombay), India's largest city. In his retirement, P. T. Borale showed up at a forum where Walter and I spoke. He was a member of the "dalits," the classless untouchables.

The 74-year-old Borale, wearing a neatly pressed white suit, introduced himself. "Since you traveled so far, I thought I should be here," he said. He told us about growing up as an untouchable, or member of the classless "dalits." Like other dalits, he performed menial jobs such as climbing coconut trees and cleaning latrines, sometimes with bare hands. He and his outcaste friends had no utensils except buckets for carrying excrement to fields and ditches at the edge of the city.

Considered outside the entire social caste system, untouchables lived at the edge of villages and often were forced to go barefoot. They often were forbidden to touch the town water pump. They had to wait with a pail until a person of caste condescended to pump water for them. Most higher castes avoided the dalits and sometimes even murdered them for attempting to enter temples or schools.

Borale described how he educated himself in his childhood by listening day after day outside open school windows as teachers conducted classes. When he was a teenager, police jailed him a few days for attempting to board a city bus. As a young adult, he managed to disguise his caste and win admittance to a small law school.

He succeeded as a lawyer, mostly serving Dalits who were physically or financially mistreated. He became leader of an organization that gradually won for the lowest castes educational and job benefits. Although the Indian government officially banned discrimination in 1955, it persisted in rural areas. Borale's reputation spread through Mumbai. In the late 1950s, poor neighborhoods elected him Mumbai's mayor. Its metropolitan area, soon to exceed twenty million residents, was India's commercial center and the world's fourth largest city.

After describing his life to Walter and me, Borale said, "Because you came from such a long distance, the courteous thing for me to do was be here." We explained that nothing we said in our prepared remarks could have matched his story.

A political party for dalits was founded in 1984.

The social barrier Borale broke helped other untouchables attain higher status. In some villages, they volunteered for a few days or weeks' training as health-care providers and midwives. A few followed in Borale's footsteps by being elected as their village leaders.

In 1997, another dalits, K. R. Narayanan, was elected India's tenth president. Mayawati (Naina Kumari), a dalits and female attorney, became chief minister of Uttar Pradesh state in 2008.

His profile highlighted by the camera's flashbulb, P. T. Borale, 74, describes to Gilleland in India how he rose from a classless "untouchable" to become mayor of Mumbai (Bombay).

23

At Lectern and Helm

My enthusiasm for teaching increased on entering a classroom if I added to my notes an element or two that had not been there in previous semesters. A new fact or idea made me feel that the entire lecture sounded fresher than it would have otherwise. Greater confidence on my part, I felt, rubbed off on students.

Two or three times in thirty years I performed a little experiment that no faculty member I knew duplicated. Because I urged future journalists to appear politically neutral in stories they wrote, I wondered if I practiced what I preached in lectures. So, I added a non-credit question to final exams of courses in which controversial political questions had been discussed in class. I asked students to designate where they thought I fell on the political spectrum from ultra conservative to middle-of-the-road to ultra liberal. The majority of students each time were wrong.

Press law, journalism history, and journalism ethics topped my list of favorites among courses taught. Others were news writing, editing, and research methods.

In the ethics course, I recommended that future journalists pursue stories with "polite aggressiveness." I, as did my colleagues, told students to never accept gifts from news sources, never stray from the facts, never plagiarize, be highly selective about joining organizations, and be circumspect about promising to protect confidential sources. Using unnamed sources is permissible only if they possess vital information that cannot be obtained elsewhere. If reporters promise to protect someone's identity, they must not violate it.

Promises of anonymity may be exchanged for information "on background" (no identification of source), "deep background" (no hint that a source exists), or "off the record" (no identification of source ever, and use of the information only if obtained from one or more others).

I recommended that future reporters exhibit non-partisan demeanors in work outside the editorial page, regardless of how they cast ballots in the voting booth.

I told students about Editor Frank Ahlgren's decision to order a prominent page position for an unfavorable police story about his son and his decision to fire a reporter for doing clandestine publicity for a patent medicine company. We discussed numerous examples of editors resisting pressure from advertising departments that sought special treatment for big clients.

The class and I discussed with pride American journalists' nearly spotless record of avoiding recruitment for either industrial or government espionage, despite the convenient cover news media jobs might provide. We studied attempts by government officials to suppress revelations of wrongdoing by passing punitive taxes on newspapers, as occurred in Utica, New York, in the 1950s.

In the press law course, my students visited law libraries to study numerous libel and invasion of privacy cases to avoid expensive torts in their own careers. They also researched the news media's long struggle for access to information that the public has a right to know. The students analyzed federal and state officials' attempts to undermine shield laws protecting sources.

They read debates that preceded relaxation of laws restricting concentration of media ownership, and they studied arguments in Congress and the Federal Communications Commission leading to demise of broadcasting's Fairness Doctrine in 1987 during the Reagan administration. The doctrine required broadcasters to provide reasonable opportunity for contrasting controversial views.

Through the years, several former students told me that my law course helped lead them to legal careers. Student Gregg Zive went to Notre Dame Law School; Hampton Young, Southwestern Law School; Sheila Caudle, Catholic University Law School; Erin Klinck, Pacific McGeorge Law School, and John McCaghren, New York Law School. All became attorneys, indicating they hoped to represent news media. Another student, Lew Carnahan, became a Reno Municipal Court judge.

Reno Municipal Court
November 15, 1989

Dear Professor Gilleland:
. . . I still recall with enjoyment the classes I took from you.

Judge Lew Carnahan

March 16, 1994

Dear Professor Gilleland:
While my exposure to you as a teacher and administrator was minimal during my years at Northeastern, the experience I had as your student in Law of the Press proved to be engaging, enriching, and profoundly formative.

The manner in which you taught and your breadth of knowledge enhanced what I found to be a highly interesting and captivating subject. My success in your class was due to your presentation of the subject, as well as my apparent natural interest, and both factors contributed to my decision to now apply to law school.

I am applying to New York Law School for September 1994, and I have completed my personal statement which I have enclosed for your reference.

Thank you for providing me with an invaluable experience, your recommendation, and for the time you took when I needed it as a journalism student.

John P. McCaghren

McCaghren sat through the last press law course I taught shortly before retiring. I turned the course over to Bill Smith, a new Northeastern faculty member with a doctorate in law, whom we hired from Penn State University.

My lectures in press law and research methods required the most preparation. But I may have received the most favorable response from a history lecture. Students seemed to like it because it provided some legal background while entertaining them. It dealt with John Wilkes of England, Eighteenth Century agitator and reformer. Wilkes had an impact on laws affecting press freedom on both sides of the Atlantic. Historians, I maintained, often failed to give Wilkes the attention he deserved.

The lecture:

John Wilkes -- rascal, loud mouth, and rabble rouser -- was big and homely. Upper-class ladies thought his speech crude and licentious. They considered him a dirty old man. But he had, within him, goodness and courage. He championed

causes in the 1700s that won popular approval in England and the American Colonies.

The son of a well-to-do whisky distiller, he was ten years old in 1735 when England received word that New York editor John Peter Zenger had won an important colonial court case that helped establish truth as a defense against a libel charge. Wilkes studied at the University of Leiden and returned home to marry a young heiress, because "she pleased my father and she was rich." The marriage did not last. His wife could not stand Wilkes' libertine habits and his hard-drinking friends. One bunch of carousers that captured his youthful fancy was known as the "Hellfire Club" and "Medmenham Monks." Dressed in religious garb, they held wild parties in an old chalk mine beneath an abandoned abbey outside London. Their worst vice may have been heavy drinking. But they spread stories about practicing demon worship, and they entertained prostitutes, whom they called "Medmenham Nuns."

Wilkes bought his way into politics, a common practice. He put out seven thousand pounds in a complicated deal that got him elected to the House of Commons as a Whig. While a Member of Parliament, he started a newspaper as a weapon against pro-royalist Tories. The poet, Charles Churchill, one of Sir Winston Churchill's ancestors, assisted Wilkes in this publishing venture.

Wilkes called the newspaper the *North Briton*. With it, he tossed sharp barbs at Tory prime ministers. He attacked the artist William Hogarth, with whom he often feuded about politics. When King George III defended England's separate peace treaty with France at the conclusion of the Seven Years War, Wilkes declared that England's military ally, Prussia, had been "basely deserted." The king's speech explaining the treaty, Wilkes said in No. 45 of the *North Briton*, was written by the king's ministers and contained falsehoods.

This irked the Tories. They issued a general warrant for the arrest of anyone connected with publication of No. 45 of the *North Briton*, which appeared on April 23, 1763.

The populace hated general warrants. The warrants did not specifically name persons to be arrested, places to be searched, or things expected to be found. About four dozen persons, nearly all innocent, found themselves under arrest by general warrant. Wilkes, placed in the Tower of London, soon gained release because of his privilege against imprisonment as a Member of Parliament. He sued a secretary of state and several other officials for illegal arrest. He won his case and received compensation for damages.

Another printer, Dryden Leach, also sued, and he won. He was among those arrested in connection with the *North Briton*. The Leach and Wilkes court decisions brought an end to general warrants in England and inspired increasing protest against their use in the American Colonies.

Remembering John Wilkes, writers of the Fourth Amendment to the U.S. Constitution prohibited general warrants in this country. Later, several states put the same provisions in their constitutions.

Wilkes faced more trouble. A government undersecretary instigated a clandestine search of his home. From Wilkes' private printing press, government officials found proof sheets of a poem, "Essay on Woman," which he co-authored with the Archbishop of Canterbury's son. It was an obscene parody on Alexander Pope's "Essay on Man." Wilkes intended the poem to be read by a few friends. His political enemy, the Earl of Sandwich, with relish, read it to the House of Lords.

When the Earl of Sandwich pontificated to the Lords that Wilkes would die by hanging or by venereal disease, Wilkes stood up and said, "That depends, my Lord, on whether I embrace your principles or your mistress."

The Lords decided that both "Essay on Woman" and North Briton No. 45 were criminally libelous and that Wilkes should stand trial. Before the trial took place, Wilkes challenged another of his adversaries in Parliament to a duel. Wilkes lost. A bullet wound put him to bed for a month. While recuperating he decided he could not receive a fair trial. So, he crossed the channel to France and exile.

Declared an outlaw by Parliament, he traveled leisurely through Europe for four years, conversing with James Boswell in Naples and the great Voltaire in Ferney, France. No record exists of what Wilkes and Voltaire talked about, but it may have been one of the great conversations of all time.

When the Whig party gained power in England, Wilkes returned home, won election to Commons from Middlesex County in northwest London area, and willingly stood trial. A court convicted him on two counts of criminal libel, fined him a thousand pounds, and sentenced him to twenty-two months in prison. Parliament expelled him -- a big news story at the time.

While Wilkes waited in prison, Middlesex citizens repeatedly re-elected him to Parliament, which refused to acknowledge each election. Parliament finally created a public furor by seating a candidate that Wilkes had roundly defeated.

Boswell wrote: "This being justly considered as a gross violation to the right of election, an alarm for the Constitution extended itself all over the kingdom."

Mobs roamed London streets shouting, "Wilkes and Liberty." Intellectual leaders quarreled over the issue. Churchill praised Wilkes; Hogarth satirized him. Boswell even dared to disagree with Samuel Johnson. Johnson wrote in a pamphlet, "The False Alarm," that liberty was not endangered merely because Parliament had kept Middlesex from being represented by a jailed criminal.

A widely read newspaper writer called "Junius" -- an alias invented to escape such prosecution as Wilkes had endured -- halted his invectives of Tories and Solicitor General William Blackstone long enough to defend Wilkes. Junius argued in letters to the *Public Advertiser* that since Wilkes had been duly elected to the House of Commons he should be permitted to represent the people who voted for him. He praised Wilkes' courage for insisting on freedom of expression. Junius wrote, "The liberty of the press is the Palladium of all the civil, political and religious rights of an Englishman."

Released in April 1770, after nearly two years in a cell, Wilkes won election as London alderman. In that post he supported attempts by newspapers to report and comment on proceedings of Parliament, which long had been forbidden. Two editors were arrested after a member of Commons, Colonel George Onslow, complained that they not only had violated law by printing reports of Parliamentary speeches, but also they had called him a "paltry insignificant insect."

The editors appeared as defendants before two aldermen, London's Lord Mayor and, ironically, Wilkes. Wilkes and the Lord Mayor, also a Member of Parliament, listened to testimony regarding the complaint and arrest. They miffed Parliament by dismissing the prisoners on a legal technicality.

Through its power to punish members for breach of privilege and contempt, Parliament committed the Lord Mayor to the Tower of London for six weeks. The action was extremely unpopular with common people. They hissed the name of King George in the streets and attacked carriages carrying Members of Parliament. The public outcry proved effective. Parliament began turning away from its tradition of barring its doors to the press. In 1771, it ceased to prosecute newspapers for reporting Parliamentary speeches, debates and proceedings.

The year 1774 turned out to be genial for Wilkes. He became Lord Mayor of London. And Parliament finally decided he could take his seat in Commons. He won election in 1779 to the lucrative post of Chamberlain of the City, which he filled scrupulously the rest of his life. In his second year as Chamberlain, anti-Catholic sentiment became so widespread in London that riots broke out. Although not Catholic, he felt its adherents to be in needless danger. He said breach of peace could not be permitted. So Wilkes, now 54, mounted a horse to lead militia in suppressing the rioters.

Historians say Wilkes maintained secret correspondence with some Colonial leaders of the American Revolution. It is on record that he championed the Revolution on the House of Commons floor. He made ten speeches in which he pleaded the Colonial cause and advocated cessation of hostilities. Because he and another Member of Parliament, Isaac Barre, stood up for the Colonies, settlers in Northeast Pennsylvania honored the two men when founding a new town. They named it Wilkes-Barre.

As a Member of Parliament until 1790, Wilkes worked for reforms in the election of members. His long struggle against various charges of libel inspired his political Whig friend, Charles James Fox, to sponsor a bill to give juries the right to decide law as well as fact in criminal libel cases. This led to enactment of the Fox Libel Act in 1792. New York adopted a similar law in 1805, and states throughout America eventually copied it.

Wilkes crusaded against a legal principle that prevented defendants from pleading truth as a defense against charges of criminal libel. His work left an impact in 1843, long after his death, when Parliament passed Lord Campbell's Act. The act made it possible to argue defense of truth, when truth is published with good motives and justifiable ends. This principle caught on in American states.

Wilkes died in 1797 at the age of 70. Before his death, Dr. Johnson finally said of him: "Jack has a great variety of talk; Jack is a scholar. Jack has the manners of a gentleman."

The Helm:

To put academe behind me for hours at a time, I bought a 25-foot Catalina sloop that I sailed off the Massachusetts coast. I named the boat "Spinoza," a nostalgic reference to the Ph.D. dissertation I now admitted I'd never write.

I moored the boat first in Scituate harbor and later at Hull. On weekends and vacations, I often took Betsy and our offspring and their spouses on day sails. When no one else wanted to go with me, I sailed alone to Plymouth, Marblehead, Manchester, or Salem.

I'd tie up in the harbor of one of these famous old fishing communities, walk downtown to a restaurant, return to the boat to spend the night, and sail home the next day. In Salem, I walked the streets of the old witch trials and sought out Nathaniel Hawthorne's House of Seven Gables.

The most adventurous outing occurred while sailing alone to Provincetown. I got half way. As I headed eastward -- serenely listening to my marine radio forecast mild rain -- a squall hit. The next twenty minutes were the longest I spent on Spinoza. I grappled with halyards and sails in an effort to keep them from ripping apart. Nearest land lay beyond the horizon, so I didn't worry about wind blowing the boat onto rocks or coastline. But stinging rain and swirling seawater poured into the cabin, soaking bunks, food and electronic equipment.

When the squall ended, I untangled the lines, re-hoisted the battered sails, and reluctantly headed home. As I did so, the marine radio finally reported the storm's arrival and departure. It said wind speed exceeded 65 knots. It felt like more to me.

I grew a beard, telling myself it was compatible with the sea and my advancing age.

24

My Final Edition

Declines in the health of the daily newspaper industry and my prostate occurred almost simultaneously. The prostate took much of the fun out of my job when I reached the age of 60. I decided two years later to call it quits.

The *Patriot Ledger*, Quincy, Mass., carried this story:

Journalism Director to Retire

LaRue W. Gilleland, director of the Northeastern University School of Journalism, has announced that he will retire June 30.

Gilleland, 62, a Scituate resident, came to Northeastern in 1981 from the University of Nevada at Reno.

"It's time for someone younger than I to take over the J-School administrative duties," Gilleland said. "The school's alumni have made their marks throughout the world. The journalism faculty is among the best. We now need a director with fresh ideas to prepare for the 21st Century."

Under his direction, Northeastern expanded its undergraduate courses and launched a graduate program in journalism.

Gilleland earned bachelor's and master's degrees in journalism from the University of Missouri. He is a former reporter for the Honolulu Advertiser in Hawaii and the Memphis Commercial Appeal in Tennessee. He also edited the Journalism Educator, a scholarly journal, and was president of the American Society of Journalism School Administrators.

He has been on the New England Press Association's board of directors since 1982. Gilleland said he considers his greatest achievements at Northeastern to be the school's 95 percent job placement rate, the school's success with the Moscow University student exchange program, and the contributions the school made to the quality of education in India.

The Smithsonian Institution and the Indo-U.S. Sub-commission on Education and Culture sent Gilleland to India three times in recent years as part of a project to improve journalism education at universities there.

Northeastern President John Curry said he was pleased with Gilleland's contributions to the university.

"He is an amazing visionary who brought top-notch quality to Northeastern," Curry said. "I think he has done the job so well."

Northeastern will form a national search committee to find a replacement for Gilleland.

After he retires, Gilleland plans to do some of the things he has never had time for. An avid sailor, he also intends to do some sailing and traveling with his wife.

The Patriot Ledger
Quincy, Massachusetts
Dec. 17, 1991

As my July 1, 1992 departure approached, students and alumni occasionally dropped by my office to reminisce and say good luck. Faculty and administrators became increasingly solicitous.

Northeastern University
May 20, 1992

Dear LaRue:

I am so sorry about your decision to retire. It seems only yesterday that you came to Northeastern University. I remember distinctly (Arts and Science Dean) Richard Astro's excitement concerning your coming.

LaRue, we owe so much to you. You have built quality programs in our School of Journalism of which I am very proud. I continue to hear from our many majors of their intense satisfaction with the quality of their education under you leadership.

I hope you can often reflect on what you have developed at Northeastern University. We are so much stronger than we were a decade ago. My sincere appreciation to a dedicated visionary for a job well done.

John A. Curry, University President

The university administration designated Nick Danilof to replace me as School of Journalism director. Mark Jurkowitz of the Boston *Phoenix* wrote:

June 14, 1992

When LaRue Gilleland arrived at Northeastern University's Journalism Department in 1981, he inherited an empire that included two or three rooms, antique manual typewriters, two full-time faculty members, and about 200 majors.

Today, as he prepares to retire as director of what's now the School of Journalism, he presides over a program that has been technologically modernized, features 12 faculty positions and about 600 undergrad and grad students, and has been divided into four concentrations that include print, radio and TV news, advertising and public relations.

In short, the highly regarded former Memphis Commercial Appeal reporter, executive director of the American Society of Journalism School

Administrators, and Journalism Department chair of the University of Nevada, Reno has put Northeastern's J-school on the map.

"He (Gilleland) took this place from nothing and made it the most vital unit of the College of Arts and Sciences," says Nick Danilof.

Or, as one observer puts it, "LaRue turned it into the kind of department a Nick Danilof would want."

Mark Jurkowitz, Boston Phoenix

The Journalism Alumni Association threw a surprise retirement party for Betsy and me at the university's elegant Henderson House in Weston. A jazz band entertained.

Making kind remarks about growth and improvement of the J-School were university administrators, faculty members, students, alumni, Editor Jack Driscoll of the Boston *Globe*, Columnist George Merry of the *Christian Science Monitor*, President David Faulknor of New England Press Association, and Valerie Sarazen, my administrative assistant.

Also attending was Patrick Purcell, Boston *Herald* publisher. Northeastern alumni working at the *Herald* had high respect for Purcell. I first met Purcell at a professional meeting where he introduced me to his boss, Rupert Murdoch, CEO of News Corp. Purcell, who had held a number of executive positions under Murdoch, was considered a Murdoch protégé.

Murdoch, when I met him, was reserved but courteous. He asked me how many students at Northeastern majored in journalism, and if the program was growing. When I said yes, he nodded approval and changed the subject.

Murdoch was soon forced by FCC rules to shed the *Herald* in order to add a Boston TV station to his Fox Broadcasting division. He sold the newspaper to Purcell for a reported price of about $270 million.

That money may have become part of carefully plotted media acquisition that soon included, among others, News Corp., Fox, Dow Jones, the *Wall Street Journal*, New York *Post*, London's *News or the World*, and an $80 billion bid to take over Time-Warner.

Murdoch had earned a master's degree from Oxford and inherited an Australian daily from his father in 1952. He soon added newspapers in New Zealand, the United Kingdom, and the San Antonio Express-News in the United States. He bought the London *Times* and in 1985 and became a U.S. citizen.

A House of Commons committee served Murdoch, his son James, and their company CEO Rebekah Brooks with a summons in 2011 on suspicion of "hacking" into government and private phones, including voice mails of a young female murder victim.

Coverage of the committee investigation was a major international story, including testimony that questioned the character and abilities of Murdoch. When witnesses were quoted as making unflattering remarks about Murdoch, his son, or Rebekah Brooks, the Murdoch media reported them accurately. I followed the story mostly in the *Wall Street Journal,* and I was impressed with the newspaper's straightforward honesty when reporting criticism of its boss.

A headline in Gannett's *USA Today* in 2014 predicted "Murdoch may spark media merger mania," involving boards of Disney, CBS, Viacom, Discovery, Scripps, Starz, and others.

As I began retirement, I decompressed with part-time jobs. Northeastern paid me for consulting work, and I taught one class a semester for a while at Boston College. Jim Willis, who headed the Boston College Communications Department, hired me. He had worked for me at Northeastern.

Meanwhile, Betsy and I watched daughter Michelle, her husband Dave Daigle, grow their family with the arrival of two daughters, Alexandra and Melissa, in Norfolk, Massachusetts, an hour's commute from Boston. Soon after, our son Ross, his wife Lynn, and their two daughters, Lauren and Eva, moved from Hingham and bought a home in the same Norfolk neighborhood. Michelle and Ross held civil engineering jobs with different federal agencies in Boston. Daughter Virginia continued to serve as a nurse practitioner in the Veterans Health Care system.

Our daughter Louise, whose married name was Lenzen, died of a liver ailment in Nevada at the age of 44. Her daughters, Jessica and Elizabeth, married and lived in Las Vegas.

In 1994, Betsy and I sold our house in Scituate and moved to the Villages, a retirement community near Lady Lake, Florida. There we turned the first page of our last chapter together -- playing golf and traveling. We joined the Unitarian-Universalist Fellowship of Marion County. I was elected to its board of directors.

Because many headwaiters couldn't spell my first name when Betsy and I arrived for "early bird specials," I adopted the nickname "Gil" in retirement. The name soon caught on with my golf buddies.

LaRue and Betsy Gilleland retired from Northeastern University in Boston to The Villages, Florida.

When Betsy and I discovered our golf games hardly improved, we started traveling. We visited forty countries in Europe, Asia, the Near East and Latin America.

On a trip to Turkey, I spent a night and day in police detention. I blamed the incident on carelessness. Betsy blamed "incipient senility." It began as Betsy and I prepared to land in Istanbul on a tour arranged through Grand Circle. I discovered my passport had disappeared from my hip pocket. I placed it there, I thought, after changing planes and going through customs in Amsterdam.

Betsy and I frantically searched around our seats and our carry-on luggage as passengers disembarked. Several crewmembers helped us look to no avail.

Inside the airport, Betsy passed through customs while I explained my plight to Turkish customs officers. They said that without a passport I'd be sent back to America on the next plane. Because no plane would leave for hours, airport police locked me in a detention room for the night. Through a wire screen I briefly communicated with Betsy before a Grand Circle guide led her and others in our group to a hotel in downtown Istanbul, about thirty miles away.

The guide promised to take her to the American Consulate the next morning in an effort to get me a new passport. We carried passport photocopies and two extra passport photos each, according to State Department recommendations. If she failed to get the new passport, Betsy and I agreed she would complete the three-week tour. But, with no passport, I wondered how I would re-enter the United States. I felt a bit like Philip Nolan, the "man without a country" who inspired Edward Everett Hale's short story of that name. Nolan succumbed in a jail in India.

Straight-back chairs lined the walls of a room confining me inside Istanbul airport. A table at one end held a coffee pot. Airport police came in every two or three hours to get a cup of coffee, glance my direction, re-lock the door, and leave.

It was a long night. I may have dozed a few minutes with my head propped against the wall behind me. To Grand Circle's credit, the guide knocked on Betsy's hotel room door early the next morning and drove her to the consulate. After she filled out papers, a consulate clerk said, "Your husband will have to come in and sign these."

When Betsy explained I was being held at the airport, the clerk said, "There's nothing we can do." An American standing nearby suggested, "Ask to see someone higher up."

Betsy did, and a consulate official told her she could take the papers back to the airport for me to sign. But he then informed her she needed three photos, not two. It was a holiday in Turkey. Shops with duplicating equipment were closed, like nearly everything else. The guide, however, knew a Turkish wedding photographer and took Betsy there. He made a third copy of my passport picture.

Meanwhile, I paid an airport attendant to buy me a couple of sandwiches. I helped myself to police coffee. Betsy and the guide returned about the middle of the afternoon with an application for me to sign. They headed back to Istanbul and obtained the passport just before the consulate closed. They returned to the airport about 7 p.m. With the new passport, I legally entered Turkey.

The rest of the trip went well. We visited Istanbul's major mosques and palaces, Cappadocia's caves once occupied by early Christians and earlier Hittites, Konya's tomb of great Sufi poet Rumi, and the ruins of ancient Ephesus. We walked around Bishop Nicholas' hometown of Myra, where he inspired the concept of Santa Claus in the Fourth Century by giving young women dowries to save them from poverty or prostitution.

On a trip to Egypt in 1997, about half way through President Hosni Mubarak's three-decade grip on power, terrorists provided some uncomfortable moments. As Betsy and I packed to depart on Egypt Air, we heard on a TV newscast that Islamic radicals had fire-bombed a bus in Cairo. The explosion occurred a block from the hotel where we had booked a room. It killed ten persons and injured nineteen. After brief hesitation, Betsy and I continued the trip.

In Egypt, we encountered heavy police presence everywhere. Near the great Pyramids at Giza, we felt their presence reduced harassment by vendors. When an aggressive vendor convinced Betsy to briefly hold a small statue he was peddling, he immediately demanded money for it. An Egyptian tour guide interceded, and enabled Betsy to walk away.

In future years, Giza vendors became more aggressive, banging on cars and pressuring tourists to make overpriced purchases. A police official told us that terrorists, with links to Al Qaeda, hoped to weaken the government by interrupting the tourist trade on which Egypt depended heavily for foreign currency.

After Betsy and I looked at some of the thousands of items in Cairo's Museum of Eastern Antiquities, including King Tut's Golden Mask, I struck out on foot alone for Tahrir Square. It soon would be the gathering spot for throngs of young people that would topple President Mubarak. The square was named for a Ninth Century Muslim general who helped the Arab world preserve mathematics and scholarship during Europe's Dark Ages.

Just off the square was the café where Muslim activist Sayyid Qutb and Nobel Prize-winning novelist Naguib Mahfouz had done much of their socializing and writing. It was called the Ali Baba (for the fictional character in Arabic literature). I was told that the Ali Baba café was where Mahfouz had stopped frequently for a cup of coffee until an Islamic extremist stabbed him in the neck – permanently curtailing his mobility and ability to write.

I'd heard the Ali Baba described as a favorite gathering place for some members of the Muslim Brotherhood, Egypt's oldest political party. Although I didn't know it, the Brotherhood soon would briefly dominate the country's politics. It would eventually lose power to a military faction, partly because of the Brotherhood's advocacy of strict Sharia law and restrictions on women. The Brotherhood, anti-Zionist and anti-Christian, helped spawn al-Qaeda terrorism in some nearby Arab countries. Its policies provoked many Egyptians to demonstrate in Tahrir Square and elsewhere.

Getting to the cafe on foot was an adventure. I found it after dodging much traffic. Inside, Egyptians talked at scattered tables. All patrons were men. Some wore western-style business suits without neckties. I asked a man seated near me if many foreigners came to the café. If his response were friendly, I intended to follow with more pointed questions about the Muslim Brotherhood. But he smiled and let me know by hand gesture that he did not understand my English.

So, I decided not to press my luck. I was acting on my own curiosity, not being paid by any news medium. So, I sat quietly listening to recorded Egyptian music and observing the customers. I sipped first a Stella beer and then a cup of strong Mediterranean coffee. Because words "beer" and "coffee" are universal, I had no trouble ordering.

Qutb had traveled to the United States in the 1920s and lived briefly in Greeley, Colorado, where he was connected with the University of Northern Colorado, shortly before novelist James Michener earned his master's degree there. In his writings, Qutb encouraged Muslim schools to concentrate on religious education only. But Mahfouz disagreed, and their friendship ended. A close association between Qutb and Egyptian President Abdul Nasser also dissolved with Qutb's arrest and execution in 1966 on a charge of involvement in a plot to assassinate Nasser. As I finished my beer, I pondered Qutb' and Mahfouz' past connection with the Ali Baba.

I paid my bill and left.

After departing Cairo by riverboat, Betsy and I traveled south on the Nile for five days. Soldiers patrolled the boat day and night. All night we could hear a soldier stomp around the moving vessel's perimeter. We stopped to see the antiquities at Karnak, Luxor, Valley of Kings and Valley of Queens. We visited Rameses II's temple at Abu Simbel before heading home.

News media reported a disturbing story of Islamic extremism six weeks after Betsy and I returned home. On the spot near Luxor in the Valley of the Queens, where we stood admiring Queen Hatshepsut's ancient temple, a half dozen extremists dressed in black opened gunfire on tourists -- mostly German, British and Japanese. About sixty died.

Almost exactly two years later, Egypt Air 990, the flight number Betsy and I had taken, plunged into the Atlantic with more than two-hundred passengers. Aboard was a tour group with Grand Circle, the company that arranged our trip. Investigators said they believed the co-pilot, an Egyptian Muslim, intentionally thrust the plane into a nosedive. He did so after struggling with other crew members. A recorder caught his voice at the last moment repeating, "I put my trust in God."

The crash, some conjectured later, may have been a prelude to the September 11, 2001, attack on New York's World Trade Center.

25

Parting Shots

The Association for Journalism and Mass Communication (AEJMC) changed the name of *Journalism Educator*, the journal I edited for seven years, to *Journalism & Mass Communication Educator*.

After I moved to Florida, James Cook of the University of Kentucky, the journal's new editor, asked me to write an article in connection with the publication's 50th year. The article appeared in the August 1995 issue. A shortened version appears below:

Journal Editor Says Predictions
Were Optimistic -- and Wrong

A 1970 meeting in Las Vegas that led *Journalism Educator* into the AEJMC publications family comes to mind today as a historic milestone I witnessed during my editorship. Also from that year I learned any editorializing about the future should be done circumspectly. Predictions I made about education in our field were optimistic -- and wrong.

Journalism Educator **had served its founder, the American Society of Journalism School Administrators, for a quarter of a century when academicians from across the country converged on a Las Vegas hotel. They and I believed JE should benefit a broader readership than it had in the past.**

The Las Vegas negotiations continued two days around conference table, swimming pool, and hotel bar. We reached agreement and drafted a proposal.

As a future AEJMC publication, *Journalism Educator* would continue to print articles on teaching, administration and research techniques, and it would

204

compile a national directory annually that also would appear in *Editor & Publisher International Yearbook.*

All AEJMC members and many libraries in the country and abroad received JE copies. The publication's impact on higher education grew.

However, a JE editorial I wrote in 1970 made some predictions about journalism/mass communication education's future that turned out to be fanciful. In the editorial, I said:

1. The old green eyeshades v. chi-squares controversy would be over in a decade. Educators no longer would debate whether students should be given writing, editing, and other professional skills *or* communications theory *or* liberal education. Educators would work out a balance.

In my retirement today, former associates around the country tell me that the debate continues and that an effective balance has been found at too few schools. Teaching good writing skills, among others things, often receives short shrift.

2. Media executives in a decade would take a more active interest in journalism/mass communication programs at nearby universities than in the past because they would recognize their own vital stake in the quality of these programs.

Such media leaders today do exist -- Scott Low, *Patriot Ledger* publisher in Quincy, Mass., and Rollan Melton, Gannett board member, among others -- but their numbers fall below my expectations twenty-five years ago.

3. Increasingly well-prepared men and women would teach in journalism/mass communication programs. A number of years of full-time media work would sharpen their academic backgrounds.

The word I receive today is that the percentage of full-time professors with extensive media experience has probably declined rather than increased. If so, this would explain in part why some media leaders do not relate well to our field in academe.

Journalism and mass communication education faces challenges to its legitimacy and scope from within the university and from outside. The challenges are greater today than ever before. The recent attempt to abolish the University of Washington School of Communication, I fear, will occur again and again in public and private universities.

Education and the media would be served well if the best print and broadcast executives educated some top university administrators. It would be in the executives' self interest to lobby universities to produce future employees with broad education and solid grounding in careful fact gathering; clear, concise writing; ethics and moral responsibility; mass communication law; and logical thinking, among others. These areas of study, the executives should state persistently, require well-structured curricula, not token courses, and teachers with academic and professional backgrounds. The limited number of institutions with such programs should be increased.

Many university administrators know something about science and the liberal arts, but little about mass communication or journalism. Some doubt journalism teaching that emphasizes lucid communication based on first-hand research has a legitimate place in the university.

I know a woman who worked for the Boston *Herald* before taking a graduate English course. Her professor and the English department chair expressed surprise and dismay that she interviewed -- actually talked to -- expert sources for a graduate paper she wrote rather than rely entirely on library research. Such professors and chairs often become university presidents.

Not all media leaders are equipped to be useful to journalism and mass communication education. A few know more about turning out Hollywood movies or operating cereal companies than they do about news publications or TV stations. These managers often see no distinction between reporting fact and producing fiction. They tend to blur the line between information and entertainment.

But so do some universities. They place such diverse fields as theater, speech, and journalism, among others, in the same academic unit. I heard about a mass communication school of few years ago that offered a course in writing the novel. A young person may benefit from a course in fiction writing, or acting, or oral interpretation of literature -- if it is taught elsewhere than in the academic unit preparing him or her to be a print or broadcast reporter, or public relations practitioner. The paths to fact and fiction, to information and entertainment, should be kept mostly separate and well-marked.

Although my predictions about education 25 years ago were wrong, I am still hopeful. Journalism and mass communication education will survive. I believe it eventually will restructure itself, state its mission more closely, and become stronger than in the past.

A good first step would be for educators to define areas of mutual self-interest with the Scott Lows, the Rollan Meltons, and other media leaders who relate well to academe. Media executives have heard more often from educators seeking grants than from educators wanting to discuss educational philosophy and common purpose.

-- LaRue Gilleland

*　　　*　　　*

Ohio State University
November 14, 1995

Dear LaRue:
A voice from your past -- you may not even remember me. But I wanted you to know that I read with delight your commentary in the autumn Journalism Educator. *It was an excellent analysis of the Grand Canyon that continues to widen between journalism and j-education.*

I wish you had been right a quarter of a century ago in predicting that the green eyeshades and the chi squares would learn to appreciate each other. Alas, it was to be a Bosnia. Now academe seems intent on an "ethnic cleansing" of media professionals. As John Wicklein, one of my former colleagues at Ohio State, tersely put it, "No pros need apply."

John Clarke, Professor

While Professor Clarke agreed with my analysis, hopeful exceptions to the cause of our pessimism have occurred here and there. Two examples: Stephen Burgard, Los Angeles *Times* editorial page editor, became director of the Northeastern School of Journalism in 2004. Jerry Ceppos, Knight Ridder Newspaper Company vice president, became dean of the University of Nevada-Reno School of Journalism in 2008.

Walter Robinson of the Boston *Globe*, Northeastern Search Committee member

207

when I was hired, led the *Globe's* "Spotlight" investigative team of eight that won the 2003 Pulitzer Gold Medal for Public Service. Its hard work interrupted by the 9/11 terrorist attack on New York's World Trade Center, the team spent months gathering information on sexual abuse charges against priests in the Boston Catholic archdiocese. Robinson, like most of the reporters, had attended parochial schools in "the most Catholic city in America."

The archdiocese, after shuffling accused priests from parish to parish in an attempt to cover up, agreed to pay victims an $85 million settlement. Cardinal Bernard Law resigned as Boston's archbishop after apologizing for letting the coverup occur. The Pope transferred him to Rome as head of the Basilica de Santa Maria Maggiore.

The Boston story produced a tsunami when newspapers in other cities got involved. Their investigations resulted in removal of 450 priests nationwide and $1 billion in legal settlements. Child-abuse in America led to similar stories about priests in Ireland, Germany, and elsewhere in Europe. By 2010, the pope called a Vatican conference to deal with the scandal and promised reforms.

Robinson demonstrated objectivity and balance. In one case, he uncovered information that questioned the honesty of a priest's accuser.

He left the Boston *Globe* to teach investigative reporting at Northeastern as distinguished professor of journalism. His courses emphasized stories requiring pursuit of a lot of documents and shunning anonymous sources. Robinson used his good relations with *Globe* editors to get many student stories published in that newspaper.

Robinson's work with students drew attention from *The Chronicle of Higher Education* in November 2009 in an article entitled, "University-Based Reporting Could Keep Journalism Alive." It favorably compared the output of Robinson's Northeastern class to that of students at the University of Missouri's *Columbia Missourian;* Columbia University's "City Newsroom," where student reporters cover Brooklyn, the Bronx and Queens; and Arizona State University's Cronkite News Service, which provides student stories to thirty Arizona media clients.

When Steven Burgard succeeded Danilof as Northeastern J-School director, Danilof remained on the faculty and wrote his book, *Of Spies and Spokesmen: My Life as a Cold War Correspondent.*

The Journalism-Speech Department merger dispute died down after I left Northeastern. As late as 2007, I received a note from Burgard saying no one had broached that idea for several years.

26

The Digital Onset

Daily newspapers openly conceded they were bruised by advent of Internet and World Wide Web in the 1990s. Publishers forthrightly described declines in advertising revenue and loss of readers to Facebook, Twitter and other social media.

Subscriptions declined so fast in a few years that the average number of copies of daily newspapers bought by each 100 households fell from an average of 140 to 50.

A Chicago *Tribune* cartoon in 2010 depicted a grandmother telling her family, "The newspaper says they plan to stop delivering letters on Saturday." Her adult son says, "What's a letter?" Her young grandson, engrossed in a hand-held electronic reader, says, "What's a newspaper?"

I never thought the future of newspapers was that dire, although the Internet's impact forced some dailies to cut staffs and percentage of space devoted to news. A few opted for less-than-daily schedules. The daily *Times-Picayune* in New Orleans reduced publication to three times a week.

The Ann Arbor *News* left its Michigan readers with only two issues a week. The *Christian Science Monitor* ceased daily print publication.

Two good newspapers I had competed against went out of business. They were the Honolulu *Star-Bulletin* and the Memphis *Press- Scimitar*.

Some other dailies also stopped publishing. Of 1,611 American dailies in 1990, only 1,387 remained nineteen years later. This shrank the pool of expert journalists who regularly visited federal, state and local government offices. Thus, reporters less frequently read voluminous public records to put tough questions to officials or invoked open-record and open-meeting laws when needed.

Also affected were wire services, television and radio that relied on newspapers for many of the story ideas they developed on their own initiatives.

Many weekly newspapers performed more profitably than dailies. Weeklies successfully entertained and informed their readers about events in smaller communities. But they often lacked resources and opportunities to do serious investigative reporting usually led by large dailies.

Quoted in *USA Today* on February 17, 2014, Internet pioneer Marc Andreessen said he was bullish about the future of the entire news industry, including dailies and weeklies. Columnist Rem Rieder called Andreessen, co-founder of Netscape, "a very smart person who clearly cares a lot and has thought a lot about journalism."

The lead in investigative stories was usually taken by journalists on large dailies. Most such stories were produced by men and women working in teams, sometimes for weeks or months. Gaining access to documents, pouring over them, and developing and interviewing sources generally requires large staffs, extensive budgets, and direction from expert editors and attorneys.

Over several decades investigative reporters exposed graft and incompetence at all levels of government, and among leaders of both major political parties. They found bribe taking in the judicial system; payoffs by rackets to police; disenfranchisement of voters by faulty apportionment; lax codes in construction of buildings and bridges; neglect in homes for the aged and the mentally disabled; resume falsification by seekers of public office; cheating by educators on student standardized tests to improve school rankings; mismanagement in charitable and religious organizations, among others. Some observers have expressed doubts that careful investigative reporting will continue in the digital age.

One of the most important investigative stories of the Twentieth Century began to surface in 1971 when a Northeastern University graduate, Nat Hentoff of the *Village Voice*, wrote that the New York *Times* was preparing a "blockbuster" involving Vietnam and the Pentagon. He mentioned the newspaper's isolation of several staffers on two floors of a Hilton Hotel to analyze thousands of pages of the Pentagon Papers, a top secret report on United States involvement in the Vietnam War. It had been prepared for the government by the Rand Corporation.

One Rand researcher, Daniel Ellsberg of Massachusetts Institute of Technology, made copies available to the *Times* because he thought the public should be informed about how the United States stumbled into the war. In forty-three volumes, the papers revealed deceptions by Democratic and Republican leaders.

When the *Times* began publishing its report, the government obtained a temporary injunction, the first prior restraint of the press in America since 1721.

The Washington *Post* and Senator Mike Gavel of Alaska entered the controversy. The *Post* assigned reporters to prepare its own series on the Pentagon Papers, and Gavel convinced the Unitarian Universalist Association's Beacon Press in Boston to print the documents in book form. Knight Newspapers, the St. Louis *Post-Dispatch*, Chicago *Sun-Times* and Los Angeles *Times* prepared to publish parts of the Papers.

After an injunction lasting two weeks, the Supreme Court finally relied on its 1931 *Near v. Minnesota* decision to reassert that the government must prove clear and present danger to national security to prevent publication. The historical information in the Pentagon Papers, the court ruled, did not meet the clear and present danger test. Meanwhile, Beacon Press published its book.

When the Pentagon Papers story appeared in newspaper and book form, President Nixon worried that his own overseas activities might not hold up well under scrutiny. He authorized a White House surveillance team, later called the "Plumbers," to come up with a list of political enemies. The list included Daniel Ellsberg.

"Plumbers" secretly entered the office of Ellsberg's psychiatrist, hoping to find information that would discredit Ellsberg. They also broke into the Democratic National Committee headquarters in Washington's Watergate apartment complex to plant listening devices. Police quickly arrested five burglars. Of several Washington *Post* police and general assignment reporters working on the story, Bob Woodward and Carl Bernstein took the lead in painstakingly connecting the burglars to the White House. A mysterious contact called "Deep Throat" helped them. The name, a fiction, came from a pornographic movie title. The real Deep Throat, a government informer, turned out to be a top FBI official.

Closely supervising its reporters was Washington *Post* Managing Editor Ben Bradlee. Keeping an eye on Bradlee was Publisher Kathryn Graham.

The New York *Times* worked to stay up with the *Post*. Both newspapers paid sizable staffs of attorneys to protect their First Amendment rights. The *Times* assigned Seymour Hersh as its primary story investigator. Of television networks, CBS led in coverage.

The climax came when a court ruled that tapes made of conversations among officials in Nixon's office had to be turned over to a judge. The court found evidence of White House coverup because eighteen and a half minutes of the tape had been erased deliberately.

The House of Representatives voted overwhelmingly to impeach the president. Nixon resigned in 1974. Forty government officials received indictments and jail time, mostly eighteen months to four years. They included John Mitchell, attorney general; James McCord, security director for the Committee to Re-elect the President; and White House staffers G. Gordon Liddy, John Erlichman, Howard Hunt, Charles Colsen, and H.R. Haldeman.

Investigative reporting connected with the Watergate story inspired career choices of many young people. In 1975, students in journalism-related majors at nearly two hundred American universities had nearly doubled in five years to more than 64,000. These figures were compiled by Professor Paul Peterson of Ohio State University for *Journalism Educator*, the quarterly journal I edited seven years.

Meanwhile, in a belated effort to cope with the Internet, some newspaper companies started their own Web sites. The first journalist I knew to supervise such an effort was Mary Helen Gillespie, a Northeastern graduate working for the Boston *Herald*.

In the mid-1990s, the *Herald* named her executive editor and vice president, supervising online reporters and "Web producers." In a letter to me, she referred to developing Web "content." "We used to call it news," she said with apologetic humor.

Some newspaper owners followed American manufacturers in off-shoring jobs to save money. The McClatchy Company hired a subcontractor in India in 2008 to edit copy and design pages for its Miami *Herald.* Pasadena Now, an online publication, announced successful outsourcing of local news coverage to part-time workers in India. From Mysore and other cities, English-speaking "reporters" telephoned Pasadena officials for news ranging from city hall debates to civic events -- even Rose Bowl preparations. New York *Times* columnist Maureen Dowd wondered how long it would be before "some guy in Bangalore was writing my column about President Obama."

Ink-on-paper began to slowly disappear from public and academic libraries. They digitized their collections and discarded bulky bound volumes of newspapers and scholarly journals.

A few observers predicted a "post-Gutenberg death of print." But such pessimism was not universal. Some said print may survive in what language historians call a "communicative shift." The first communicative shift, they said, occurred about five thousand years ago when spoken language successfully adapted to the introduction of writing or script. Script survived another shift -- invention of the printing press -- about five hundred years ago. Print later adjusted to radio and television.

Some optimists believe lost advertisers may return to print because they recognize it can emphasize their messages in a way television and the Internet cannot. Advertisers and other readers may prefer print media's reputation for investigative reporting. Readers may enjoy the feel of turning pages of a newspaper as they drink their morning coffee. They may appreciate priority among news stories presented by a sya editor's page makeup and headline placement.

Another hopeful harbinger of print's eventual adaptation to the digital age: The 2008 opening of the Newseum on Pennsylvania Avenue in Washington, D.C.

The half-billion-dollar Newseum leadership came from Gannett's Al Neuharth. Margaret Engel, Alicia Patterson Foundation director, selected many of the Newseum's artifacts to showcase American news media's proud past and to look optimistically to the future. Engel was a Missouri J-School graduate and former Des Moines and Washington, D. C., reporter.

Meanwhile, journalism schools -- and J-programs using the name "mass communication" -- made a valiant effort to add courses dealing with the Internet and Web.

"Convergence," a new term in journalism education, meant turning out graduates possessing more diverse skills than in the past. Journalism schools combined the study of digital-online applications in ways intended to prepare graduates to work in any medium -- print, Internet, TV, radio, and non-fiction book.

Northeastern University's Bill Kirtz reported a new twist in Poynter Online on

October 30, 2008. He pointed out that many traditional journalists see the non-fiction book as providing opportunity to escape newspaper cost and space cutting. They turn to non-fiction book writing as their "last best home," Kirtz said.

Memorabilia

Newspaper columns:

October 29, 2007
UNR: A University that Changes Lives

The University of Nevada changed my life in ways that you'll
never find listed in the literature the admissions office sends to
prospective students.

I won't be at Homecoming this weekend, but, as the 30th
anniversary of my graduation from UNR approaches in
December, I'm convinced that applying to the University of
Nevada was the most fortuitous decision I've ever made. . . .

Two people I met at UNR made all the difference in the world to
me. The first was the woman who would become my wife. . . .We
met in a journalism class, and she saw something in me that I
still can't comprehend. We celebrated 28 years of marriage a
week ago and have raised three terrific children. LaRue Gilleland
also saw something in me that I wasn't aware of. Gilleland was
the chairman of what was then the Journalism Department at
UNR. He would go on to serve as chairman of the same
department at Northeastern University and then as the first
director of its renamed School of Journalism. . . .

Just two classes short of a degree, I stopped at Gilleland's office
one day in the summer of 1977 to talk about an internship. "I've
been thinking," he said. "You're a pretty good writer. You
should try interning at a newspaper. It'll do you good even if you
never work for a paper."

Sure, I replied with little enthusiasm.

It seemed like a small thing at the time -- I would spend a couple
of months working at a small weekly in Gardnerville -- but the
result was tremendous. A guy whose goal for years had been

nothing more than to spin records on a radio station had found a profession -- some would say, a calling. (Gilleland also would recommend me for a job as a Congressional press secretary.)

So, 30 years later, I have to thank my wife and LaRue Gilleland.

Steve Falcone, Columnist
*Re*no Gazette-Journal

*   *   *

1994
Editor Praises J-School
Management Course

Future reporters are learning at Northeastern University what makes for success as future editors.

The course is listed as "Publication Production and Management." It means simply: how to manage a newsroom. It is required of all print journalism majors.

LaRue Gilleland, former director of the School of Journalism at Northeastern, instituted the course because he felt it would be useful someday in a reporter's career. Time and again, reporters are promoted to editorial (read it management) positions and suddenly find themselves immersed in a sea of human relations decisions rather than being involved in writing stories or editing copy.

These newly promoted editors were probably proficient in covering fires, investigating crimes or maybe interviewing celebrities. Now they find these skills are suddenly not demanded of them anymore. They are fish out of water. Gilleland's course helps prepare them to make personnel management decisions. . . .

Most editors today applaud Gilleland's foresight.

Bill Coulter, Editor and Publisher
Clinton (Massachusetts) Daily Item

Letters:

Thomas A. Parker
Exclusive Management
Madison, Tenn.
March 23, 1959

Dear Mr. Gilleland:
It was so nice of you to call yesterday. Enclosed is the clipping on the seagulls. I thought you would get a kick out of this story.

As I told you over the phone, I was not upset over this story as I do not know of any birds having ever bought any of Elvis' records. Surely we will not lose any record sales over this story. It is possible, however, that we may even sell some extra records of the same tune used to scare the seagulls, to a good many of the people who have been trying to get rid of seagulls.

We could retitle the tune SPECIAL SEAGULL REMOVER.

Sincerely,
The Colonel

Aug. 4, 1965

Dear Professor:
Now that I am finally graduated, I want to thank you for making journalism come alive and providing a true inspiration for me.

Too many teachers present their subjects in a boring, uninteresting manner, but this was never the case in any of your classes. I feel I obtained not only the knowledge available in the courses but a desire and thirst for greater knowledge.

Jim Maine, UNR Graduate

June 3, 1965

... You are a brilliant professor and a very talented, interesting lecturer. The University of Nevada is indeed fortunate to have you on its staff.

La Vaughn Gosting, UNR Graduate

Oct. 15, 1968
I just want to tell you that I think you are a great (for lack of a better word) teacher. Last semester I had a very poor teacher. He created no enthusiasm. Probably because he had none himself. I was so shocked at the first day in your class. The difference was utterly unbelievable. I wish that there were more teachers and people like you.

Lucy Munden, UNR Student

Niagara Falls (N.Y.) Gazette
April 14, 1969

Just a note of congratulations on your recent appointment as editor of **Journalism Educator,** *which I noticed in the April issue of Quill.*

According to my calendar, it has been almost nine years since I worked under your direction in the newsroom at the University of Missouri School of Journalism. That experience has proved helpful to me in many assignments. . . .

I was working late one night when I received a fatal accident report from the Highway Patrol. When I arrived at the scene the driver was dead. He was a young man of 26 who was killed after his car struck a curb, swerved off the road, and skidded 250 feet before striking a tree. My J-School education and your advice about probing for a story really paid off, LaRue.

Other papers and radio stations treated it as a straight fatal. I checked with a priest who lived at the university, near the scene of the accident. It was just a hunch, but it paid off. I found out the young man was a student and also that he had to be in his dormitory by 10:45 p.m. The accident happened at 10:40 p.m. The Gazette made a lot of mileage out of the story. I emphasized the student was apparently trying to beat the deadline.

I also found out by further checking that he had been a Korean War veteran with a remarkable record as a jet fighter pilot.

It made a good story, LaRue, and I was aware later that I had put into practice some valuable tips you gave me at J-School. Thanks again.

Donald E. Glynn, Reporter

The Sacramento (California) Bee
I really appreciate your lectures on stocks and bonds in Advanced Reporting now. I'm doing a series on women in the market and talking to brokers. You have to know what they're talking about.

Candy Pearce, Reporter

San Rafael, California
September 26, 1973

Since going to work for the San Rafael (Calif.) newspaper I have had quite a bit of good front page copy. . . .

They recalled three councilmen here in an unexpected overthrow.

Thought you might like to see that some of the law library experience that you pound into the heads of law of the press students comes in handy. I think some of the background you gave me helped out in this particular instance.

Bill Roberts
Marin Independent-Journal

February 6, 1975

Sitting in the cafeteria or the Library restaurant, you can hear the various comments about teachers and classes: "He's great no matter which class he has." "He is the first professor I've had who really cares about the students." "If you can't get into is class this year, wait until you can. It'll be worth it." "For some reason, it doesn't really matter which class you take if the teacher is good."

Based on these criteria and comments from friends and former students, I would like to nominate the following as the 'teacher of the year 1975-76': Professor LaRue W. Gilleland, journalism, and Professor Donald W. Winne, managerial sciences.

Marc Cardinalli, Student
(Letter to Sagebrush, UNR newspaper)

Harrah's Hotels/Casinos,
April 30, 1975

Mr. Gilleland is one of the most knowledgeable journalism teachers from whom I've had the pleasure of taking a course. The high standards he expects of his students and the interest he takes in preparing them for their respective careers will make him an asset to leadership at the university.

Jonnie M. Clasen, Publicist

Nevada Bell Public Relations
May 1, 1975

Congratulations on your new status as departmental chairman-elect. A better choice couldn't have been made.

Mike Cuno, Mike Hodges, Jim Riley

Nevada Legislature
May 1, 1975

Congratulations on your election as Chairman of the Department of Journalism. Since my days as a student there, I have felt you were the best professor in the department.

Steve Coulter, Assemblyman

Nevada State Journal
May 15, 1975

. . . I know from private conversations in the past with both students and professors that you are held in high esteem. Perhaps even more significant is the fact that the same can be said for the working Press in Nevada and environs.

Paul A. Leonard, Editor

KORK-TV, Las Vegas
May 15, 1975

Just a brief note of congratulations on your selection as the new chairman of the Department of Journalism. I know the department will continue to grow and maintain its excellent reputation under your leadership.

Regardless of whether or not we are ever able to work together, I hope you will feel free to call on me for any assistance I can ever give to the department.

Dave Cooper, News Anchor

May 28, 1975

I wanted you to know that I used your GOSS technique during the spring semester and found it very helpful. I had an interview at the Bureau of Land Management in which I ended up doing 90 per cent of the talking and my news source doing only 10 percent.

Later I saw instructor Joan Elder who reminded me of your GOSS technique. I went back and did the interview again. This time I did 10 percent talking and 90 per cent listening. I got a good story. You had taught me the GOSS technique in J-221 Newswriting, but I guess I didn't understand it them. Perhaps you can use this personal testimony from me with other students.

Desmond Powers, UNR student

Murray, Kraft and Rockey, Inc.
Anchorage, Alaska
June 24, 1975

Congratulations on being named chairman of the Department. Needless to say, I think it's great that your fellow instructors have recognized your talents and abilities. The University of Nevada should also be grateful.

I can well remember the many hours of classroom instruction I received from you, and I know that the entire school will benefit by your selection.

Bruce Pozzi, Director Public Relations

University of Missouri
Nov. 21, 1975

I propose an article for **Journalism Educator** *on the University of Missouri School of Journalism's new training program in state* *capital reporting that has proven to be both self-sustaining and an educational success.*

This fall, we set up a news bureau at the capital, Jefferson City. A young, full-time faculty member directed the reporting of six graduate students and a number of undergraduates. . . .The news bureau offered copy to Missouri newspapers. . . .

Incidentally, I have been using your GOSS formula in my news classes with excellent results.
Ernest Morgan, Journalism Professor

Congress of the United States 1976
I still feel that the Department did an outstanding job of preparing me for the "real" world. I will always be thankful for your instruction in the classroom and your guidance outside the classroom.

John E. Brodeur, Press Secretary
Office of Representative Jim Santini

El Informador
Guadalajara, Mexico
June 1, 1978

I have much to tell you about. The competition bought all the government's newspaper chain and left us as the only really independent newspaper in this Mexican state. We have decided to venture into the newest and most sophisticated means of producing a newspaper and have bought the Harris 2500 Series of computerized equipment to publish El Informador.

I believe we will be the most modern plant south of the border, and something to be proud of. We will not increase our circulation now, but we will produce a better paper. I think we will now have time to work a little more on quality of newspaper information.

That's why I, a former student of yours, asked you for the books; I need help to better the editorial page.

Jose L. Alvarez del Castillo, Editor and Publisher

Rhinebeck, New York
October 10, 1978

I never could have been a reporter had it not been for you. You gave me a push when I needed it, and you made me believe in me. That's the best thing anybody can do for another person. Thank you! Thank you!

Mimi McAndrew

Klamath Falls (Oregon) Herald & News
December 7, 1978

For some reason I find myself constantly returning to the local law library here to pour over the many volumes in an effort to see what's legal on a variety of fronts.

I take this opportunity to join the many others who have voiced appreciation over the years for the library exposure the press law class offered. I would not have the foggiest idea of what I was doing without it.

Martin Bibb, Reporter

Saint Bonaventure University, New York
May 2, 1979

Dear Search Committee:
Professor LaRue W. Gilleland, chairman of the Department of Journalism at the University of Nevada, has asked me to address you on his behalf as a candidate for the position of chairman at

Northeastern University. I am honored to do so.

I have known Professor Gilleland for more than ten years. My impressions concern his ability as a scholar and as administrator. You are probably aware of his development of the GOSS interviewing technique that has been well received in both the academic and professional fields.

Indeed he has an enviable professional background all of us prize so much as faculty members in journalism education.

His skills came to the fore in his editing of Journalism Educator, *before his tenure a pitiful publication that he developed into perhaps the most well-read among journalism scholars, including some in the theoretical areas.*

I am not in a position to evaluate first hand Professor Gilleland's record at Nevada, but all reports I have had, including at least one from a former administrator, indicate he has gained the respect of many others in journalism education for his work in Reno. He is known throughout the country.

LaRue Gilleland is the kind of person Northeastern would be pleased to have as its leading journalism administrator. I assure you I would say the same in regard to my own institution.

Russell J. Jandoli, Head
Mass Communication

Gardnerville, Nevada
May 10, 1979

To: Journalism Search Committee
Northeastern University, Boston

Mr. Gilleland has taught at UNR for 16 years, and served as department chairman. I knew him as one of his students 10 years ago. He had the respect of faculty and students alike in those days. Nothing has happened to diminish that respect. He has grown, and as chairman of the department has added new luster to Nevada's journalism school.

He was my favorite instructor in college, and there are scores of graduates who feel the same way about him. They respect him as a teacher and as a man. He has high integrity. He is a thorough professional.

I am general manager of a publishing company that has earned high marks for editorial excellence with its newspapers. I can tell you that those of my former classmates who have achieved some professional standing since graduation remember LaRue Gilleland with fondness and deep respect.
Nevada's loss will be your gain.

Tom Wixon, General Manager
Carson Valley Publishing Co.

May 15, 1979

In my position as associate dean, Professor Gilleland and I worked together relative to the College Courses and Curricula Committee which he so ably chaired for five years. Inasmuch as this committee functions as the screening group for all courses and curricula changes, the recommendations of this committee are a significant function in the College of Arts and Science.

Underlying all of Professor Gilleland's characteristics as a successful journalist and department chairman is the fact that he is a very fine human being in the best sense of the word. LaRue, along with his lovely wife, Betsy, would be an asset to any journalism department.

Edgar F. Kleiner, Associate Dean
Arts and Science

Reno, Nevada
May 30, 1979

LaRue Gilleland has the leadership qualities we dream of finding, but seldom do.

He is a great teacher and outstanding advocate of what is best for his students and his staff.

He is oriented to change, and is expert at managing change before it manages him.

He has a warm and agreeable leadership style, uses a participative approach and can make difficult decisions on a timely basis.

He not only is a great journalism educator, but he's going to be even greater.

He and his wife, Betsy, are comfortable in any social setting and his wife is a great asset to him in all ways.

For 16 years I have seen him in many settings. He has been a champion in each instance. He gets from me the highest marks as educator and friend and constructive critic.

Rollan Melton, Board of Directors
Gannett Company

Napa Valley College, Calif.
June 3, 1979

I've been reading about you in **Editor & Publisher** *and wanted to send you a note to say congratulations! I will always appreciate my education at the University of Nevada. Since I left, I was co-owner and publisher of a small weekly in northern California and, after moving back to Napa, went into public relations.*

Thank you for your role in my education.

Betty Malmgren, Community Relations Officer

June 9, 1981

To: Raymond Gross, President
New England Press Association
This letter will help introduce a man who has been a very good friend of Nevada journalism for many years and who soon will be moving into your area.

He is LaRue Gilleland, who leaves the University of Nevada, Reno the end of this month to become chairman of the J-Department at Northeastern University.

LaRue has been a prominent figure in Nevada journalism for 17 years. We are going to miss him very much as he has been of great service to our Association, helping us with a variety of projects over the years, ranging from professionally-run seminars to assistance with our Better Newspaper Contest, a yearly event where entrants are judged in 27 different categories of newspaper work.

LaRue was singled out for a high honor during our April 1981 annual convention when he was presented with a plaque commending him for his many contributions and dedication to the Nevada State Press Association.

It's an old cliché, but our loss certainly will be your gain. We hope you will make him feel welcome in your part of the country and will call upon him should the occasion arise. He is a willing worker, very cooperative, extremely congenial and, we feel sure you'll like him as we have.

Pete Kelley, Secretary/Manager
Nevada State Press Association

Yerington, Nevada
October 31, 1980

I read with great interest and disappointment the announcement concerning your leaving the University of Nevada for Northeastern University in Boston.

Nevada will miss you, and we will surely miss you. It is hardly necessary to tell you that I always felt you were the best professor in the J-Department during my years there and I know many other students who felt the same way. I was very glad to see you appointed chairman of the department in 1975 and I am sure the department has continued to grow and improve under your leadership.

Jim Sanford, Editor
Mason Valley News

Medford, Massachusetts
June 22, 1988

You really helped me last week. I can't thank you enough for taking time to get my career moving on the right track. My new résumé is circulating throughout Massachusetts, and it would make you proud. Again, a million thanks to a man who made the job-hunting process fun again, again, and again!

Cecilia "Dea" Lahiff, N.U. student

Christian Science Monitor
May 19, 1991

You are certainly well thought of both at the university and within the journalism profession. You have brought the journalism program at Northeastern to a high level. It is something in which all of us who studied at NU can take pride. I know the understanding and support of your dear wife has contributed, in no small way, to this accomplishment.

George Merry, Columnist

Needham, Massachusetts
October 30, 1991

I don't know if anyone ever tells you this, but I think you're doing a great job. I really enjoy being here. I'm pleased with all my classes. It's good to feel you're getting your money's worth. I don't know if they'll be able to replace you.

Kevin Philip Lavelle, N.U. student

The News
Southbridge, Massachusetts
Dec. 10, 1991

I would like you to know how much one small-town editor appreciates the leadership role you have played in the region's journalism community. At a time when most schools in New England haven't even given lip service to diversity, you have focused on opportunities in journalism education and in journalism for people of color.

Your participation on the NEPA board for a decade has put you on the frontline of the industry's ethical and economic issues. You've been a champion of press freedom. I have known few journalism educators so willing to tackle the tough issues journalism faces.

Loren Ghiglione, Publisher

Dec. 19, 1991

Somehow I missed the article in the NEPA Bulletin about your planned retirement.

Nevertheless, I wanted to underscore the kind words from Loren Ghiglione. You should be proud of the success of the journalism program under your leadership. There's quite a difference between what you have now and what Northeastern had when I was a student there.

I am sure we will be seeing each other between now and June, but I didn't want to let the year run out without expressing my best wishes and congratulations.

John S. Driscoll, Editor
The Boston *Globe*

Minneapolis, Minn.
December 31, 1991

. . . I salute you on a career that has reached from coast to coast. May you have many happy years in retirement.

Paul Swensson, American Press Institute

The Heart Center
Manchester-Nashua, New Hampshire
April 1, 1992

As a former student and advisee of yours, I can safely say that you had a great influence on my studies, providing invaluable advice and insight during my years at Northeastern. Your know-how in the classroom helped me to learn a lot about the field and grow as a scholar and professional.

The combination of top-notch classroom training along with the practical benefits garnered from the Co-op program, really have helped further my professional growth.

Christopher R. Dugan, Marketing/Public Relations Director

May 22, 1992

You have done a remarkable job moving the Northeastern University journalism program ahead. You deserve much credit for molding the program into one of the finest schools of journalism in the country. In doing so, you have helped enhance the reputation of all of us older grads as well.

You can look back with pride on a solid record of accomplishment. It has been my privilege to have worked with you over the years. Your leadership will be missed by all of us connected with the university.

Paul G. Keough, Deputy Regional Administrator
United States Environmental Protection Agency

Santa Rosa, California
January 3, 1992

I read about your upcoming retirement in **Editor & Publisher,** *and I have to admit I did so with very mixed feelings. On one hand, I'm delighted that you will be able to enjoy a well-deserved retirement. However, I think the field of journalism is losing one of its very best educators.*

It seems like only yesterday when it was the Fall of 1963 at the University of Nevada. You were a brand new professor and I was taking my first journalism class. You really made it interesting and exciting and convinced me this is what I wanted to do. A couple of years later, you gave me the only "D" I ever received in college. But I have to admit that it spurred me on to better achievement.

I suppose we have both put on a few miles since then, but I always remember those days and how much I learned from you. I'd sure like to get together for a visit one of these days.

Michael J. Parman, Publisher
The Press-Democrat

West Warwick, Rhode Island
June 8, 1992

Just thought I'd drop a line to congratulate you on your retirement and thank you for all the battles you fought on behalf of Northeastern University's journalism students. You won wars which not only benefit Northeastern's crop of reporters and editors, but which benefit the entire American press circuit.

Thank you again for your dedication to NU's Journalism School during the past decade and to our profession during the past 40 years. Northeastern is a better university for having known you.

Karen A. Bordelau, Managing Editor
Kent County *Daily Times* **(Class of 1982)**
Boston Phoenix

September 10, 1992

I wanted to thank you for your help and encouragement, and for your effort to get me the Paul Hirschon scholarship. I also wanted to say this is a fantastic program.

Although I had six years with newspapers before starting graduate work, I still learned so much here that I did not know before, such as in law and ethics.

So many working for newspapers don't have this knowledge.

It's a great program you built, and you put together an excellent staff. Among other things, they all have a good sense of humor, which is a credit to you. My experience here has been so important to me. I will always be a booster of this program.

Tim Sandler, N. U. Alumnus

Northeastern University
June 18, 1992

As your impending retirement date approaches, I want to share with you our deep appreciation for all your skill, for all your energy, and for all of your hard work in making our School of Journalism what it is today -- a very visible and excellent center of journalism education within higher education.

You have transformed a very small department into a major school of journalism. You will leave behind a tremendous legacy of accomplishment and achievement of which you must be justifiably proud. But your legacy goes far beyond your accomplishments for the J-School.

You have brought quiet reason and thoughtful contribution to many a discussion in the Council of Chairs and elsewhere, for which those of us who have been privileged to work with you are truly appreciative.

Robert Lowndes, Dean of College of Arts and Science

December 11, 1992

Probably your last act as director of the School of Journalism was influencing me to come here. When I stopped by your office in late June, I was considering three schools -- Northeastern, Boston

University, and Syracuse.

It was the time you took with me, and the interest you showed, that convinced me to enroll at Northeastern, and I'm very pleased that I did. You also pointed out that Boston is an important media center.

I just got out of an editing final, and my head is swimming. Your program has been even more challenging that I expected.

Peter Lieb, N. U. student

*   *   *

Northeastern magazine, describing my 1981 arrival at the university, carried this paragraph in 1993:

In one of Gilleland's first directives at N.U, he had the vending machines removed from the department's lobby. It was a small step, but to him an important one.

"It gave the wrong atmosphere to prospective students, parents, and visiting media," he says. "That was not a proper entry way." Gilleland never lost his reporter's instincts, though he has spent the last thirty years in higher education. His eye for detail -- and journalist's vision of the bigger picture -- have served him well as an administrator.

A tongue-in-cheek item about my departure, written by journalism faculty members who had served under my directorship, also appeared in *Northeastern* magazine:

Colleagues of LaRue Gilleland couldn't resist lampooning the retirement of the much-loved J-School director last year.

Under a scathing headline, the mild-mannered Gilleland

farcically fires these parting salvos: "I've spent the last thirty years listening to stories about . . . critically ill siblings and stolen backpacks from students who couldn't get term papers in on time. Then I had to deal with all those whiny faculty members. God, I've never met a more spoiled, self-centered, culturally elite bunch of insignificant blowhards in my time."

From N. U. Admissions Office literature (2005):

I first came to Northeastern unannounced on a campus tour with my mom. I stopped in the School of Journalism, and the director at the time, LaRue Gilleland, was willing to meet with me. That personal interest is why I chose to attend Northeastern.

Rhondella Richardson, Weekend Anchor
WCVB-TV, Boston (N. U. Class of 1990)

From books:

Sonny's Story: a Journalist's Memoir
by Rollan Melton
Board of Directors, Gannett Company

. . . I want here to tell the potential executives who escaped before I could sign them up that I regret not enlisting them. The most striking example is LaRue Gilleland, a big-league talent. It hurt bad that I couldn't land him. (p. 210).

News Clippings:

THE WEATHER

(Weather Bureau forecast,
8:30 p. m.)

Honolulu and Vicinity: Continued
fair with moderate trades Wednesday and Thursday.

24 hour data (Airport): Temperatures,
Max. 84, Min. 73; Rainfall, trace.
(Details, Page 7.)

The Ho

To Reach All Departments
Telephone 52977

Oct. 8, 1952   96TH Y

Freed of

Inventor to Show 'Intoximeter' Here

By LA RUE GILLELAND

The "intoximeter," the result of a facetious suggestion and an instrument which has saved auto accident victims suffering from concussion, shock, and overdose of carbon monoxide from being jailed for intoxication, will be demonstrated by its inventor at 7:30 tonight in the police station classroom.

Dr. Glenn C. Forrester, 57, Niagara Falls, N. Y. chemist who invented the instrument, will give a lecture and demonstration to which the public is urged to attend. The city prosecutor, doctors of the city and county emergency hospital, lawyers, reserve police officers, and the press also have been invited.

* * *

DR. FORRESTER explained in an interview yesterday afternoon that the intoximeter idea had something of a humorous beginning. A friend made a tongue-in-cheek suggestion that the chemist make pellets to absorb liquor odors on the breath of a person who came home from an all-night binge.

"I did just that and put them to work experimentally with the Buffalo, N. Y., police department," he said.

However, it soon became apparent more than pellets were needed, he said. Innocent persons suspected of driving while intoxicated were held unduly long while the pellets were sent to a chemist for analysis.

* * *

"OVER 50 physiological conditions such as shock and insulin deficiency give rise to many superficial symptoms of drunkenness, and the need for an on-the-spot test became urgent," Dr. Forrester said.

He pointed out that eight witnesses of an auto accident in a major West Coast city signed statements that in their opinion the driver of an involved car was drunk. It was later proved the driver was suffering from brain concussion.

"My next step was to combine what I had already developed and an on-the-spot test into the intoximeter," he said.

The intoximeter, which costs $4, is a sealed cylinder about the size of a large flashlight. It contains, among other things, a balloon assembly, three glass tubes, and containers for chemical absorbents of carbon dioxide and alcohol.

* * *

"ANY OFFICER can be trained to use the instrument," Dr. Forrester asserted. "It can give an immediate answer so a man is not held unnecessarily, and yet leaves the real job of deciding on alcoholic influence in the hands of a competent chemist."

Dr. and Mrs. Forrester arrived in Honolulu Thursday night by Pan American Airlines.

INTOXIMETER DEMONSTRATED — Dr. Glenn C. Forrester, New York inventor of the intoximeter, a means of determining a suspected drunk driver's intoxication or sobriety, demonstrates the instrument in his Halekulani hotel room. Blowing into a purple colored chemical in a tube, he explains that if the fluid changes color within 40 seconds during a routine test, some auto driver has imbibed too much. (Advertiser photo.)

Australian LifeSaving Team Here

Australia's seven-man life saving team, believed the world's greatest, was taken on a whirlwind police-escorted tour of the city yesterday afternoon after their BCPA Airlines plane landed in Honolulu from Sydney.

The Australians will teach islanders their surf rescue methods and try to promote volunteer beach patrols in Hawaii patterned after Australia's famous system.

AFTER A GREETING at the airport by scores of onlookers a caravan of convertibles containing city officials and Lions Club members sped the all-star team to the Hula Bowl where they paraded at the end of the football game.

They were guests of the Aloha Week King and Queen, their colorful attendants, and chairman Ralph I. Price last night at the annual Aloha Week Hawaii inauguration dinner at Niumalu, Nuuanu Valley.

YOUNGEST MEMBER of the team is John Bloomfield, a 19-year old Sydney university student from New South Wales. The six-foot two-inch swimmer was also a ski champion in Australia in 1950 and 1951.

Oldest man on the team is Arthur Parkyn, 41, a Queensland school teacher. Parkyn, a graduate of Queensland University, is an expert boatsman.

Harry Clarke, 28, is an advertising executive with the Newcastle Morning Herald. He won six life saving championships in Australia's Northern District and is captain of the visiting team.

BRIAN WHITING, a 21-year old oil company employe, six-feet three-inches, has placed in ski events. Whiting is a consecutive winner in surf board races.

Alec Norton, of Tasmania, is the business manager for a transport company. Married and the father of two children, he is six-feet two-inches.

A 25-year old policeman, Thomas Jennings, has long been a member of championship teams from South Australia. Last season he was a judge at one of Australia's popular surf life saving carnivals.

DONALD MORRISON of Western Australia, the shortest man
(Continued on Page 6, Col. 2)

AUSTRALIA'S SURF LIFE SAVERS ARRIVE—Pictured shortly after they arrived at Honolulu airport yesterday from Sydney, are the seven members of Australia's surf life saving team and some members of the greeting committee. Standing left to right: William Walkley, Sydney oil man who financed the trip to Hawaii; Judge Adrian Curlewis, president of the Surf Life Saving Association of Australia; Mrs. William Walkley; Brian Whiting, team member; Mrs. Elsie Ross Lane, executive secretary of Aloha Week; John Bloomfield, team member; Donald Lucas, team manager; and Ralph I. Price, chairman of the Waikiki Lions reception committee. Kneeling left to right: Team members Harry Clarke, captain, Arthur Parkyn, Don Morrison, Alec Norton, and Thomas Jennings. (Advertiser photo.)

CONTINUED From Page 1

Australian Life Saving Team Here

on the team, has won the Australian surf belt championship three times in five years. The surf belt job is one of the most difficult on the team. Morrison is 5 feet 10 inches.

The manager and instructor of the team is Donald C. Lucas. An outstanding surfer himself, he is a top consulting engineer for an Australian company.

On board the plane which landed yesterday was William Walkley, president of Ampol Petroleum, Ltd., of Sydney, the man who put up $8,000 to pay the team's traveling expenses.

MR. WALKLEY offered to send the team to Hawaii last July after he saw a little girl drown at Waikiki beach.

The president of the Surf Life Saving Association of Australia, Judge Adrian Curlewis, was on hand to welcome the team at the airport. He arrived in Honolulu Wednesday.

At 10 a.m. this morning, the team will be picked up at the Central Y.M.C.A., where they will stay for the next three weeks, to make an island tour, stopping at various spots to be greeted Lions clubs.

After appearance on station KGU at 7 a.m. Monday, they will start to work teaching islanders Australia's life saving technics at the Waikiki Natatorium.

March 19, '53

Girl's Tragedy Spurs Drive Against Dope

By LARUE GILLELAND

After listening to a story about an unloved little island girl who became a drug addict, We the Women yesterday voted unanimously to endorse a bill before the legislature which would tighten up the territory's narcotic laws.

The story about the teen-age child was told by Dr. Teru Togasaki, Honolulu physician, at a noon meeting of the club at the YWCA. Without identifying the girl, she cited the case as an example of what can happen when laws to stop narcotic traffic are too easy.

The little girl is grown now. She's 23. During the few years she has spent time jail, the territorial mental pital, a girls' detention ho and just walking the street

When she was only 17 she Dr. Togasaki, "My life is en I have nothing to live f Six years later she feels same way.

* * *

SHE IS NOT an unusual c The federal government mated there are 300 to 500 addicts in the territory. doesn't include users of juana. They are in a clas themselves.

Why did the pretty, haired girl grow up the way she did? Dr. Togasaki explained it something like this: A narcotics salesman took advantage of her feeling of being unl by her parents. He led her to

believe there was one way she could become the most popular girl in the world—at least in her mind—and sold her some dope to prove it.

* * *

HY IS A DOPE peddler un d to do this sort of thing Honolulu? Frank Gibson

CONTINUED From Page 1

Tragedy Spurs Drive on Dope

deputy attorney general, answered that one for We the Women. "The risks involved aren't great enough," he said.

Selling narcotics to an innocent child in Honolulu carries no heavier penalty than violating a traffic law, Mr. Gibson said. They are both defined as "misdemeanors" in Hawaii.

Dope peddlers from the West Coast are actually encouraged to come to Hawaii because a person convicted of selling dope here only spends about three to six months in jail, Mr. Gibson pointed out.

* * *

WE'VE GOT TO make the penalties so heavy that selling narcotics here won't be worth the risk," Mr. Gibson said.

Mr. Gibson pointed out that persons can't be dope addicts unless they can acquire dope. He aid the purpose of the new bill was to help shut of the supply at its source by making peddlers think twice before they take a chance on selling their product.

Where the existing law lists one year in prison as a maximum penalty for selling narcotics, the proposed legislation increases the penalty to 10 years at hard labor for the first offense and 20 years for the second.

AMONG OTHER things, the proposed bill would include several more narcotics under the definition of "habit-forming drugs" and require doctors to report addiction cases to the department of health.

239

March 29, '53

$4 Million in Highway Projects Now Underway

By La RUE GILLELAND

When men began work early this month on a nearly three mile stretch of the Moanalua Rd., ewa of Honolulu, the number of highway projects under way on Oahu reached seven. An eighth project, Waipahu Circle on Kamehameha highway, is temporarily at a standstill due to a steel shortage.

The cost of all this is more than $4,255,000, and most of the projects are due to be completed this fall.

One of the most expensive single contracts is one of the most recent, Moanalua Rd., which will cost $1,104,021. The contractor is James W. Glover, Ltd., who went to work on the road March 2.

WHEN THE JOB is completed, Moanalua Rd. will be a four-lane divided highway extending two and three-fourths miles from a point near the entrance road to Tripler hospital to Aiea naval hospital road.

However, this project is one of two that will not be finished this fall. Contractor Glover will need about a year and a half to finish the job.

The most expensive of all the island highway jobs is the first unit of the mauka arterial. It will cost $1,510,982. The first unit of the public works department giant lies between Isenberg St. and the Old Waialae Rd. The contract calls for overpasses for the arterial at University Ave. and Kalo lane. Oct. 13 is the completion date Contractor J. M. Tanaka is shooting at.

* * *

THE FIRST unit of the new Nuuanu Pali highway will amount to $540,086. It will extend about one and a third miles from the Castle ranch office at the Kalanianaole-Kamehameha intersection to the top of the hairpin turn.

Since this job started there have been 130 days that were "unworkable." Due to weather and "extras," necessary items that showed up after the contract was signed, the date this unit of the highway is completed is expected to be postponed to sometime this fall. Moses Akiona is the contractor.

A Waipahu Circle project, one of five of its kind, is designed to replace the old circular track at this important intersection with Kamehameha highway with a traffic pattern of new modern design.

The project, totaling $163,947, was halted Feb. 9 when steel could not be obtained for two bridges. The job is 40 per cent finished. J. W. Glover is the contractor.

* * *

WAIAWA CUTOFF is another of the Waipahu Circle projects. The other three have been completed. Unless Waiawa cutoff gets into trouble like its companion project, or runs into a lot of unworkable days, it will be completed in October. Oahu Construction Co. is the contractor.

Kamehameha highway from Kaneohe Bay drive to Kaneohe town is being widened from two to four lanes. The highway distance between these two points is close to seven miles. The contract calls for a new bridge and a change in the channel of a stream bed so the stream will pass under the bridge at its new location.

The cost for this maneuver, plus the highway, will be $278,097. Inter-Island Contracting Co. expects to do the job by September or October.

* * *

TWO OTHER units of the mauka arterial are also under way. Contractor J. M. Tanaka expects to complete the second unit between Alexander and Isenberg Sts. by Nov. 2. Hawaiian Dredging Co. is building bridge over the Palolo-Manoa stream on old Waialae Rd. The bridge will become part of a ramp serving as a one-way approach onto westbound lanes of the new six-lane mauka arterial. Scheduled completion date is July 7.

240

Former Athlete, Orator New TH Treasury Head

By LaRUE GILLELAND

The Territory's new 47-year-old treasurer sat down at his desk last week, casually dipped his pen in an inkwell, and signed his name, Kam Tai Lee, to a $1,000,000 check.

Then Mr. Lee looked up, thought a moment and said, "After 16 years in the banking business, it's the biggest check I've signed."

It was his third busy week as head of Hawaii's treasury. As treasurer he now has custody of more than $42,000,000 and his office employs about 50 persons in its four bureaus. He resigned as vice president of the Liberty Bank to take the job.

* * *

BORN OF CHINESE parents in Waikane, Oahu, Mr. Lee was educated in the islands and attended the University of Hawaii. He was a popular man on the campus in the 1920s. About the only university organization he failed to join was the Association of Women Students. He missed that one, as he put it "because I couldn't qualify."

Mr. Lee also was a university track star and orator. He ran the 220-yard low hurdles and the 100-yard dash. His time for the 100-yard was 10.2 seconds. Soon after he became a freshman he entered an oratory contest against upperclassmen and came out with first prize, $100 cash.

"That money kept me in the university for nearly six months," he said.

* * *

HE LATER edited the year book and the campus paper, Ka Leo O Hawaii. After graduating in 1929 with an A.B. degree and a major in political science, he became a successful Honolulu business man.

In 1937 he entered the whirlwind of Republican politics. That year he was elected to the house of representatives and stayed there until 1943.

While a representative he was sponsor of the territory's first unemployment compensation measure, today a $23,000,000 fund. He also introduced the territorial scholarship measure which is still in effect. The act permits six students in the Territory to attend the University of Hawaii each year without paying tuition.

Mr. Lee's Republican political philosophy is clear-cut. "Gov-

ernment should be run as cheaply as possible, yet efficiently," he said.

He and Mrs. Lee have four children. When he accepted the position as treasurer, he automatically acquired such weighty titles as Hawaii's fire marshal, commissioner of securities, ex-officio insurance commissioner, and bank examiner.

* * *

THIS MEANS, among other things, that he sends out deputies and takes charge of fire investigations when arson is suspected, licenses stock brokers, makes sure no one sells bogus securities, sees that no loan firm chisels anyone with high rates, certifies new corporations to do business in the territory, and acts as head salesman of territorial bonds.

In his spare time Mr. Lee likes to relax with bowling and photography. At home in the evening he is usually found in his darkroom. He owns seven cameras.

* * *

HIS BOWLING average has been about 160. Last Sunday afternoon he was running up a good score at Kapiolani Bowl when he was interrupted by a phone call. The new treasurer was needed at a legislative hearing.

MILLION DOLLAR CHECK—Kam Tai Lee, who became treasurer of the territory on March 31, signs a $1,000,000 check as part of his new duties. Mr. Lee succeeded Sakae Takahashi. The check will transfer tax money to the territory's general fund. (Advertiser photo.)

241

Politics Charged As Sherretz Gets Post

After electing Ransom D. Sherretz executive secretary of the territorial employes retirement system, the board of trustees of the system wound up a meeting with a few hot words yesterday afternoon when it was asserted that Governor King previously had called four of the board's seven members into his office and asked them to cast their votes for Mr. Sherretz.

THE MEETING broke up with William P. Meyer, a candidate for the job, saying he was "astonished" that political considerations were involved in a civil service appointment. Mrs. Helen G. Murphy, a Republican board member indicated the governor's action had caused her to turn "Democrat." Board member Fred Ohrt walked out after asserting, "I'm through being lectured by Mr. Meyer."

It all came about this way: Early in the meeting at the Keelikalani building the board nominated two men for the job out of a list of five persons who had passed civil service examinations with high scores.

THE NOMINEES were Mr. Meyer, investment analyst for the retirement system's $67,000,000 fund for the past nine years, and Mr. Sherretz, former director of personnel and classification for the city and county civil service commission. Mr. Meyer has long had his eye on the job, which would have been a promotion for him and $100 a month more pay.

For many minutes the board discussed the pros and cons of each man's qualifications. Then Mrs. Murphy, a new member of the board from Maui, said she had heard a report that Governor King had contacted four board members and told them to see that Mr. Sherretz became executive secretary.

MRS. MURPHY, an elementary school principal representing the Hawaii Education Assn. on the board, scanned the faces around the table and asked, "Is it true?"

Board member Theodore F. Trent answered, "I'm sure he wouldn't call me into his office, I'm a Democrat." Most of the others laughed at that and assured Mrs. Murphy that the report was groundless.

Someone wanted to know where she had heard the rumor in the first place. She looked across the room at James R. McDonough, HEA's executive secretary, and said Mr. McDonough told her.

The HEA earlier had written the board that it endorsed Mr. Meyer. Mr. McDonough told the board members he felt his source of the report was "reliable."

A VOTE WAS CALLED for on the two nominees by Chairman Henry A. Nye. When the ballots were counted, Mr. Sherretz had won—four votes to three.

As the board was adjourning, Mr. Meyer, who had stepped out of the meeting when nominations came up, returned and said he had a statement to make. He pulled a notebook out of his pocket and read:

"First I want to say that the result of this meeting is not a surprise to me since I spoke to the governor this morning and learned from him that he had asked four trustees to support Mr. Sherretz. He explained also that there were political considerations in this appointment, that I had not been promised the job of executive, and that he felt he had to support Mr. Sherretz."

MRS. MURPHY put her hand to her forehead while Mr. Meyer continued: "While I was astonished that there were political considerations in any appointment to a civil service classified position, I did thank the governor for his candor."

Mrs. Murphy stood up and said, "Gentlemen, I am keenly disappointed." She reminded the board members that she had asked them if the rumor was true and that they had led her to believe it was not.

"I've been a Republican for a long time," she declared, "but as of now I'm a Democrat."

Mr. Trent extended his hand and said, "May I be the first to welcome you to the Democratic party."

CHAIRMAN NYE told Mr. Meyer that his job as investment analyst would not be affected by the board's selection of Mr. Sherretz as executive secretary. Mr. Meyer would continue in the same job he has held for the past nine years.

$183,800 DOPE SEIZURE HERE

The Honolulu Advertiser

Hawaii's Territorial Newspaper

LATE NEWS FINAL

ON OAHU 5¢   OTHER ISLANDS 10¢

97TH YEAR, NO. 33,544.—HONOLULU, HAWAII, U.S.A., SATURDAY, JULY 25, 1953.   18 PAGES

The Weather
(Weather Bureau forecast, 9:20 p.m.)
Honolulu and vicinity: Generally fair, but with partly cloudy periods, occasional showers during night. Moderate to fresh gusty trades.
24 hour data (Airport) Temperatures, max. 82, min. 73, rain, trace. (Details, Page 3)

Honolulan
Is Arrested
By Customs
Narcotics Found In
False Bottoms Of

Honolulan Is Arrested By Customs

Narcotics Found In False Bottoms Of Luggage on Return From Hong Kong

Customs inspectors seized more than $180,000 worth of opium and heroin found hidden in secret compartments of luggage belonging to Sau Hong Lee, 2238 Pacific Heights, shortly after he stepped off a plane at Honolulu airport yesterday afternoon from Hong Kong.

Lee, listed in the city directory as a general contractor and builder, was arrested at 4:30 p.m. He was taken to the Honolulu police station last night for questioning and will appear before a U. S. commissioner today.

WARDE C. HIBERLY, acting collector of customs, said the narcotics was concealed in false bottoms of five leather traveling bags. He estimated the bags contained 25 pounds of smoking opium, worth $175,000, and two ounces of heroin, valued at $8,800.

Lee, 43, is married and the father of four children. He has been suspected by Honolulu police as having an "interest" in narcotics. Mr. Hiberly said police had warned the customs office to give careful attention to the contractor when he returned from his Hong Kong trip.

WHILE INSPECTING Lee's luggage, Customs Agent Noah H. Coon became suspicious when he noticed the bags weighed more than they should for the amount of clothing and other items inside. He and Lloyd B. Guy, another agent, thrust a knife into the bottom of the one bag and found that it had a false bottom.

When they withdrew the knife there was opium on the blade.

LEE, KNOWN to police as "Small Snake," has a gambling record that reaches back to 1932. Since that time he has been arrested 24 times on gambling charges, and has been convicted 12 times.

The last conviction came in 1947 when he was fined $100. Bail forfeitures and acquittals account for the disposition on the other 12 arrests.

Lee also testified as a prosecution witness during the 1947 police bribery trials.

Persian In Tree Is Starving Out Shoemaker Clan

By LaRUE GILLELAND

Consider the plight of Mr. and Mrs. Finas Shoemaker of 3715 Rockwood:

Their starving Persian cat has been perched high up in a tree for a week.

Their neighbors are hopping mad because the cat cries at night and the Humane Society and the Fire Department have failed to do anything about getting it down.

Their four daughters are upset and will not eat because they feel sorry for their hungry pet.

Mrs. Shoemaker said the neighbors held a back yard conference yesterday and decided to make a protest to Henry Loeb, city commissioner-elect.

It all started last Saturday when the cat, which seldom had been out of the house before, apparently was chased up the tree by another cat, and then refused to come down.

Neither Mr. Shoemaker nor his neighbors has a ladder long enough to reach the animal, which is clinging to a limb more than 25 feet above the ground.

Men from the Humane Society took a look at the cat yesterday but told the Shoemakers to telephone the Fire Department because the Humane Society doesn't own the equipment needed for such a job.

"But when we called the Fire Department we were told the department wouldn't come out just to get a cat out of a tree," Mrs. Shoemaker said.

"We don't know who else to call. I guess the poor thing will just stay up there and starve. What can you do? There's nobody in Memphis to get it down!"

Meanwhile, the four children—Mildred, 13, Billie, 9, Linda Sue, 5, and Barbara, 4,—are on a hunger strike.

Producer Here To Boost Movie, 'Animal World'

(Picture on Page 30)

By LARUE GILLELAND

Irwin Allen, Warner Bros. young Oscar-winning producer who is enthusiastic about his work and sensitive of his receding hairline, checked in at the Gayoso yesterday to beat the tambourines for his unusual technicolor epic, "The Animal World."

The picture tells a life-and-death story of animal life—from its first appearance two billion years ago in primeval seas to the present—in 81 minutes.

It opens Wednesday at Warner Theater. There are no human actors.

"This is one of our leading players," said Mr. Allen as he held up a model of Tyrannosaurus Rex, a giant lizard believed to be the most destructive creature that ever walked on earth.

"A mechanical reproduction of the model, which will appear 30 feet high on the screen, will breathe, fight, bleed and eat. Our researchers have even made the texture of his skin look realistic."

Three thousand technicians worked three years to make the other dinosaurs — Brontosaurus, Stegosaurus and Triceratops—accurate in appearance. Scientists, naturalists and photographers filmed scenes of present-day animals in 27 countries, he said. Three million feet of film were exposed.

The 39-year-old bachelor said the same photographic methods and technical care were used in this picture as in "The Sea Around Us," for which he won an Academy Award.

"Oh, I'll admit the animal picture was planned to get families away from their television sets and to make money at the box office. But there is another satisfaction. The film teaches something—teaches the story of life."

'I Just Went Crazy,' Says Woman Who Shot Husband

(Pictures on Page Two)

By LARUE GILLELAND

A slim, 25-year-old woman admitted she shot her jealous husband to death yesterday morning as he lay half-clothed on a bed reading a magazine at 226 South Cleveland.

John David Yarbrough, an unemployed carnival worker, died instantly at 7, a.m. with a 38-caliber bullet wound in the right side of his stomach. He was 34.

His wife, Mrs. Fay Treadway Yarbrough, mother of three of his four children, will be arraigned at 9 this morning in City Court on a charge of murder, according to Homicide Capt. W. W. Wilkinson.

The shooting occurred in the living room of the apartment of Mrs. Lellah Mae Johnson, a bookkeeper, whom the couple had been visiting for three weeks since the close of the Mid-South Fair where he had worked.

Tells Of Quarrels

Mrs. Johnson, who called police, said she was in the bathroom when she heard the shot.

Mrs. Yarbrough said her husband was jealous of her and they had quarreled so much "I just went crazy."

Police said she took the automatic pistol from her husband's suitcase and walked to the bed where he was thumbing through Billboard, an amusements trade magazine, to find a carnival job.

"He saw me point the gun at him," she told police.

She said he told her, "Cock it, baby," apparently not thinking she would shoot. Then she pulled the trigger.

Mr. Yarbrough was lying on his back clad in shorts when police found him. A Thompson Bros. ambulance took him to nearby Methodist Hospital where physicians said he was dead.

'Had Wonderful Time'

Mrs. Yarbrough, wearing a green skirt and sweater at Police Headquarters, answered detectives' questions calmly.

Police quoted her as saying, "I definitely loved him but we quarreled ever since I married him seven years ago because he was jealous of me."

She said she and her husband had gone dancing Wednesday night and "we had a wonderful time until we got home and then he accused me of not loving him."

She said he woke her at 5:30 a.m. yesterday and "started arguing again and wouldn't let me sleep."

Mrs. Conrad Vigland, apartment manager who lives across the hall, said she was planting a flower in the back yard when Mrs. Johnson came to the door and shouted twice, "Mrs. Yarbrough's shot her husband!"

Mrs. Vigland said, "There was silence a few seconds and then Mrs. Yarbrough began screaming inside the apartment. Then we began to hear the noise of the ambulance siren."

Police said Mrs. Johnson was letting the couple stay with them because they had mutual friends in Birmingham, Ala. Mr. and Mrs. Yarbrough planned to leave Memphis as soon as he found a job.

David B. Yarbrough of 1153 South Perkins, the slain man's father, said his son had three children by his present wife and a fourth child by a previous marriage which ended in divorce.

Wounded In War II

Mr. Yarbrough was born in Birmingham and came to Memphis when a child. He was a graduate of Tech High. He was in the Merchant Marine service and Navy in World War II. He was on a merchant ship in 1942 when it was torpedoed off the coast of Brazil and was wounded in 1944 while serving on a destroyer off Casino, Italy.

He was an office worker with Tennessee Coal & Iron Co. in Birmingham until a strike closed the plant. He returned to Memphis last month to work in a concession at the Mid-South Fair.

He leaves his wife; three sons, John Yarbrough and Anthony Yarbrough, who were with their parents in Memphis, and David Yarbrough, who is staying with Mr. Yarbrough's grandparents, Mr. and Mrs. J. P. Jones of Birmingham; a daughter, Juanita Yarbrough, also staying with Mr. and Mrs. Jones, and his father.

Cosmopolitan Funeral Home has charge.

SOPHISTICATED LADY—Nita Kochman, 9-year-old daughter of Mr. and Mrs. J. S. Kochman of 3180 Toby Lane, put herself in a little girl's dream world yesterday when she visited the Cotton States Fashion Exhibit at the Peabody. She dressed up in a big hat, high heels and fur and posed with a mannequin for all to see.

PRETTY MODEL — Mid-South buyers looked on approvingly as Miss Mary Lou Johnson (right), a senior at Ole Miss, modeled a coat at the four-day fashion show. Seated from left are Mrs. Jack Stubbs of

Holly Springs, Miss., and M. B. Williams of Water Valley, Miss. Standing are Mr. Stubbs (left) and Harold Williams of Water Valley. About 5,000 buyers are expected to attend.

WHAT STYLE!—Two youngsters have fun trying on samples of the many new boys' wear items displayed at the fashion show by Bill Landau (center), an exhibitor from Kansas City. The boys are Sammie Zalowitz (left), 6-year-old son of Mr. and Mrs. Lester Zalowitz of 4220 Minden Road, and Stanley Potts, 8, son of Mr. and Mrs. Avon Potts of Corinth, Miss. —Staff Photos by Barney Sellers

Milady Will Pay A Bit More For Gayer, Frillier Styles In Holiday, Spring Wear

Exhibitors Here Say Trade Brisk — Synthetics Appear As Other Fabrics With Adornments —'Flapper Era' Starts Comeback

By LARUE GILLELAND

Southern women can expect to dig a bit deeper into their pocketbooks to buy the "gayer and frillier" fashions to be offered for the holiday and spring season. And clothing retailers will do a brisk business.

This was indicated at yesterday's opening big Cotton States Fashion Exhibit at Peabody.

"Looks like the market is going to be as good if not better than last year's," said Robert I. Wolff, vice president of Cotton States Fashion Exhibitors and a representative of Selmore Garment Co.

"Business is good. I've already shipped as much this year as during all of 1955," said Joshua Bresler, representative for O&B Shoe Co. of Atlanta.

Rise Not Noticeable

A check with salesmen and buyers at the exhibit, which is not open to the public, showed this consensus: "There will be a slight increase in retail prices but they will be hardly noticeable."

Here's what women will find when they go shopping: Dacron dresses that look like cotton, synthetic arnel that looks like silk and rayon spuns which have the feel of fine Irish linens.

Dresses from these materials will have a lot of adornments—ruffles, lace, tuckings and sometimes a few touches of rhinestones.

Women will find that some of the styles of the gay 1920s are coming back.

Ralph Rolle, national sales manager for Max Wiessen & Sons, pointed to a lame' dress of the flapper era and said, "This is going to be a top seller."

Lines Are Straight

He held the dress up. It had straight lines and a bright sheen. It looked like something out of "This Side of Paradise."

"This style dress will sell from $14.95 to $49.95," Mr. Rolle said.

One of the newest designs in footwear is a low but well shaped dress shoe.

The shoe has the same appearance of a high spiked shoe but the heel is only 1¼ inches long. The shoe was designed for teenagers but older women are asking for it also.

Mr. Bresler said the "skinner," a plain, flat pump, and the "contessa-type shoe," originated in Italy, are expected to be popular.

There's something rather elegant and original in costume jewelry. It's called Aurora Borealis, or the "Northern Lights." Necklaces, bracelets and earrings are set with multi-colored stones, each cut in such a way it changes hue when light strikes it from various angles.

New Earring Trend

Shoulder duster earrings — that means they're so long they touch a woman's shoulder — and swing back earrings are predicted to become increasingly good sellers.

"The public is looking for something different and we're trying to give it to them," is the way Al Schechter, owner of Algert Jewelry Co. of Cincinnati, summed it up.

There's a swing back to the Gibson Girl in lingerie, too, with sheath-line and can-can petticoats.

Old fashioned "granny gowns" and night shirts made like the ones grandpa wore and "ski suit" pajamas, designed to take the place vacated by red flannel underwear, are the approaching "rage" in sleepwear.

About 5,000 buyers from the Memphis trade area are expected to attend the show before it ends at 4 p.m. Wednesday. About 600 lines of nationally advertised merchandise are being exhibited on the third, fourth and fifth floors of the hotel.

Short Hairdos Of Flapper Era Here To Stay

By LARUE GILLELAND

April 15, 1957

Those short-cropped but graceful new hairdos many women are sporting nowadays were influenced by the flapper era. And —like 'em or not—you're going to see more and more of the same.

That's the word from Robert Fiance, an expert who can't help but get tangled up in his work occasionally. He's one of the nation's top hair stylists.

Mr. Fiance was in town yesterday to conduct an eight-hour long forum for 400 men and women beauty operators from the Mid-South at the Holiday Inn on South Third.

Trend 25 Years Old

"The latest trend in hair styles goes back at least 25 years," said the owner of Robert Fiance Hair Design Institute of New York.

How do you describe the style?

"It has soft dips and swings, a short length and often gentle waves at the side of the face or over the forehead."

The big difference between the old style and the current trend is that the furrows or waves will not look as "hard and deep" as they did then, Mr. Fiance said.

Egg-headed and block-headed women should not be downhearted. Mr. Fiance — who switched to hair styling after studying physical science in college because he figured he could make more money — said any woman's appearance can be improved by the right hair design. No matter what the shape of her head or how plain her features, it can be done.

Art Of Illusion

"By the art of illusion, you can make something look like what it is not. By altering a line, you can add weight or take it off and make a woman look youthful or older," he said.

But all in all modern women have it pretty soft. Mr. Fiance pointed out that more than 2,000 years ago Chinese women gave themselves permanents by wrapping the ends of their long hair in sticks and boiling them in water for about nine hours. Egyptian women plastered their wrapped hair in mud, then sat under the sun to let it bake.

The forum was sponsored by Union Beauty Supply Co. at 1276 Madison.

Sack Dress Fad Will Be Around For Some Time

(Picture on Page 28)

By LARUE GILLELAND

—AP Wirephoto — Jan. 10, 1958

Like it or not, mister, you're going to see more and more women wearing those baggy sack dresses.

This will be no short-lived fad. Fashion designers are determined to put sex into the chemise.

That's the word from Cotton States Fashion Exhibitors who opened a four-day show of spring and summer merchandise yesterday at the Peabody.

Sales Are Increasing

"Sales of chemise dresses have been increasing rapidly," said George Sapira of New York, an exhibitor. "It's a style that lets you know there's a woman under the dress."

More than 600 of the nation's top lines of fashions in men's, women's and children's wear are on display. Two other shows also are in town. They are the King Cotton Fashion Exhibit at the King Cotton and the Tri-State Fashion Exhibit at the Tennessee Hotel.

Market visitors will see something new in women's swim wear. Knit suits of cotton, wool and orlon will be "the thing" this season. Perhaps one of the most unusual creations is a suit made of aluminum thread and lastex. It's said to fit well and is lightweight.

Fine Line Drawn

Cotton suits with big floral prints also will be popular. These may be bought with matching coats for lounging on beach or pool side. Most suits will have "cowl necklines" and deep V-cut backs.

Robert Middleman of Knoxville, Tenn., another exhibitor, said many aluminum and cotton suits will retail for less than $20.

There'll be only a fine line between raincoats and regular coats now. The reason for this is that manufacturers have learned how to make any fabric water repellent.

Despite the growing interest in the straight-lined chemise dresses, the old-stand-by pleated skirts and sheath skirts will continue to be big sellers. But they're being made in off-beat colors, such as orange, lime and robin's egg blue.

What a lot of men don't realize, according to Mr. Sapira, is that the chemise is not as shapeless as they think.

"Most chemise dresses are only sack-like at the waist. They fit pretty well elsewhere."

About a thousand buyers from throughout the Mid-South are expected to attend the show at the Peabody. More than 500 will

---

Clock Watched On License Trip —140 Minutes

By LARUE GILLELAND

Feb. 22 '57

Whew!

'It sure takes a lot of time driving to get a driver's license in Memphis.

Made a mock run yesterday from my house in Whitehaven to the Highway Patrol office at 5540 Poplar to the Courthouse and back, just like I'd have to do if I were actually getting a license.

It took two hours and 20 minutes.

Times Checked

This was my timetable:

1:42 p.m.—Left Whitehaven in my six-year-old car.

2:04 p.m.—Cruised past the Fairgrounds on Southern. (The Fairgrounds is where city and state officials have been talking about moving the Highway Patrol office.)

Arrived at the patrol office on Poplar at 2:23 p.m. Walked in, drank a Coke and talked to the officers while a black-haired woman was taking her examination. (A man who accompanied her got bawled out for trying to help her with a written question.)

Sgt. Fred Scott said he thought it would be a good idea if the county sent a clerk there to issue licenses every day. (Clerks are there on Saturday mornings.) He said room for a desk for the clerk couldn't be found. Then people wouldn't have to drive from one end of the city to the other to buy a license.

But he had no objection to the proposed Fairgrounds location.

12 Miles

2:48 p.m.—The black-haired woman left, so I left. Arrived at Poplar and Second at 3:18 p.m., after driving 12 miles from the patrol office. Then I spent 15 minutes in the Courthouse watching a man buy his license. Then I drove home.

I figured the whole thing could have been done in an hour and nine minutes—or half the time—if the patrol office and a place to buy licenses were both at the Fairgrounds.

Former Memphis Musician Is Mysterious Spy Witness

Feb. 24 '57

By LaRUE GILLELAND

A pudgy Russian-born musician familiar to Memphis vaudeville fans in the 1920s turned out to be a key cloak-and-dagger figure yesterday in an international spy ring.

Boris Morros, who attained fame as a movie producer after leaving Memphis, will be a star Government witness against three alleged Soviet agents, it was announced yesterday in New York.

Morros' bald head was a familiar sight as he directed music at the old Palace Theater at 81 Union in 1926-27. He is now believed in hiding somewhere in Europe.

The Government wouldn't say yesterday for whom he was working — Russia or the United States. There was speculation on whether Morros was a spy who had defected to the West, an FBI "plant" or a "double agent" working for both sides.

Morros

The 60-year-old naturalized American was referred to 14 times in a Federal Court indictment against Jack Soble, 53, his wife, Myra, 52, and Jacob Albam, 64, arrested in New York Feb. 3.

Colorful Career

The trio is charged with passing secrets to Soviet agents in New York, Paris, Zurich and Vienna.

Morros, who often played piano recitals for the Beethoven Club and the Nineteenth Century Club, has had a colorful career.

Before the Bolshevik Revolution in 1917, he was said to have conducted the Imperial Russian Orchestra in St. Petersburg. It was reported he fled with his wife and infant son to Paris because the new regime resented his "czarist connections."

He came to this country in 1922 as a poorly paid musical director of a popular French revue, "Chauve Souris."

Hollywood Producer

Morros was brought here from New York four years later to direct music for Fanchon & Marco, vaudeville promoters. In 1927 he was made musical director of the old Publix theater chain.

He later went to Hollywood and produced such successful films as "Carnegie Hall," "The Flying Deuces," "Lysistrata," and "Tales of Manhattan."

Morros revisited Memphis in the 1940s.

David Rosenthal, longtime stage manager of Ellis Auditorium, yesterday recalled Morros as a man who spoke poor English "but he was a genius with music."

NEGRO HELD IN DEATH OF WEST MEMPHIAN

March 11 '57

Escaped Convict Seized In Field, Gun Nearby—Denies Killing J. W. Orman

By LARUE GILLELAND

A Negro escaped convict was being questioned at Crittenden County Jail in Marion, Ark., yesterday in connection with the shotgun slaying of a West Memphis service station attendant Saturday night.

Thomas Walker, 49, a Blytheville farmer, was arrested at 7 yesterday morning in a plantation cotton field three miles south of West Memphis. Police Chief Bud Holland made the arrest after receiving a telephone tip Walker was seen burying a shotgun beside a gravel road near the plantation. The 12-gage shotgun was found partially buried with its double barrel sticking out.

Services For Victim Today

Services for J. W. Orman, the victim, will be at 2:30 this afternoon at Citizens Funeral Home in West Memphis. Burial will be in Crittenden Memorial Park.

Mr. Orman, who was 64, was shot in the chest about 10 p.m. Saturday at Cates Esso Service Station on Highway 70 and Hulbert Road.

A Negro appeared outside the front door with a shotgun and told Mr. Orman to "stick 'em up." The attendant slammed the door in the Negro's face and the gunman fired once through the front door. Mr. Orman died en route to Crittenden Memorial Hospital.

Sheriff Cecil Goodwin, who is directing the questioning, said Walker admitted burying the gun but denied having anything to do with the shooting. The gun was unloaded when found.

Buried Gun From Fear

Walker claimed he buried the gun after hearing about the shooting because he feared having the gun found in his car, according to the sheriff. The Negro said he escaped from Indiana State Prison in 1952 while serving a life term for armed robbery.

The Negro told Sheriff Goodwin he had used the shotgun Friday morning to kill a chicken at his farm home. The gun was in his car, he said, when he went to Osceola Saturday to see a friend, John Smith.

Unable to find the friend, he started back toward Blytheville but discovered he was traveling the wrong way when he got almost to West Memphis. He then had car trouble and spent Saturday night in his car near the city, he said.

Chief Holland said the suspect fits the general description of the slouchily dressed gunman witnesses saw at the shooting.

Sheriff Goodwin said an empty 12-gage shotgun shell was found beside a sporting goods store near the service station.

Increase Noted In Bums Begging On Main Street

By LARUE GILLELAND

There are so many beggars in downtown Memphis the beggars are starting to complain.

Bob, a 50-year-old pauper who "works" North Main Street, put it this way:

"You gotta talk fast when you see somebody because he may try to bum you before you bum him."

Bob was one of five beggars who asked this reporter for handouts during a two-and-a-half-hour walk downtown. Most of them were on Main between Court Square and Exchange.

Four said they were from out of town. All agreed the competition here is rough.

"There are more bums around here than on Market Street in St. Louis, and that's saying something," grumbled Bob at the corner of Poplar and Main. "Why, I've been two blocks up and down this street and only got 16 cents. One guy tried to give me a Spanish nickel."

The men, all about middle age and wearing shabby clothes, were willing to talk at length after getting a quarter.

None of the out-of-towners had been here more than three weeks. They said they were from De Kalb, Miss., Dyersburg, Tenn., Nashville and St. Louis.

Most claimed to be veterans and were quick to point out a scar or missing hand or foot as proof of having been wounded.

The man from Mississippi and the two from Tennessee said they came to Memphis looking for work. They said jobs are scarce at home.

"I'm a crackerjack mechanic," said 40-year-old James at Main and Adams. "I was working in a garage in Nashville but it went out of business so I came here. Couldn't find a job here so I got drunk and landed in jail two days ago. Just got out."

City Judge Beverly Boushe said there has been an increase in the number of "transients" arrested by police and arraigned in City Court in the past few weeks.

"There's no question in my mind, there's been a larger number of beggars from out of town in City Court lately," said Judge Boushe. "Most say they are just passing through Memphis and few can pay their fines."

The judge said fines in such cases are usually about $11. If a man can't pay his fine, he must work it out at $2 a day at Shelby County Penal Farm.

C. M. Traylor, night clerk at Union Mission at 107 Poplar, said there was an increase about a month ago in the number of men asking lodging at night. He said he has noticed a decline during the past week, probably due to warmer weather.

"Warmer weather is definitely a factor," Mr. Traylor said. "When the weather is not too cold, the men often sleep along the river bank."

CIAL APPEAL FINAL

MORNING, SEPTEMBER 8, 1957   144 PAGES   PRICE 20 CENTS

Faubus Says Guard Will Keep Negroes Out Of High School Despite Ruling By U.S. Judge

State And Federal Conflicts Are Dramatic But Not New

By LARUE GILLELAND

The conflict between Federal and state authority in Little Rock is dramatic but not new.

Americans have experienced remarkably similar incidents before—once in Memphis.

Let's look at history:

During two hectic pre-election weeks in 1938, Tennessee's Gov. Gordon Browning threatened Memphis with an invasion of 1,000 National Guardsmen. He was stopped by a Federal Court injunction.

Governor Browning claimed he had the right to use the troops because the Shelby County political organization under E. H. Crump was scheming to put him out of office by "stealing" the election with invalid votes.

The political organization charged Governor Browning's purpose in sending troops would be to discourage citizens—particularly Negroes supporting Prentice Cooper—from voting.

Hotly Worded Order

Federal Judge John D. Martin halted further movement of the state troops poised at Jackson, Union City, Dickson and Dyersburg with a hotly worded injunction.

Judge Martin said: "I direct the marshal of this court, his assistants and all citizens' aid that may be necessary, to restrain the threatened action, to repel this invasion of troops unlawfully ordered."

Governor Browning reacted with the statement: "The idea of letting a Federal judge deter me from handling troops as I want is silly and absurd."

But two days before the election Governor Browning withdrew the troops. And he lost the election to Mr. Cooper by a landslide.

Earlier Examples

There were two earlier examples of armed resistance to Federal authority. One was in Texas during the "hot oil" depression days of 1931. The other was in Pennsylvania a century and a half ago.

But Texas and Pennsylvania gave way before the power of the United States Supreme Court. Their defeats may be precedents for Gov. Orval Faubus of Arkansas, who is using the National Guard to try to prevent racial integration in Little Rock's Central High School.

In the Texas case, Gov. Ross Sterling invoked martial law to

Continued on   18,   ol. 1)

deal with "insurrection, tumult, riot and a breach of peace" in several East Texas counties. He did this in an effort to override a Federal District Court order.

The trouble came about because of state conservation regulations limiting the production of oil. Well owners challenged the regulations as unconstitutional and the District Court decided in their favor.

Peace Never Threatened

Governor Sterling (who incidentally was the businessman Memphis' Sterick Building is partially named for) instructed the state militia to enforce the production limit despite the court order.

The matter went to the Supreme Court, which upheld the District Court and found that there was never any real threat to peace.

Chief Justice Charles Evans Hughes declared in effect that a governor could call out troops to prevent violence, but a Federal Court could itself determine whether there was likely to be violence, and thereby overrule the governor.

The Pennsylvania case reached its climax in 1809 when Chief Justice John Marshall ordered the state to give Gideon Olmstead a British ship and cargo he and three other men had captured in 1778.

The Pennsylvania Legislature had claimed most of the prize for the state because a ship belonging to the state had brought the British vessel into the port of Philadelphia after Olmstead had captured it.

Called State Militia

Gov. Simon Snyder called for the state militia to prevent enforcement of the Supreme Court decree. President James Madison told the Governor:

"The executive is not only unauthorized to prevent the execution of the decree sanctioned by the Supreme Court of the United States, but is expressly enjoined, by statute, to carry into effect any such decree, where opposition may be made to it."

Olmstead received his prize money.

251

SHOP TALK — Four newspapermen discussed the front page Little Rock integration story yesterday at the Peabody where they were guests of the Kiwanis Club in connection with National Newspaper Week. They are (from left) Gordon Hanna, managing editor of The Commercial Appeal; Kenneth Johnson, the newspaper's bureau chief in Little Rock; J. Z. Howard, managing editor of the Memphis Press-Scimitar, and LaRue Gilleland, reporter for The Commercial Appeal.

Little Rock Newsman Blames Crisis On Unyielding Stands

Many newsmen who covered the Little Rock integration crisis feel it might have been avoided if Federal and state governments had been willing to compromise a bit, a veteran reporter said yesterday.

Kenneth Johnson, chief of The Commercial Appeal bureau in Little Rock, told the Kiwanis Club how he and five other staff writers of this newspaper gathered the facts and wrote what probably will be the year's biggest news story.

A large segment of newsmen from throughout the country believes "a little giving and taking from both sides might have stopped the head-on collision which eventually did result," he told a luncheon meeting at the Peabody.

Introduced By Hanna

Mr. Johnson was introduced by Gordon Hanna, managing editor of The Commercial Appeal. Mr. Johnson and other newsmen were guests of the club in connection with National Newspaper Week.

They included J. Z. Howard, managing editor of the Memphis Press-Scimitar, LaRue Gilleland, reporter for The Commercial Appeal, and Tom M e a n l e y, Press-Scimitar reporter.

Mr. Johnson already was on the scene at Little Rock's Central High School when more than 200 reporters from many states and foreign countries began descending upon the city after Gov. Orval Faubus called the Arkansas National Guard.

"Regardless of how you feel about the Governor's actions—whether you praise or condemn him—he has hit upon something that has been working up to a crescendo in Southern minds for months.

Give Voice To Feeling

"He gave articulation, I believe, to what might be described as a feeling that the South was being kicked around.

"One man in Little Rock told me recently he thought the thing which actually set the stage for the controversy was the civil rights fight in Washington which preceded the outbreak of trouble in Little Rock.

"He appeared to feel it was just a question of where the big fight would break out in the South—that if it hadn't been Little Rock it would have developed somewhere else."

Mr. Johnson said Governor Faubus has become a spokesman for persons opposing integration and those who have felt the Federal Government was getting too big.

There were some lighter moments during the trouble. Mr. Johnson told of a newsman from Great Britain who stopped a burly member of a mob in front of the school and asked:

"I say, ol' boy, precisely what is it you don't like about this integration thing?"

Burly Negro Slain On Beale After Wounding Policeman

Man Called 'Mean' By Acquaintances Scuffles With Officer When Questioned And Grabs Gun —Shot By Patrolman's Partner

(Pictures on Page 41)

By LARUE GILLELAND

A wounded policeman's partner fatally shot a berserk Negro during a sudden gunfight yesterday at Beale and Hernando.

The husky Negro had shot Patrolman George W. Hutchinson, 30, of 153 Oakdale, in the right leg and hand with the policeman's own pistol.

Patrolman T. A. Robertson, 29, fired three bullets into the gun-wielding Negro as dozens of bystanders watched.

The slain man, who had become "wild with rage," was identified as Jesse Parker, 47, of 158 Pontotoc.

The shooting occurred at 11:15 a.m. when the policemen stopped he Negro to question him. They said Parker, walking at the southwest corner of the intersection, appeared to fit the description of a man who had been in a quarrel earlier in the morning at 280 Gayoso.

Mr. Hutchinson, who was in good condition at Methodist Hospital last night, said he got out of the squad car and asked, "What's your name?"

Fight Described

Parker yelled, "Get away from me!" Then he grabbed Mr. Hutchinson and both men tumbled into the gutter.

"He grabbed me for no apparent reason," Mr. Hutchinson said.

Mr. Robertson said he jumped from the car and was helping Mr. Hutchinson subdue the heavy, six-foot Negro when Mr. Hutchinson's revolver fell from its holster.

"He suddenly became like a wild man and was as strong as a bull," Mr. Hutchinson said. Parker broke away from the officers, picked up the gun and said, "I'll kill you, you . . ."

Mr. Hutchinson grabbed the barrel and the Negro fired twice, putting one bullet through the policeman's right hand and another through the flesh of his right thigh.

Fired Three Times

Mr. Robertson said he then drew his own pistol and fired once.

"He turned and waved the pistol at me, so I shot two more times. Then he fell."

Parker died en route to John Gaston Hospital. A Thompson Bros. ambulance took Mr. Hutchinson to Methodist Hospital. Mr. Robertson received scratches and bruises but was not treated.

A Negro witness, Joe Faulkner, 67, of 275 South Third, said, "If the officer hadn't shot the colored man, I believe he would have shot both officers."

Miss Marie Robinson, clerk at Gattman's Department Store at 205 Beale, said, "I saw the Negro get killed. I looked out in time to see him and the officer scuffling."

A big crowd gathered at the scene and traffic became jammed.

The wounded patrolman's father is Capt. E. L. Hutchinson, head of the Detective Di-

(Continued on Page 18, Col. 1)

vision's check forgery squad. Captain Hutchinson, who has been with the Police Department since 1937, said, "My son is going to be all right but I am worried about his wife. She's expecting a baby soon and this may upset her."

Captain Hutchinson has another son, E. L. Hutchinson Jr., who is a deputy sheriff.

Mr. Robertson

Mr. Robertson, a veteran of hand-to-hand combat in Korea, said, "This reminded me of the old days with the Seventh Division and I'm sorry it had to happen. Today was the first time I've had to pull my pistol since 1952 when I joined the police force."

Chief J. C. Macdonald said Mr. Robertson probably saved Mr. Hutchinson's life when he shot the Negro.

Homicide Capt. W. W. Wilkinson said Parker was described by other Negroes on Beale Street as a "mean colored man."

Captain Wilkinson said he believed a bullet hole found in the front of Pantaze Drug Store at 209 Beale, where the fight occurred, was made by the bullet that went through Mr. Hutchinson's hand.

Police said Parker had a record of previous arrests in Memphis and Detroit for fighting, disturbance and unlawfully driving another person's auto.

Mr. Hutchinson, resting in his hospital bed last night, said, "If the Negro had just answered my question like I asked him to, this would never have happened."

Police said it turned out Parker was not the man involved in the quarrel on Gayoso.

Reporter Drawn In Tunnel By Hypnotic Spiral Wheel

By LARUE GILLELAND

It was like being drawn into a tunnel.

The hypnotist said it would feel that way as I watched the slowly revolving spiral wheel.

I could think of nothing else. There was nothing else. Only that wheel. And the turning. The pull forward.

The hypnotist had captured my attention. That's what he had to do first.

Then he asked me to stand in the middle of a room, close my eyes and imagine a thick board against my back, head to heel.

Confidence Increases

He painted a word picture of this board and how it felt against my spine. I could feel it. My emotions were involved. My confidence in the hypnotist increased.

He suggested the board was hinged to the floor and rocking back and forth on that hinge. The next thing I knew, I was rocking.

Then he suggested my eyes were getting heavy. And they were. He painted more word pictures. Repeated them in different ways.

There I was. Couldn't get my eyes open. Couldn't get 'em open. That's what the hypnotist said would happen. He said you won't be able to open your eyes. No matter how hard you try they won't open. And they didn't. Until he said, "Relax."

The hypnotist was Joe G. Prescott of 3439 Philsdale, who was instrumental in founding the Mid-South Hypnology Association about four years ago.

Principles Useful

Purpose of the organization is to help do away with false notions about hypnotism and to promote its use in mental therapy, as an anesthetic in medicine and dentistry and to show how it can be used effectively by anyone in everyday life.

Mr. Prescott, who is supervisor of the Memphis agency of Penn Mutual Life Insurance Company, said the principles of hypnosis are applied by all good salesmen.

And, whether they know it or not, the principles are used by the best parents and teachers and everyone who gets along well with other people.

Mr. Prescott, who has been studying hypnosis since 1939, believes it is a science which can be a great benefit to humanity.

RENO EVENING GAZETTE
A NEWSPAPER FOR THE HOME
Page Four   Monday, April 8, 1968

'He Stood Tall That Night'

Professor at Nevada Recalls King Interview

EDITOR'S NOTE: A meeting with Dr. Martin Luther King, long before he had reached his summit of world attention, is recalled by LaRue Gilleland, associate professor of journalism at the University of Nevada. Prof. Gilleland is a former staff writer for the Commercial Appeal in Memphis. He wrote this account for the Reno Evening Gazette.

By LaRUE GILLELAND

Martin Luther King, boyish and rather short, stood tall that night in the eyes of his people.

His own modest self - confidence reflected in their black faces. It was near the beginning of his career — almost a dozen years ago in Memphis.

Only 27 then, the Negro minister had brought his new crusade for racial equality for the first time to the city in which he was destined to die.

The hot South Memphis auditorium was crowded with hundreds of Negro men, women and children waiting for a message of hope.

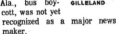

I was the only white man and the only news reporter present. Dr. King, despite his part in the 1955-56 Montgomery, Ala., bus boycott, was not yet recognized as a major news maker.

GILLELAND

I probably would not have gone to the meeting at all if the program had not included Jackie Robinson. The Negro baseball player had come to town with Dr. King.

Though I went mainly to see the Dodger star, I gave my attention to a Baptist preacher.

Already a commanding orator, Dr. King appeared to induce happiness as he spoke. To the multitude that night he was like some young Mohandas Gandhi, a symbol of power and beauty beyond their individual lives.

He was poised, handsome, and well-educated with his recently acquired doctorate from Boston.

He told his listeners that acceptance of the first Negro in major league baseball had been "the mere start of a glorious new era for our race."

"There will be Jackie Robinsons in politics, in business, in the theater, and in every occupation and profession in this great land," he said.

Dr. King found time to talk with me before and after his speech. I was only a year younger than he. But I discerned at once his far greater inner strength. I was white. He was black. He was the superior man.

He spoke to me of Rosa Parks, the seamstress who was arrested after she refused to give up her seat to a white man and move to the back of a Montgomery bus.

Dr. King explained how he, an obscure Montgomery pastor, met the night after Mrs. Parks' arrest with 50 Negro leaders of the city to discuss the case.

The decision they made was momentous, although, he told me, it didn't seem so at the time. The whole Negro community of Montgomery would boycott the buses in mass protest.

Out of that unfolded all the Negro protests and demonstrations since, including the march Dr. King, who was killed by a sniper Thursday, planned to lead in Memphis today.

It also was out of the Montgomery boycott that Dr. King became the spokesman for Negro aspirations through "non-violence."

As we talked in the crowded Memphis auditorium that night years ago, the sensitive young Negro minister put me at ease with a ready smile and the quiet, friendly way he answered questions.

It was as if Dr. King did not want a stranger to feel uncomfortable amid a multitude whose skin was of different color.

255

Gazette
Column
Honored

A column reflecting on the late Dr. Martin Luther King Jr., written for the Reno Evening Gazette's editorial page readers by University of Nevada journalism Prof. LaRue Gillieland, has been held up to the nation's newspapermen as a fine example of bringing perspective to the news.

The column, published on the Gazette's editorial page April 8, is reproduced in the June issue of The Quill, the magazine of Sigma Delta Chi, journalists' society.

Gilleland, a former staff reporter for the Commercial Appeal in Memphis, where King was gunned down April 4, recalled interviewing King in the Tennessee city at a civil rights meeting in 1956 before King was nationally known. Gilleland was the only white person in the crowd of several hundred.

"As we talked in the crowded Memphis auditorium that night years ago, the sensitive young Negro minister put me at ease with a ready smile and the quiet, friendly way he answered questions," Gilleland wrote. "It was as if Dr. King did not want a stranger to feel uncomfortable amid a multitude whose skin was of different color."

The Quill published Gilleland's story in connection with a story by Hillier Kreighbaum, professor of journalism at New York University. Krieghbaum called upon the press to do more interpretive reporting and praised newspapers that make the effort, citing the Times perspective coverage in the King assassination.

Gilleland has been a journalism professor at Nevada since 1963, teaching courses ranging from news reporting and editing to philosophy about press responsibility.

June 6, 1968

256

Problems With Tough Guys

Elvis' Hassles Remembered

EDITOR'S NOTE: After four men attempted to steal Elvis Presley's body from a cemetery in Memphis, the Gazette-Journal invited LaRue W. Gilleland, a former Memphis newspaper reporter who knew the singer and his early hassles with strangers, to write a story. Gilleland is chairman of the Department of Journalism at the University of Nevada-Reno.

By LaRUE W. GILLELAND

Elvis Presley's voice hit a sour note that cold, rainy night we sat in his parked Continental on a Memphis side street — while police looked for him.

"What'd I do wrong this time?" he asked.

It was our third encounter in 1956-57. At 22, he had just gained stardom by radically altering pop music. At 27, I covered the night police beat as a reporter, showing up each time Elvis got in hot water. Tough guys liked to pick on him.

"They say you pulled a gun on a young Marine," I said.

Elvis stared at me. His lip quivered slightly, then curled. We were there together because an editor on my newspaper, the Memphis Commercial Appeal, had called Elvis' unlisted phone number, suggesting he meet me on an out-of-the-way East memphis street.

I arrived, turned off my lights and waited. In a few minutes, Elvis parked behind me. I walked to his car and got in.

The March rain beat harder on the roof of his Continental. "Heck," he said, "I thought the Marine knew I was kidding. I'll show you the gun."

He reached past me and opened the glove compartment. Inside lay a pistol.

"Pick it up," he said.

I hesitated.

"Go on, pick it up."

LARUE W. GILLELAND
... reporter

I did. It was a toy.

Elvis explained that several girls had stopped him earlier on a downtown street to sign autographs when the Marine, who apparently had been drinking, walked up and said:

"You bumped into my wife as she came out of a restaurant two months ago. She told me all about it. I want to get it straightened out right now."

Sensing trouble, Elvis pulled a Hollywood prop pistol he'd used in a recent movie from beneath his coat.

"You don't want to start trouble with me, do you?" he said. The Marine backed off, then called police from a pay phone.

Watching Elvis' face in dim light coming through his car window from a nearby street lamp, I told him, "My city editor says the police are looking for you. Don't you think you'd better take this toy pistol to them? They

know you didn't start any fights in the past."

We shook hands. He drove away in the downpour, heading for police headquarters. I had a story to write.

"If Presley becomes paranoid someday," I thought to myself, "he'll have good reason."

Walking back to my car, I recalled our first meeting five months earlier. Elvis had rocked two service station attendants with his fists, then rolled to legal victories over them in a courtroom.

That incident occurred when Elvis drove into a Memphis Gulf station and a crowd of teen-agers surrounded his car. The station manager, complaining his gas pumps were blocked, told Presley to move. Hemmed in by the crowd, the singer waited.

Elvis climbed out and knocked the manager about 10 feet with a blow. The manager got up and drew a knife. Another station attendant swung at Elvis and missed. I arrived just as police broke up the fight.

I talked briefly with Elvis at police headquarters while he and the service station attendants were booked for assault and battery. Assigned to cover Memphis City Court the next day, I heard the judge tell Elvis: "The testimony points to the guilt of the other two men. I'll dismiss you." People in the courtroom applauded.

When Elvis walked onto the street from the courtroom, motorists waved and pedestrians begged to be photographed with him. A little gray-haired woman stood in front of Elvis and said, "I'm just an old lady, but I like you, too."

Elvis reached down and took her face in his hands. He told her, "You look like you're 25 years old to me."

As he drove away, she turned to a woman standing next to me and said, "Isn't he a dandy?"

257

Cover design by Lauren Gilleland
Communications Design Major (2018)
Pratt Institute
Brooklyn, NY

Back cover excerpted from Northeastern University
Magazine, May 1992, pgs 27-28, by Laura Bennion

Fonts

Cover and chapters: CarbonType, by Vic Fieger
Body: Garmond

Made in the USA
Lexington, KY
27 April 2018